Morality

Morality

An Anthropological Perspective

Jarrett Zigon

Oxford • New York

First published in 2008 by
Berg
Editorial offices:
1st Floor, Angel Court, 81 St Clements Street, Oxford, OX4 1AW, UK
175 Fifth Avenue, New York, NY 10010, USA

Berg is the imprint of Oxford International Publishers Ltd.

Library of Congress Cataloguing-in-Publication Data

Zigon, Jarrett.
    Morality : an anthropological perspective / Jarrett Zigon.
      p. cm.
    Includes bibliographical references and index.
    ISBN-13: 978-1-84520-658-1 (cloth)
    ISBN-10: 1-84520-658-4 (cloth)
    ISBN-13: 978-1-84520-659-8 (pbk.)
    ISBN-10: 1-84520-659-2 (pbk.)
    1. Ethics—Cross-cultural studies. 2. Anthropology—Psychology.
3. Anthropological ethics. I. Title.

GN468.7.Z54 2008
170—dc22

2008025876

British Library Cataloguing-in-Publication Data

A catalogue record for this book is available from the British Library.

ISBN 978 1 84520 658 1 (Cloth)
ISBN 978 1 84520 659 8 (Paper)

Typeset by JS Typesetting Ltd, Porthcawl, Mid Glamorgan
Printed in the United Kingdom by Biddles Ltd, King's Lynn

www.bergpublishers.com

Contents

Introduction

Morality is a concept that has been of philosophical interest for over 2,000 years. Rarely, however, did these philosophical explorations take much notice of the everyday moral lives of actual, living people (some important exceptions are: Brandt 1954; Ladd 1957; Nordenstam 1968). In other words, moral philosophy tends to consider the concept of morality at an abstract level. At the beginning of the twentieth century sociocultural anthropology as we know and practice it today began to shape itself. In contrast to philosophy, modern anthropology took on the task of describing and analyzing the everyday life experiences and conceptual worlds of different peoples around the world. Yet, as several have argued, until recently there have been very few explicit anthropological studies of local moralities (Wolfram 1982: 274; Pocock 1986: 7; Faubion 2001a; Laidlaw 2002; Robbins 2007; Zigon 2007).

This, no doubt, is a contested claim. For many anthropologists will say that in having studied, for example, the various religious, gender and kinship systems from around the world, they have been studying morality all along (Parkin 1985: 4). This, however, is a question of definition. According to those anthropologists who would claim that the discipline has, at least to some extent, been studying morality all along, it would seem as though they would agree with Ruth Benedict's claim that morality "is a convenient term for socially approved habits" (1956: 195). Unfortunately, such a definition does not differentiate morality from any of the other concepts anthropologists generally use. For if morality is just another term for socially approved habits, then morality becomes a synonym for, for example, religious practice, ritual, reciprocity, or kin relations. It is a central contention of this book that it is this confusion of definition that has stood in the way of a more subtle and in-depth anthropological study of moralities.[1] In exploring various examples of anthropological approaches to the study of moralities, we will leave behind this confusion and set out a more focused approach to this study.

This book, then, is an exploration of the anthropology of moralities. Its main task is to forge a new path for this important line of research. This will require new and more precise definitions of what is to be studied. For I think it is fair to say that the history of our discipline has shown that it is only with this kind of focused

---

1. Wolfram points out that this confusion of definition stems from anthropology's theoretical foundations in Durkheimian sociology and Durkheim's confusion and poor philosophizing on morality (1982). This point is also made in Laidlaw 2002 and Robbins 2005.

study that our methods are appropriate. But new paths always depend on what was already there. Because of this, it is important that we carefully consider the various anthropological studies that claim, to varying degrees, to be studies of morality. Therefore, a significant amount of what follows in this book will be an overview of these studies, including three case studies that explore the work of three anthropologists in more detail. While I focus on the most recent works in the discipline, it will be important to mention those few earlier anthropological studies of local moralities that serve as the foundation for this new disciplinary focus.

What will become clear almost immediately as we begin this exploration of the literature is that very few of these studies were originally conceived as anthropological studies of local moralities. In itself this is not a problem, for it is quite common and even expected that the fieldwork experience will bring about new and unexpected discoveries and analyses. Nevertheless, because morality is an undertheorized and confused concept within the discipline, it often leads to, in my view, one of several misuses. One misuse is that which I have already mentioned, namely, that morality is conflated with, in the words of Benedict, "socially approved habits." As we will see, this has its roots in the late nineteenth- and early twentieth-century social theories of Emile Durkheim, whose ideas still hold much influence in the social sciences.

A second common misuse of the analytic concept of morality is to impose some Western philosophical view of morality onto the everyday moralities of the people we study. Because anthropology has not yet provided a view of morality that goes much beyond Benedict's definition, we often rely on some version of a Western philosophical view. Thus, for example, it is not uncommon to come across Habermasian rational communicators, Taylorian agents, or Aristotelian social virtuosos in the anthropological literature. While there is no doubt that anthropologists of moralities have much to gain with engagement with moral philosophy, imposing these philosophies more or less in whole onto anthropological data and the lives of our informants does little to move the discipline forward or, more importantly, to adequately describe the moral lives of the people we study.

A third misuse of the concept of morality is the imposition of the anthropologist's personal moral views onto the lives of the people they study. This is particularly true for some Marxian and feminist anthropologists who, although I agree with their views to a great extent, unfortunately too often seem to analyze their data through preconceived theoretical lenses. Throughout this book we will have ample opportunity to see each of these misuses of the analytic concept of morality in the works we consider. As I have already said, I suggest one reason why these misuses are so common is because so few anthropological studies begin as explicit studies of local moralities. Therefore, one way of avoiding these mistakes is to engage in anthropological studies of local moralities from the start. For in doing so, the anthropologist is forced to consider more thoroughly just what it is she means by morality. It is my hope that this book will help in this consideration, and in the final chapter I will offer a guideline for conceiving of morality and the moral lives of our interlocutors in a more subtle manner so as to help bring about this kind of more focused research and analysis.

To summarize, then, this book will be an exploration of the anthropology of moralities. It is my contention that despite claims to the contrary, this is a very recent explicit and more sophisticated research agenda for anthropologists. Therefore, this book will focus on more recent anthropological (as well as a few other social scientific) works that take morality as either their explicit and intended focus of research, or use morality as an after the fact analytic concept. Because the latter works still remain more common, we will have an excellent opportunity to see the differences and respected merits of both approaches.

Let me also add that this book is not a work on the ethics of anthropology as a discipline or its research methods. There are already numerous works that address this important issue (for example, see: Cassell 1980; Fine 1993; Robben and Sluka 2007). Rather, this book is, to the best of my knowledge, the first to provide an overview of the work that has already been done and suggests ways to move ahead in the increasingly important anthropological study of local moralities. The question of the book, then, is not how we as anthropological researchers should morally engage with the peoples we study, for that is the realm of the ethics of anthropological fieldwork, but instead how the peoples we study conceive of, negotiate, and practice morality in their everyday lives.

This does, however, raise the important question of the distinction between morality and ethics. Ethics has its origins in the ancient Greek word *ethos*, meaning way of life or custom and habit, and morality comes from *mos*, which is simply the Latin translation of *ethos*. Here, of course, it is easy to see why Benedict's definition might be appealing. But it is important to note that there has been over 2,000 years of philosophical discourse on the concept that has taken it well beyond this simple view. This discourse cannot be simply dismissed out of hand.

More to the point, as this word origin suggests, with few exceptions, there has been very little distinction either philosophically or anthropologically between morality and ethics. It should be pointed out, however, that increasingly ethics has come to be associated with the proper and expected way of doing a certain profession, such as, the ethics of anthropological research or medical ethics or business ethics. Despite this distinction of professional ethics, there is generally little other distinction made (for an example of a social theorist who does make a distinction, see Bauman 1993). Because of this, throughout this book while discussing others' work, I too will make no distinction between morality and ethics and will do my best to keep to the term used by the author about whom I am writing. Nevertheless, because I believe a real distinction between these two terms is in fact helpful for the future of an anthropology of moralities, in the concluding chapter I will offer what I see as a helpful distinction between morality and ethics.

Some Early Works in the Anthropology of Moralities

Discounting late nineteenth- and early twentieth-century evolutionary anthropology, which produced a good deal of text on the evolution and development of morality cross-culturally – one example of this is Marett's "Rudimentary Ethics," in which he argued that there are two stages of society, the first stage is that of non-moral custom and habit and the second of rational decision-making where morality appears in society for the first time – it is difficult to find ethnographic works that explore the moral worlds of local peoples explicitly and in depth. This, as I have already mentioned, is a contested statement; it is, however, one that I believe is true if we consider morality to be more than "socially approved habits." K. E. Read, an anthropologist who did one of the first focused anthropological studies of morality, agrees. Read argues that the failure of anthropologists through most of the twentieth century to explicitly study local moralities is twofold (1955: 235–47). First, he suggests, there was a general reaction against the evolutionary theories that often made a priority of showing the superiority of Western morality and civilization, and therefore, it was a theme and concept that became, if you will, taboo. Second, Read argues that the fact that modern anthropology was modeled on the natural sciences led to the eschewing of the study of those things considered to be non-objective, such as morality. If Read is correct in his twofold explanation, which I believe he is, it is interesting to note that it has only been after the so-called interpretive and humanistic turn in anthropology in the last twenty years or so that anthropologists have begun to explore with more subtlety the moral worlds of their informants.

Despite this lack of ethnographic focus on morality, there are still some important works we can look to as having made an attempt to consider the moral worlds of local peoples. One of the earliest examples is that of E. E. Evans-Pritchard's work on witchcraft among the Azande (1968[1937]). I will discuss this text in more detail in Chapter 2, but for now it is important to note that Evans-Pritchard saw witchcraft as central to the moral value system of the Azande, and as he put it, "'It is witchcraft' may often be translated simply as 'It is bad'" (1968[1937]: 107). Although Evans-Pritchard does not go into much detail about the moral world and its concepts of the Azande, by showing that witchcraft can be interpreted as a moral concept he laid the groundwork for decades of anthropological research on witchcraft.

An even earlier work that is often cited as an anthropological exploration of a local moral world is Malinowski's book on crime and custom among the Trobriand Islanders (1926). In response to the general perception of his day that so-called savages lived in a lawless and anarchic state of being, Malinowski argued that the Trobriand Islanders lived in a well-ordered society without the need for institutionalized law akin to that of Euro-American societies. This could be shown, so he argued, by discovering and analyzing "all the rules conceived and acted upon as binding obligations, to find out the nature of the binding forces," and to classify "the norms and rules of a primitive community" (Malinowski 1926: 15). While this may sound like Malinowski would go on to do a very interesting analysis of the moral conceptions of the Trobrianders, Read rightly points out that despite his remarkable descriptions of nearly every important institution and organizational aspect of Trobriand life, he actually says very little about their morality (Read 1955: 236). Again, one must wonder if this is due to a simple devaluation of the topic of morality within the discipline of anthropology, or because of a general misunderstanding of the concept that too often conflates it with, for example, economic exchange, such as reciprocity, or religion (Read 1955: 235).

This confusion seems to have only gotten worse in a work by Christoph von Fürer-Haimendorf (1964). In a single chapter entitled "Values and Moral Concepts," von Fürer-Haimendorf covers the basics of what he considers Nepalese Sherpa moral beliefs, which it should be pointed out seem to be synonymous with their religious beliefs, etiquette, and values, mostly in terms of wealth accumulation. While it is certainly laudable that von Fürer-Haimendorf should attempt to describe the morality of the Sherpas, it is clear that he found it difficult to distinguish the moral world of these people from other aspects of their social life. But it would be a mistake for the anthropologist of moralities to believe that morality is synonymous with, or even always related to, religion, let alone etiquette or the value of wealth accumulation. In defense of von Fürer-Haimendorf, he was writing at a time when it was still common in anthropology to attempt to provide a full and systematic depiction of small-scale societies. This is an untenable task that anthropologists no longer attempt. While there is certainly much that we can learn from works like that of von Fürer-Haimendorf, such as his incredibly detailed descriptions for one, what is perhaps most interesting about this work is the pitfalls it warns us to avoid in our future attempts at an anthropology of moralities.

Just one of those pitfalls is the listing of what locals believe to be moral virtues or transgressions. Von Fürer-Haimendorf gives us a list of thirteen such transgressions, but reassures us that he could provide us with pages of lists (1964: 276–7). Indeed, this was the time period of lists or collections of facts. Mostly they were provided by those, such as Linton (1952 and 1954), Murdock (1965), and Redfield (1957), who were arguing against cultural and moral relativism in one way or another. These "lists" (I use scare quotes because they were not all actual numbered lists like that of von Fürer-Haimendorf) were of the supposed universals or cross-cultural similarities that could support an anti-relativist position. But such lists and collections only add to one of the biggest of the misunderstandings and confusions about morality within the discipline, that is, that morality can be codified in terms of principles and rules (this will be covered in more detail in the next section). As I will try to point out throughout the rest of this book, morality should not be considered as such.

Such lists and collections were offered as a critique of relativism. While in the next section I will discuss in more detail both cultural and moral relativism and their central role in the history of modern anthropology, here I will briefly consider how some of their defenders have considered morality. As I have already pointed out several times, Ruth Benedict, one of relativism's first and strongest defenders, defined morality as "socially approved habits," and it was this very broad notion of morality that has for the most part been accepted by moral relativists and, in fact, anthropologists in general. Because relativists see morality in this way, and because these habits differ between societies, there must be, so relativists conclude, different moralities for each society. This is something to be considered further in the next section, but for now we simply want to understand that moral relativists generally agree with Edward Westermarck's claim that different moralities exist between different societies if "a mode of conduct which among one people is condemned as wrong is among other people viewed with indifference or enjoined as a duty" (1906: 742). This position, combined with that of Benedict, is succinctly put in Raymond Firth's relativist definition of morality, a definition which can without much hesitancy be said to characterize the still prevalent view of many anthropologists: "Morality is a set of principles on which [judgments of right and wrong] are based. Looked at empirically from the sociological point of view, morality is socially specific in the first instance. Every society has its own moral rules about what kinds of conduct are right and what are wrong, and members of society conform to them or evade them, and pass judgement accordingly" (Firth 1951: 183). In such works as these, morality was treated as just one aspect of the more general concept of cultural relativism, and because of this, morality was not treated in explicit detail where it seemed like anthropologists had an excellent opportunity to do so.

This opportunity was finally taken up by K. E. Read in his groundbreaking and still important article on morality and personhood among the Gahuku-Gama of Papua New Guinea (1955). In this piece, Read takes an interpretive approach to Gahuku-Gama conceptions of morality and in so doing explicates their moral world in relationship to their ontological view of human persons. In addition to this, he attempts the very unrelativist task of comparing Gahuku-Gama moral conceptions of personhood with those of what Read calls the Western European conception. While Read claims that the latter conception views persons as morally equal and having moral value independent of status, Gahuku-Gama conceptions view moral value and difference in terms of the status and role of the persons involved. Thus, moral value and hierarchy change from context to context. Morality for the Gahuku-Gama, then, is contextual, shifting, and to some extent negotiable. As we will see throughout this book, Read's analysis of the Gahuku-Gama has been significantly influential for how some anthropologists of moralities today consider the moral worlds of their informants. That is, his emphasis on the moral person, context, and shifting and negotiable moral positions has proven vital to the way morality is now considered by some anthropologists.

Another important work for anthropologists of moralities, but one not very well known in the discipline in general, is *Anthropology and Ethics* by Edel and Edel (2000[1959]). In their pioneering work on the subject, Edel and Edel raise the question: "By what mark shall we know 'the moral'?" In attempting to answer this question, they make a distinction between what they see as the two predominant approaches to this question. They call these two approaches Ethics Wide and Ethics Narrow. Ethics Wide, so they argue, "assumes that moralities are part and parcel of the whole field of human endeavor and striving" (2000[1959]: 8), and as such, inquires into human values and notions of the Good. With such a broad definition, however, it is difficult to make a distinction between Ethics Wide and the anthropological concept of culture, and they make no argument for why the former is preferable to the latter.

Ethics Narrow, on the other hand, limits moral inquiry to particular phenomena. Edel and Edel conceive of this as a cross-cultural investigation of obligation and duty, that is, of questions of *ought*. Recent anthropological studies of moralities, however, suggest that focusing on the *ought* may confine morality to its Western conception. For instance, Howell suggests that a cross-cultural study of moralities is better served by focusing on the acting individual's process of moral reasoning during which choices are made between alternative possible actions (Howell 1997: 14–16). Ultimately, however, Edel and Edel suggest that an Ethics Wide, much like the study of culture in general, is too broad, and Ethics Narrow is too limiting for considering the often complex configuration and possibilities of moralities. In the end they conclude that only a cross-cultural empirical study of the family resemblances of personal, cultural, and human practices that constitute a moral configuration can lead to an adequate study of moralities (Edel and Edel 2000[1959]: 11). While it seems to me that Edel and Edel fall into the same anthropological trap of considering various spheres of social life, such as family relations and economic transactions and exchange, necessarily part of this so-called moral configuration, they have importantly pointed out the necessity of focusing our anthropological investigations of local moralities on the minutia of everyday life.[2] That is to say, an anthropology of moralities is best served by, to borrow from the Edels, narrowly focusing on particular practices or spaces of moral interactions.

These practices and spaces are what Howell, in the introduction to her important collection of ethnographies of moralities, calls pegs (1997). Howell argues, and the essays in the collection show the importance of this, that anthropological studies of moralities must focus their attention on a very particular practice or space in order to discern the kind of subtle detail that makes up people's moral lives. This collection is the first of its kind to bring together essays each of which focus on local moral worlds. It must be pointed out, however, that the original fieldwork for these essays was not

---

2. I want to be clear that I do not dismiss the possibility that local moralities can be intimately intertwined with such things as kinship and family relations, gender relations, economic exchange, and religion. I simply want to emphasize the necessity of being very careful about assuming that these are necessarily part of the moral realm.

conceived as research focused on local moralities, and for that reason they may have some of the shortcomings we will see in many of the works discussed throughout this book. One question that always has to be raised when reading such works is: just how much of what the anthropologist tells us about a local morality would the local people agree to call morality? In other words, is it truly local morality, or has it become so by means of after the fact analysis. It will be important to keep this question in mind as we move from example to example in this book.

Having said this, this collection edited by Howell remains a central text to the new anthropology of moralities. What makes it so significant for future anthropological studies of moralities is that it shows the necessity of studying local moralities in terms of their particular practices, the spaces in which these practices unfold and the conceptions that underlie them. Thus, for example, we are able to see how football is an important moral ideal and space for Argentineans, speech-acts are important moral practices in both rural England and Mongolia, and personhood is a central moral concept in different African communities. These studies differ from those mentioned above (except for that of Read's) in that they do not conflate the moral with other aspects of social relations, such as gender or religion. While these latter concepts may in fact be important for an understanding of local moralities as analyzed in some of the essays in this collection, the authors do not make the mistake of equating, for example, local gender relations with morality as such as others have done. Instead, some aspects of gender relations make up just one part of a larger moral world. This is an important move forward.

One reason why this collection is so successful is that it focuses on the processes of local moral reasoning. That is to say, unlike previous works on moralities these authors do not conceive of morality as a code or a set of principles and rules to be followed or transgressed, rather morality is variously conceived by different authors as, for example, a form of embodied dispositions, cultural scripts, or moral choices intimately tied with emotions and feelings. Each of these positions, despite the differences between them, focus on morality as a realm not of rule following, but of lived experiences that feed back into one another in a continuing process of re-evaluation and enactment.

These, then, are some of the most important contributions to anthropological considerations of local moralities. As can be seen, some are more useful than others for moving forward with our studies. Still, it is always important to know from where we have come so as not to repeat our journey. In the next section, then, I will take a closer look at relativism, both cultural and moral, and its importance to the development and current state of anthropology. The critical stance I will take in this next section is not meant to suggest we should move away from relativism, as I will make clear at the end of the section, but simply to point out its weaknesses and to show the necessity of revising our idea of what we mean by this central concept within our discipline.

Relativism

There is little doubt that cultural relativism is one of the central tenets of sociocultural anthropology. Indeed, it is difficult to find an anthropologist, despite its many criticisms from outside the discipline (see Geertz 1984), who does not accept to some degree one version or another of cultural relativism. Melville Herskovits, one of the earliest anthropological voices and defenders of cultural relativism, has described it as the precept that all judgments "are based on experience, and experience is interpreted by each individual in terms of his own enculturation" (quoted in Hallpike 2004: 15). Therefore, the broad concept of cultural relativism is a kind of umbrella term for the more specific versions of, for example, cognitive, epistemological, and moral relativism. Before turning to a more explicit description of this latter concept, I will give a brief outline of the significance of cultural relativism in general to sociocultural anthropology.

Cultural relativism is both methodologically and theoretically central to modern anthropology. The origin myth of the discipline, or at least the American version, credits Franz Boas with establishing its centrality. Although it has been well argued that cultural relativism need not be as methodologically vital to good anthropological fieldwork as anthropologists contend, and, in fact, that Boas himself was not a relativist (Cook 1999), this origin myth guides the vast majority of anthropologists in their research and analysis. Because relativism claims that the knowledge, beliefs, and practices of each society "are a matter of convention and are not rooted in absolute principles that transcend time and place" (Hatch 1983: 3), it is not possible to compare and contrast them in a way that ranks them in any judgmental order of better or worse, or superior or inferior. For this reason, then, the social evolutionary methods and theories of the nineteenth century are rejected and today anthropologists rarely do much cross-cultural evaluative analysis.

While it is generally claimed that the overwhelming empirical evidence collected by modern anthropologists shows the truth of cultural relativism, this, in fact, may not exactly be the case. For there is little doubt that cultural diversity was well known long before anthropologists began their in-depth field research at the beginning of the twentieth century. Montaigne, Locke, Rousseau, and Kant all wrote about the different traditions found around the world and throughout time, but perhaps the first and most famous of the chroniclers of cultural diversity was Herodotus in ancient Greece. It is clear, then, that cultural diversity has been well known for thousands of years. So then, if it is not the empirical evidence collected by twentieth-century anthropologists that led to the rise of cultural relativism as the central tenet of sociocultural anthropology, what is responsible for its position?

If we can, at least for the moment, accept the argument of John Cook that Boas was not a relativist, but instead simply argued for the significance of trying to understand the actual beliefs and motives of local peoples and the importance of not being seduced, as the social evolutionists were, by superficial cross-cultural similarities (Cook 1999: 71), then we can say that cultural relativism only found its true proponents in Boas's students. These students, and most particularly Ruth Benedict and Melville Herskovits, came to intellectual maturity in the post-World War I years. This war saw the kind of barbarous slaughter of human life that is modern warfare for the first time, and the death and destruction that it left in its path left many with the feeling that the Euro-American world, which they had in the late nineteenth century thought of as the pinnacle of civilization, was in fact more primitively murderous and morally backwards than the small-scale societies around the world they had once thought of as far inferior to their own society. This was indeed an age of skepticism. And it is this widespread societal skepticism, a skepticism which also spread into intellectual and academic thinking, that Elvin Hatch credits with the ascendancy of cultural relativism in anthropology (1983: 50). It was during this time between the two great wars that cultural relativism had its heyday and became ingrained in anthropology both methodologically and theoretically. While there is no doubt that the enthusiasm that hit the United States and most of Western Europe after the victory over Nazi Germany in World War II led to some serious questioning of cultural relativism, and one of its aspects, that of moral relativism, was certainly questioned after the atrocities of the Nazis, cultural relativism remains today nearly unquestioned among the ranks of anthropologists around the world.

But what of moral relativism? How has that fared among anthropologists? At first glance it appears to have remained, for the most part, just as strong within the discipline as the more general concept of cultural relativism. As a graduate student I came into the discipline with a background in moral philosophy and had desired to continue with anthropological studies of morality. Although I did receive significant support from some, I also heard a wide array of relativist-like responses and skepticisms – from the dismissive claims that there is no such thing as morality to study, to the political-economic claim that morality was nothing more than an ideological expression of the power and economic structures of society, to the more cultural claim that morality surely differed from culture to culture so I best be able to ground it in a purely local description and explanation. It remains clear to this day that to a great extent moral relativism is the expected and assumed moral theory of the anthropological discipline.

But as some of these responses also suggest, there is some doubt about the doctrine of moral relativism. Beginning in the 1960s, anthropologists have increasingly expressed moral criticism and outrage over such perceived immoral practices and injustices as the Vietnam War, racism, gender inequality, circumcision and female genital mutilation, economic inequality, and American foreign policy in the post-September 11 age, among others. Therefore, there appears to be a kind of tension within anthropology. For while the vast majority of anthropologists still maintain the doctrine of moral relativism to some degree, many also clearly make moral criticisms of the world around them. While this tension may be the result of the generally undertheorized notion of morality within the discipline or the tendency of anthropologists within their work to assume their own definition of morality while discussing the so-called "moral lives" of other peoples, this is clearly not the place to try to account for it. I merely want to point it out, as this tension will remain clear throughout the various works we explore in this book.

Although this tension clearly exists in contemporary anthropology, there is no doubt that moral relativism remains the most common moral theory in the discipline. It is, perhaps, a bit too generous to call this a moral theory, as it is probably better described as an assumed perspective within the discipline. For as we will note throughout this book, morality has not been a traditional topic of specific focus for anthropologists, but instead a side issue that is called upon for analytic purposes when thought to be needed. One of the goals of this book is to bring this undertheorized use of the concept to light and to suggest ways in which morality can be more subtly and interestingly considered by anthropologists.

Still, as I have said, moral relativism remains a kind of default perspective on the question of morality within the discipline. It is assumed for the most part to be true. As the authors of the introduction to a special edition of a well-known psychological anthropology journal put it, there is an "obvious cultural and historical diversity in moral systems" (Fiske and Mason 1990: 131). This obviousness, as I have said above, supposedly comes from the wealth of empirical data collected by anthropologists over the last century. There is, of course, no doubt that there is a vast array of cultural diversity across time and space, but what is often not recognized is that until recently there have been very few explicit anthropological studies of local moralities. Therefore, one of the clear misunderstandings made by many anthropologists is to confuse local non-moral values and practices with morality (Hatch 1983: 66–7; Cook 1999: 87, 137). For example, in Fiske and Mason's introduction to the special edition on moral relativism, each of the examples they used to illustrate moral relativism was an example of differing cross-cultural relations between family members. I believe it is fair to say that the question must be asked: why should we consider family relations, e.g. the relationship between a mother and a child, morality? These kinds of relations are certainly not what have traditionally come under the rubric of Western moral theory and philosophy. They are, however, central to some non-Western moral philosophies, most famously Confucianism. Perhaps local people consider this a moral issue? Or is it perhaps possible that anthropologists conflate what is locally considered appropriate and expected familial relations with what we would call morality? These are the kinds of questions that we must ask if we are to engage in an explicit anthropology of moralities.

Richard Shweder, an anthropologist who has argued well in defense of relativism, disagrees. He argues that "cultural differences are often differences over what is obligatory from a moral point of view" (Shweder 1990: 209). These cultural differences about which he is speaking are often the kinds of differences I just mentioned with the example of familial relations. They are moral differences, so he contends, because local people feel objectively obliged to follow certain practices which, as he puts it, are locally considered as expressions of natural law and discoverable through reason. Without going into much detail, for it will be a topic of discussion in the next chapter, it is interesting that Shweder's defense of moral relativism rests on the concepts of "natural law" and "reason," both of which have their origins in ancient Roman and Greek moral philosophy and were more fully developed in medieval Christendom. Yet, somehow Shweder finds it appropriate to use these concepts to defend the very idea of a non-universalistic notion of morality.

Be that as it may, let's consider some examples to help us think about the claims of these authors. I think it is safe to say that most people in the United States would say that a father, or better yet, a good father is obliged to occasionally go outside and play with his child. For example, let us say that a good father should teach his son how to throw and hit a baseball. But what happens if a father does not do this? The child may eventually learn to play baseball by other means, become a teenager, play the sport well and even become a local baseball star. To add to the father's neglect of teaching his son to play baseball, he now does not attend this son's games either. Many people might say that this is a bad father who seems to show little interest in his son. But does this make the father immoral? Has he broken some cultural moral code? It is important here not to be confused by the terms "good father" and "bad father." "Good" and "bad" need not have moral reference. I think it is fair to say that most would say that this is not a moral issue. There may be a culturally felt obligation for a father to play games or teach a son to play baseball, for example, as well as to show an interest in the son's interests and successes, but this obligation does not amount to a moral issue. But yet, many anthropologists and social scientists will try to tell us that analogous relationships in other societies do amount to moral issues (see, for example, Fiske and Mason 1990; Shweder 1990). I will not go further with this critique, for this is an issue that will arise throughout this book. Therefore, the question of just why a particular issue should be considered a moral issue is something that should remain in the mind of the reader. For the answer to this question will not only help us consider the validity of moral relativism, but more importantly for our purposes it will help us discern appropriate themes for anthropological studies of local moralities.

The assumption of many moral relativists is that while morality does in fact differ from society to society, there is only one morality, or at least one predominant morality, within a particular society. Thus, much like the traditional notion of culture, which conceived of culture as a bounded and basically homogeneous unit of belief and practice, a notion which has been much criticized in the last few decades, moral relativists usually appear to consider morality as homogeneously bounded within particular societies or societal groups (Shore 1990b). For anyone who has done explicit anthropological research on moral belief and practice, this is clearly not the case. As Shore puts it, his own research illustrates "how the presumed homogeneity of an ethical tradition can be exploded by careful attention to conflicted ethical discourse" within a particular society or social group (1990b: 220). For example, Shore's research on ethical dilemmas and ambivalence in Samoa (1990a) and my own research in Moscow, Russia, on the relationship between personal experience and moral conceptions both show that there are a range of moralities within any particular local setting. Perhaps, then, traditional moral relativists are not radical enough in their positing of moral difference.

I have already pointed out how Shweder uses moral concepts from ancient and medieval Europe as the basis for arguing for moral relativism. A similar critique can be made for Elvin Hatch's defense of moral relativism. Hatch provides a very interesting historical overview of moral relativism within anthropology and at times is deeply critical of it (1983). However, true to the tension within the discipline I mentioned above, despite his critical position vis-à-vis moral relativism, Hatch ends up defending what might be called a weak version of this doctrine and does so using concepts that are deeply embedded within the Euro-American politico-historical context.

Hatch essentially sees moral relativism as a doctrine of cross-cultural tolerance. This tolerance is meant to go both ways. Not only are Western peoples supposed to be tolerant of the moral lives of non-Western peoples, but so too are the latter to be tolerant of our ways of life. For Hatch, this notion of tolerance, which he sees as essential to moral relativism, is closely linked with freedom. By freedom Hatch means that "people ought to be free to live as they choose, to be free from the coercion of others more powerful than they" (1983: 144). This freedom from coercion includes both freedom from alien peoples and powers, and freedom from the powerful persons and institutions within a particular society. Moral relativism, then, in Hatch's view seems to be little more than the secular-liberal view that individual persons are by their very nature (Shweder might say according to natural law) free to do as they please as long as it does not harm or act to coerce another, only taken to the level of society as a whole.

While this may in fact be something with which many of us at first glance would have little difficulty agreeing, the question again must be asked how the position of moral relativism can rest on two interrelated concepts, tolerance and freedom, that are intimately entwined with a political and moral doctrine that arose in the nineteenth- and twentieth-century Euro-American world. One is indeed left wondering about the validity of a moral theory that claims there can be no absolute and universalistic conception of morality, and that moral values cannot be imposed on other societies, and yet seems to rely so heavily on a certain moral vocabulary that is deeply embedded in a particular socio-historic-cultural context. Perhaps, then, the vocabulary needs to change.

This is just what John Cook suggests (1999). Cook is a philosopher who is intimately familiar with the anthropological and ethnographic literature concerning relativism. Applying philosophical methods of conceptual analysis to this literature, he offers an impressive critique of moral relativism. His critique is fourfold:

1. anthropologists for the most part have misunderstood and misapplied the concept of morality in their work;
2. because anthropologists have tended to project, despite their best efforts to remain objective, their own ideas onto the motives and practices of the peoples they study, anthropologists have created similarities that are better thought of as differences;
3. by relying on the notion of enculturation as a defense of relativism, anthropologists have portrayed human persons as near automatons;
4. relativists are not radical enough because essentially they have the same narrowly conceived view of morality as do moral absolutists.

I have already discussed the first of these critiques, that is, that anthropologists have generally misunderstood, confused, and misapplied the concept of morality; therefore, I will not discuss it further here. I will, however, consider the remaining three critiques in more detail.

The second critique of anthropological views of moral relativism made by Cook is that because anthropologists have tended to project, despite their best efforts to remain objective, their own ideas onto the motives and practices of the peoples they study, anthropologists have created similarities that are better thought of as differences. This is what Cook calls the Projection Error. As Cook puts it, the Projection Error "consists of thinking, on account of their similarity, that the actions of an alien people are actions of the *same* sort as actions that might occur in – or that one is familiar with from – one's own culture" (Cook 1999: 93, italics in original). It is this error of conflating two different kinds of actions for the "*same* sort" of actions that leads one to conclude that what is considered morally wrong in one society is considered morally appropriate in another, that is to say, to make a morally relativistic conclusion.

One example Cook gives is that of the well-known fact that Eskimos are known to leave their elderly parents behind to freeze to death (1999: 102–3). The relativist argument runs like this: if someone in our culture should leave his elderly parents to freeze to death, he would be prosecuted for murder. But the Eskimos find this practice perfectly acceptable and even the elderly people accept this as the right thing to do. Therefore, there are different moralities between our culture and the Eskimos. Cook argues that the Projection Error which occurs in this argument is that what the Eskimos do is interpreted as the same act as if an American purposefully left their grandmother on the back porch to freeze to death. But this is not the case at all. If an American did this, his motives would certainly be to murder or at least to cause great harm to his grandmother. The Eskimo, on the other hand, is not murdering the elderly people, but acting out of kindness. Due to the harsh conditions in which they live, elderly people often have a very difficult life. Therefore, leaving them to freeze is an act of kindness in that it relieves them of unnecessary suffering. It is, then, more akin to assisted suicide for the terminally ill than it is to murder. Despite the religious and legal barriers to this practice in our own society, assisted suicide is considered by many to be a morally kind act. Cook, then, argues that it is often a lack in properly understanding the *motives* behind actions that leads to the Projection Error of seeing similar acts where in fact they are quite different. Moral relativism, Cook concludes, is a result of this error.

The third critique Cook makes of moral relativism is that by relying on the notion of enculturation as a defense of relativism, anthropologists have portrayed human persons as near automatons. Melville Herskovits is perhaps the main proponent of enculturation as one of the founding reasons for and soundest defenses of relativism. As Herskovits put it in describing relativism, the "force of the enculturative experience channels all judgments" (1958: 270). Because, in the relativist's view, all judgments, as well as all knowledge, beliefs, perceptions and practices, are culturally learned, Cook argues that there is little, if any, room for internal moral critique of a society. For if everything is culturally learned, there is no freedom or choice or place from which to judge those very learned behaviors and ways of being (Cook 1999: 36–8). Indeed, if it were true that all of our judgments, knowledge, beliefs, perceptions, and practices were culturally learned, that would more or less render us cultural automatons who were trapped within what Hallpike calls the tyranny of culture (2004: 31). Herskovits himself seems to acknowledge this unfortunate consequence of relativism when he writes: "There is, indeed, some reason to feel that the concept of freedom should be realistically redefined as the right to be exploited in terms of the patterns of one's own culture" (quoted in Hallpike 2004: 31). In other words, Herskovits saw quite clearly that the centrality of enculturation to moral relativism leaves little or no room for internal moral criticism or debate, and therefore, for no possibility of change. As we know from innumerable examples, this is clearly not the case.

The fourth critique of moral relativism by Cook is that relativists are not radical enough because essentially they have the same narrowly conceived view of morality as do moral absolutists (1999: 125–30). Cook makes four points regarding this. First, moral relativists, like absolutists, represent "morality as being concerned only (or at least primarily) with actions." In doing so, some of the most important moral material, such as thoughts, beliefs, and emotions, is entirely left out of moral theorizing and analysis. This will be quite clear in the majority of the anthropological examples we will discuss in this book. Second, both moral relativists and absolutists describe morality as consisting of moral principles and rules. For example, in describing moral relativism Hatch writes: "It is the *content* of moral **principles**, not their existence, that is variable among human beings" (Hatch 1983: 9, italics in original, bold indicates my emphasis). Or Fiske and Mason on the commensurability issue: "there must be some sort of consistent, predictable *mechanism for resolving* *the conflicting claims* of two or more moral **principles**. This may be a coherent set of lexical **rules**, or it may be some other kind of mediating set of application **rules** that specifies which **principle** is applicable to a given issue in a specified context" (1990: 134). Or Shweder on the importance of formulating a position that there is more than one rationally defensible moral code: "Every moral **code** that is rationally defensible (to the extent that any moral **code** is rationally defensible) is built up out of *both* mandatory and discretionary **concepts** and **principles**" (1990: 210). We should also remember Firth's definition of morality from the last section, where he defined it in terms of a "set of principles," "moral rules" and "right" and "wrong." As can be seen from these examples, Cook is right to point out the assumption by most relativists, an assumption also held by most absolutists, that morality does in fact consist of a set of rules, principles, codes, and concepts (for further critique on the conflation of morality and rules, see Wolfram 1982).

Third, Cook points out that both moral relativists and absolutists treat "the words *right, wrong, good, bad*, and *ought* as the primary moral terms" (1999: 130, italics in original). Again, this is something we will see throughout this book, and I agree with Cook that we must get away from it. I will come back to this presently. Fourth, Cook also points out that both relativists and absolutists share the idea that our supposed moral principles are "external, non-personal in their origin" and that this "implies that one's role in morality is limited to that of following rules (or applying principles) which one had no hand in fashioning." This too I will address presently, but it should be pointed out that this is closely related to Cook's critique of enculturation. For if all moral judgments are culturally learned, then clearly no individual person has any part in their own moral lives. Again, this is something with which it is difficult to agree.

Here I would like to briefly further explore Cook's final two points, that of the shared moral vocabulary of both moral relativists and absolutists and the non-personal nature of morality assumed by both of these positions. The first point, the need to expand or change our moral vocabulary, comes from close attention to the ways in which moral debates and dilemmas are dealt with in everyday life. Rarely do we hear people talking about what is good or bad or right or wrong. Certainly this is true for my own research on the moral conceptions and articulations of people living in both Moscow and St. Petersburg, Russia. Instead, everyday moral talk tends to use such descriptive words as fair and unfair, dishonest, cruel, steal, and lie. It is even not uncommon for moral articulations to come in phrases or narratives. And as Cook puts it, if one does make a statement such as "Well, it's just wrong," then we might very well think that this person is unable to articulate his own position or that his position is in the end indefensible (1999: 134). If relativists could adopt this new descriptive moral vocabulary, then it would put them in a better position not only to describe local moralities more adequately, but also to separate themselves from moral absolutism. It is just this kind of vocabulary I suggest anthropologists of morality take up.

The second point is on the non-personal nature of morality. As we have seen, the standard relativist position is that one's morality is acquired by means of enculturation. As such, each person has no part in shaping their own moral lives. But as Cook points out, "it is a serious moral deficiency in a person to be unable to reflect on and reexamine attitudes and practices that he or she was brought up to accept unquestioningly" (1999: 137). Consider our attitude toward the young Nazi soldier who attempts to defend himself by claiming he was only following orders, or perhaps more appropriately, the young slaveholder in the mid nineteenth-century American south who is unable to reflect on the immorality of slavery despite the abundant criticism of this practice all around him. We do not accept their excuses for not being morally self-critical, so then, why do we feel compelled to be more lenient about this with non-Western peoples?

It is perhaps impossible to be morally self-critical if we conceive of morality as a set of principles and rules that must be learned and followed. But if instead morality is conceived of, as I will try to argue throughout this book, as the acquired attitudes, emotions, and bodily dispositions of a person throughout their life, then it becomes easier to see how in fact one can be morally self-critical. If morality is conceived in this way, it is still possible to say that morality is a social practice, for it is with social groups and in being social with others that persons have the kinds of experiences that lead to the acquisition of these attitudes, emotions, and bodily dispositions that we can call morality. This morality, however, does not consist of principles and rules, but instead is a bodily way of being in the world that is continually shaped and reshaped as one has new and differing life, that is, social experiences. Thought of in this way, then, a moral person can be both morally self-critical as well as critical of her social world. It is just this kind of morality that I will try to point out in the various works that I discuss in this book, even if the authors of these works do not view morality in this way. Therefore, while doing my best throughout this book to present the works of various authors as they themselves have presented them, I will continuously be questioning whether a better analysis of their research may have been based on a more experiential view of morality.

One important concept, which I will introduce throughout the book, that will help us understand the importance of this experiential view is what I call a moral breakdown (Zigon 2007). The theory of moral breakdown makes a distinction between morality and ethics. While this distinction will be made clearer in the closing chapter, I will briefly outline it here. Morality, on the one hand, is a kind of habitus or an unreflective and unreflexive disposition of everyday social life. This embodied morality, is not thought out beforehand, nor is it noticed when it is performed. It is simply done. It is one's everyday embodied way of being in the world.

Morality can also be considered at the discursive level. That is to say, we can speak of morality as those public and institutionally articulated discourses, such as those of an organized religion or state structures, of what is considered, by the speaker of this discourse, as right, good, appropriate, and expected. This discursive morality, then, is publicly articulated and influences the moral lives of those persons who have some kind of social relationship with these discourses, but they should not be considered as being representative or deterministic of any actually lived embodied morality.

Nor should this discursive morality be considered as representative or deterministic of the kinds of ethics persons perform. Ethics, then, is a kind of reflective and reflexive stepping-away from the embodied moral habitus or moral discourse. It is brought about by a moral breakdown or problematization (Foucault 1984: 388). This occurs when some event or person intrudes into the everyday life of persons and forces them to consciously reflect upon an appropriate ethical response. Ethics, then, is a conscious acknowledgment of a moral breakdown, or what we can also call an ethical dilemma, which necessitates a kind of working on the self so that one can return to the unreflective and unreflexive comfort of the embodied moral habitus or the unquestioned moral discourse. It is in the moment of moral breakdown, then, that morality, as both lived and embodied and discursively articulated, becomes a conscious question or dilemma and leads to a person or persons ethically working to overcome this question or dilemma.

This theory forces the anthropologist to find moments of moral breakdown to study. When we speak of moral breakdowns we can no longer simply speak about the morality of a person or group of persons, instead anthropologists of moralities must focus upon the problematization of morality. For it is at the intersection of morality and ethics, at this breakdown, that it becomes possible to see how morality plays a role in the everyday lives of the people we study. Once again I will remind the reader that this distinction between morality and ethics, and the moral breakdown that is vital to this distinction, is one that I make. It is not articulated by the authors whom I will discuss throughout this book. So when I make this distinction or discuss a moral breakdown, this will be my own interpretation offered to make a work more understandable, and not one offered by the original author.

Having said this, then, it is clear, despite my criticism of moral relativism, that to some degree I am in fact myself a moral relativist. I would, however, have to say to the degree that it is possible I am a radical relativist with a touch of universalism. I too, then, feel that tension that I described above. For while I do believe that the process of becoming moral persons is to a great extent universally shared by all persons, and this is a process about which I will say more in the conclusion, I maintain a position of radical relativism in my stance that moral dispositions are personally acquired by means of social experiences. That is to say, in a very real way, I maintain that each person to some degree has their own morality based upon their own experiences. It is the fact that experiences are limited within a range of possibilities structured by a socio-historic-cultural context that makes these various and differing moralities recognizable and translatable to others. It is to this process of recognition and translation that anthropologists of moralities must be particularly attuned.

It should be clear, then, that I do not consider there to be either one morality shared by all persons within a society, or anything we can objectively and definitively say is moral or belongs to morality. This is true despite my use throughout this book of such misleading terms as "morality," "the moral realm," and "moral world." These terms are used primarily because we lack a vocabulary that would allow us to avoid their use. They are also the terms commonly used in much of the material discussed in this book. Therefore, with much caution, I too use these terms. Nevertheless, the reader should keep in mind, and I try to make this clear as often as possible, that I believe it is much more useful to think of moralities as either the public and institutionally articulated moral discourses found in every society, or the negotiable and contextually manifested embodied sensibilities that have been shaped over a lifetime of experience within a socio-historic-cultural range of possibilities. Throughout this book, then, when I speak of moralities it is this that I have in mind.

Outline of Book

The strategy of this book is to review recent attempts at an anthropology of moralities in order to, on the one hand, assess the various ways in which this has been done, and on the other hand, to find positive aspects of these various approaches in order to suggest how we can move forward in this important anthropological study. In order to do this, it is important to first consider the main philosophical approaches to morality that have been central to moral philosophy for the last 2,000 years, as well as how some of the founding figures of the social sciences conceived of morality. This, along with a discussion of the more recent social philosopher Michel Foucault, will be vital for understanding how anthropologists have approached morality in their own research and analysis. We will consider these foundational works in Chapter 1.

Chapters 2 through 6 will consider how anthropologists have studied morality as it is related to various more traditional anthropological topics: religion, law, gender and kinship, medicine and health, and language. Breaking the chapters down in this way is of course dangerous, for it risks suggesting that morality should be associated, in full, with one or all of these particular topics. As I have already made clear above, this is one of the main mistakes anthropologists have thus far made in their studies of local moralities. Instead, we should realize that local moral worlds at one and the same time transcend any one of these particular realms and also are *partly* informed by them. For example, morality as conceived by many of my own informants (who are rehabilitating injecting drug users at a rehab center run by the Russian Orthodox Church in St. Petersburg, Russia) is certainly partly informed by Church doctrine and priests' lectures and advice, but this is only part of it for them. For some, gender also plays a role, for others it doesn't. The job of the anthropologist is to discern by means of deep ethnographic research what does and does not make up the moral world of their informants. However, because many of the anthropological studies so far done on moralities do in fact focus on one of these main anthropological themes, I have decided to break up the chapters in this way. As we move through the chapters we will have an opportunity to see both the positives and negatives of such an approach.

In the concluding chapter, rather than providing a summary or conclusion of the book, I will take the opportunity to suggest how we can take what has been learned and use it to improve both our theoretical and methodological approach to the study of local moralities. This will be done by making a real distinction between morality and ethics and showing how this distinction is vital for future research in the anthropology of moralities.

Part I
The Philosophical and Theoretical Foundations
of the Anthropological Studies of Morality

–1–

The Philosophical and Theoretical Foundations of Social Scientific Studies of Morality – From Plato and Aristotle to Durkheim, Weber, and Foucault

In many ways the original question of philosophy is: what constitutes the moral sphere? Since Western philosophy's origins in ancient Greece, morality has been a central concern of philosophers. Because philosophers have been struggling over questions such as what constitutes the moral, what is the good life, and, indeed, what is the good, for over 2,000 years, anthropologists of morality could benefit from a thorough understanding of this philosophical history. Due to limitations of space, however, this is not the place to introduce this history to anthropologists. Nevertheless, in the first section of this chapter I will provide a brief overview of the four main theories of moral philosophy. These overviews are in no way comprehensive and serve only as the most basic of introductions in order to provide a background for anthropologists who may not be familiar with these theories and their respective traditions. They also serve as a background for better understanding the context in which Durkheim and Weber's social scientific theories of morality were created, as well as the ethical writings of Michel Foucault. I will turn to these theorists in the later sections of this chapter.

Philosophical Theories of Morality

Virtue Theory

If it is true that theories of morality reflect the sociohistorical context in which they are conceived, this is particularly so for virtue theories. To some extent this is the point of virtue theory. For unlike the other predominant moral philosophies we will discuss, virtue theory is specifically focused on individuals' character and how this character fits best into a social context (Pence 2000: 256–7). While these theories often address the relation between virtues and society, they tend to have two major shortcomings. First, the society to which their authors tie the virtues is often an idealized or utopian society, and thus a society that does not, and indeed, most likely will never exist. Second, and perhaps closely related to the first and certainly

23

true of all the moral philosophies we will discuss in this chapter, the authors seem to be unaware of their own sociohistorical assumptions of moral behavior and how this significantly influences their moral theories. Because of this unawareness, then, the virtues posited by these philosophers tend to be particularly esteemed virtues in their own societies, but written about as if they were only to be realized in a state of idealized social relations. It is for this reason that virtue theory must be considered with caution. For what at first glance may seem particularly appealing to anthropologists may in fact be so only because it is a reflection of our own closest held assumptions.

As its name suggests, virtue theory focuses on the description of particular virtues that are posited as characteristics of living a good life. Some of the virtues that have consistently been upheld by philosophers of this tradition are courage, temperance, wisdom, and justice. Since its beginnings in ancient Greece, virtue theory has generally claimed that these virtues become imbued in a person by two means. First, by means of rational decision-making. To act virtuously, so it is argued, is the most appropriate way to act in a given situation and this is obvious to any rationally thinking person. It is through the proper use of reason that one can act virtuously. But one is not always able to reason and think in the ethical moment. Oftentimes due to time constraints, one is unable to rationally consider the best course of action. It is for this reason that most virtue theorists argue for some kind of embodied virtuous disposition. In other words, the virtuous person is not the one who must always rationally consider the best way to act in each situation. Rather she is the person who already "knows" how to act in any situation she may encounter. This is so because she has already, through a lifetime of ethical training, acquired the virtuous dispositions that allow her to act ethically. That is, she can act virtuously because she has the embodied character of a virtuous person. Only after the fact, if need be, can she reflect on her actions and rationally know that she acted appropriately because it was the rational, that is, virtuous thing to do. In this way, then, to speak of embodied virtues is to speak of an embodied rationality.

Although virtue theory has its Western philosophical roots in the teachings of Socrates and the writings of Plato, it was Aristotle in his *Nicomachean Ethics* who is most closely associated with this ethical theory. Arguing against the ethical doctrine of Plato, which posited an abstract Form of the Good and Justice as the end of a virtuous life, Aristotle argued that what is virtuous can only be determined in specific situations. Because what might be considered courageous in one situation might be considered reckless or cowardice in another, individuals must exercise practical reason in order to discern the appropriate way to act in each situation. It is only after years of such discernment that one acquires the bodily dispositions of a virtuous person. For Aristotle, whether one acts virtuously in any given situation due to the use of practical reason or by means of an already acquired virtuous disposition, to act virtuously is always to act according to the mean. This is his famous doctrine of the mean. By this Aristotle meant that what counts as virtuous in any given situation is the mean between two extremes of possible action. Thus, as already pointed out, to act courageously is to act according to the mean between recklessness and cowardice in any given situation. Again, what action constitutes this mean differs in each situation.

For centuries virtue theory fell out of favor in philosophical circles, but at the end of the twentieth century it has made a comeback. One of its main proponents is Alasdair MacIntyre. MacIntyre has taken up Aristotle's notion of the good, which both define as "the goal, purpose, or aim to which something or somebody moves" (MacIntyre 1998[1966]: 57). While Aristotle focused on the means by which an individual could achieve the highest possible good for any human being, which he called *eudaimonia* often translated as happiness, MacIntyre focuses his attention on the ways in which individuals can achieve their own particular good within the context of their own lives. Because these lives are always lived within a particular community made up of even smaller groupings of peoples, MacIntyre argues that one's life can only have meaning by means of actively participating in and cultivating the practices of these particular communities and groups. Thus, the good or the *telos* to be sought for each person depends upon the practices, communities, and traditions to which they belong. Therefore, the virtues that lead to the good life for a doctor are different than the virtues that lead to the good life for a plumber. Nevertheless, because each belong to the same greater community or society, they will still share some notions of which practices and how they are to be performed can help constitute the good life.

As will be seen, virtue theory is unique in the philosophical tradition in tying what counts as ethically good to a social context. As a theory, virtue theory appears promising for anthropological studies. And it is certainly true that several anthropologists have recently turned to some version of virtue theory to help explain the moral (e.g. Hirschkind 2001; Widlock 2004; Mahmood 2005). Nevertheless, the question is rarely asked if this is actually the way in which individuals either conceive of or perform their moral lives. Indeed, before so quickly adopting virtue theory for their own purposes, anthropologists need to consider if this theory adequately explains what we find in our research, or if it simply conforms to our own assumptions about the social nature of morality. As with all anthropological questions, this can only be answered through research.

Natural Law

Although often associated with Christian ethics and jurisprudence, natural law theory has its origins in the pre-Christian world of Stoic thought. Its clearest and certainly most influential proponent was the Roman lawyer Cicero. For Cicero, as with the other Stoics, the natural law unifies all being – from the lowest animals to the gods. Moreover, "since there is nothing better than reason, and it is found both in humans and in god … we humans must be considered to be closely allied to gods by law" (Cicero 1999: 113). The natural law, then, is manifest in human nature as reason. The natural law for humans, however, is not simply any use of reason, for reason can just as well be put toward evil ends, but true "law is right reason, consonant with nature, spread through all people" (Cicero 1999: 71). Thus, natural law theory unites all of humanity as moral beings through the right use of reason.

If Cicero is the most important Stoic natural lawyer, then certainly St. Thomas Aquinas had the most influence on natural law theory in general. By combining Christian theology with the Roman legal tradition – particularly the natural law tradition of the Stoics – and the philosophy of Aristotle, Aquinas provided a philosophical foundation for natural law theory. The result was not only the foundations of a rationalized Christian ethics, but also the basis for the eventual secularization of the natural law tradition. I will here briefly outline the main principles of Aquinas's theory.

According to Aquinas there are four manifestations of law. These four laws are, as is consistent with Aquinas's more general theory, unified and interrelated. For it is the eternal law of God that orders and is imprinted upon all of being, and therefore, is the principle law of all creation. Human beings as rational creatures "are under divine providence in a more excellent way than the others since by providing for themselves and others they share in the action of providence themselves" (Aquinas 1988: 46). This rational participation in the eternal law is what Aquinas calls the natural law. For Aquinas, though, this rational participation is limited by human nature. Therefore, the natural law is the eternal law to the extent that it is within the nature of humans to participate in it. The third kind of law is in turn derived from the natural law – this is human law. Human laws are those laws which accord with natural law and are created to govern human communities. Any law that is not arrived at by right reason and does not accord with the natural law is not human law but a corruption of law. Lastly there is divine law. Divine law is necessary because it is beyond the capacity of human nature and natural law to guide humankind to its ultimate end, that is, to eternal bliss. Therefore, revealed divine law is necessary for this achievement.

What concerns us here, however, is Aquinas's notion of natural law. As was already said, natural law exists because of the imprint of the eternal law on all human beings equally. As created beings in the world, humans are subject to the same law of the order of being as all others. This law, to simplify just a bit, can be narrowed to the "natural inclination [of each being] to their proper actions and ends" (Aquinas 1988: 46). The unique rational capacity, at least unique in this world, of humans allows them a privileged access to this law and the ability to know and strive to reach their end. The natural end for humans is happiness through the exercise of the virtues. However, this is not happiness in a hedonistic sense, for when Aquinas says happiness he simply means, as did Aristotle, the ultimate end. With this use of happiness Aquinas suggests along with Aristotle that we fully realize our humanity not through the pleasures of this world, but through the rational accumulation of virtuous dispositions.

The first precept of the natural law is that "good is to be done and pursued, and evil is to be avoided" (Aquinas 1988: 49). This is indeed a vague and general precept that raises many questions for moderns on the nature of good and evil. But Aquinas believed that it was proper to be so. For the "precepts of the natural law are related to the practical reason as the first principles of [logical] demonstration are related to the speculative reason" (1988: 48). It seems that he envisions moral human action as a deduction from first principles to the specifics of the situation.

Aquinas, then, presents a theory of natural law that is not a simple rule- or law-based system. Similar to the virtuous person of Aristotle, the acting individual in each case must discover how best to implement the natural law in the moment. It is through the right use of reason that Aquinas and most natural lawyers argue this is to be done. Because natural law is shared by all persons as rational beings, this theory unites all humans in their ability to be moral. But its influence goes further. Because all persons are said to be endowed with this natural capacity, so too are they endowed with certain rights. It is this notion of rights as a necessary consequence of natural law that has been most influential not only in latter day moral philosophy, but also in national and international politics.

Deontology and Kant

Unlike the other theories we are discussing, all of which to some extent are concerned with the consequences or the ends of human action and behavior, deontological theories of morality are not. Taking its name from the Greek *deon*, or duty, deontology focuses on a rather narrowly focused set of rules, laws, or constraints, which all persons are obliged to follow. Deontological theories, then, are prescriptive. The philosophers who espouse this position argue that humans already know which acts are morally wrong, and thus are obliged not to make these transgressions. Notice, however, that this position is not concerned with the consequences of acts. Thus, for example, we already know that it is morally wrong to intentionally tell a lie. Therefore, we can never do so even if by telling this lie we can relieve the suffering of the person to whom we lie, or to be a bit more provocative, if we could save the lives of the person to whom we lie and his family. In other words, for a deontologist it is morally wrong to tell a lie even if this lie could save the lives of an entire family, but it is morally correct to tell the truth even when we know beforehand that this lie will lead to the death of that family. It is for this seeming unconcern with consequences, and what might be called situational sensitivity, that has led many to critique deontological theories of morality. Yet, deontology remains one of the dominant moral theories in contemporary philosophy, and as we saw in the introduction, the notion of rules and codes that come from deontology have been very influential on anthropological views of morality. This is so mainly because of the overwhelming importance of Immanuel Kant to modern philosophy and his contribution to moral theory.

Kant argues that the failure of past moral philosophers has been a result of searching for moral principles in experience, and as a result, propagating false foundations for morality. Kant sees propositions such as moral sentiment, happiness, and "the ends justify the means" as problematic because they are based on experience and therefore conditional. Kant believes that in order to secure morality against such conditional foundations it must have an a priori source that renders it universal and necessary. By universal and necessary it is meant that morality must hold true for all humans as rational beings at all times and places. It is for this reason that an a priori morality often dictates an action that is counter to the inclinations. For the inclinations are conditional and drive the will to act according to the particular situation of the moment. Whereas, Kant argues, a universally valid moral law must be followed in every instance regardless of feeling, inclination, context, or consequence.

According to Kant, then, morality is only possible when the will determines action in accordance with the moral law. Since the will is reason in its practical use, the will is properly thought of as self-determined when it follows this law. But how is it possible that the will can determine itself, and indeed must do so in order to make morality possible? Morality is possible because all rational beings through the faculty of understanding are endowed with a conception of law. This law properly understood is the law of nature, which is the understanding's ordering of sensibility. In other words, it is this ordering of sense data that makes experience possible. It is because of the understanding, therefore, that rational beings have an a priori notion of law in general. That is to say, reason is endowed with the *form of law*, such that, all rational beings are able to conceive of the formula of a possible law. In other words, as endowed with the conception of the form of law in general, rational beings for practical purposes may consider themselves lawmakers in their ability to fit their subjective maxims to the form of law.

Since humans are impure rational beings, they will often act according to subjective maxims that are conditional. It is for this reason that they must be commanded to follow the law. This command, which takes the form of a categorical imperative, is not the moral law itself, but merely indicates the conception of the form of law. This conception allows the will to act according to the law as if it knew the law in itself. But reason does not give the moral law a definite content; for the moral law has no referent in the sensible world, thus, it may never be known in experience. Reason simply gives the formula for the form of law in general by which the will may conceive of a possible moral law. This formula is the categorical imperative, of which there is only one, although it has several formulations. The categorical imperative is: "Act only on that maxim whereby thou canst at the same time will that it should become a universal law" (Kant 1949: 38).

What does this imperative mean? Simply put, a will must consider its maxim *as if* it were a law of nature. That is, confirm the maxim's compatibility with the form of law. Such a maxim could actually become a law of nature if the will had the ability to make it so. According to Kant the simplest way to decide if a maxim could become a law of nature is by testing it against the law of contradiction. No law of nature can contradict itself; therefore, neither can any maxim that a will considers a moral law. An example of a maxim that may be tested by the form of law is the following: to make a promise I know that I will not be able to keep. This maxim is quickly discovered as an immoral act when I attempt to consider it as a universal law of nature for all rational beings. For if it were the case that to make a lying promise was a universal law of nature, this would simply result in the absolute dissolution of all promises; since if all promises were lies, there would in fact be no promises at all. It is therefore evident that my maxim, that I may make a lying promise, could never become a law of nature because it breaks the law of contradiction. Thus, this maxim will never produce a moral act. The categorical imperative, therefore, commands the formula with which all subjective maxims must be tested. This test determines whether the subjective maxim conforms to the form of law, that is, a maxim must be capable of being conceived of as a law of nature in order for it to have validity as a moral act. It is in this way that Kant speaks of moral agents as self-legislating and autonomous.

But what is the motivation to act according to this form of law no matter the consequences? Kant claims that respect is the only proper motivation for morality. Respect, so says Kant, is a self-wrought, rational feeling that all persons have only for the moral law. But it is odd that Kant, who so meticulously constructs a moral theory founded on rational nature, would have its proper employment depend upon a feeling. Kant claims, however, that respect is not a feeling of the same kind as the feelings of inclination or even moral sentiment. It is properly understood as an a priori and rational feeling. The feeling of respect is brought on by the recognition by an individual that his will is subject to something beyond the conditional inclinations of his sensibility. This self-wrought feeling is, simply put, respect for the moral law. Respect comes about, however, through the recognition of the subordination of the will to a law. By means of this recognition self-conceit, or self-interest, "breaks down" and becomes humiliated (Kant 1996: 94). As such, the feeling of respect more closely resembles pain than pleasure. In this sense, it is interesting to consider respect as a feeling brought forth through the recognition of a lacking or a nothingness; a feeling, perhaps, more astutely described by Heidegger with the idea of being guilty "as being-the-ground for a being which is determined by a not – that is, being-the-ground of a nullity" (1996: 261). In any case, for Kant it is ultimately a feeling closely resembling pain that is the only proper motivation for following the moral law and thus acting morally. It is interesting to contrast this idea with the utilitarians, to whom we will turn next, and their concern with pleasure and happiness.

Consequentialism

While the deontological theories of morality are concerned with intentions, consequentialism, as its name suggests, is concerned with the outcome of individual
acts. Intentions may be important, but what really counts for moral behavior, so
consequentialists argue, are the results. Consequentialism, then, "is the view that
whatever value an individual or institutional agent adopts, the proper response to
those values is to promote them" (Pettit 2000: 231). Two of the values that have been
central to consequentialist theories are pleasure and happiness. A consequentialist
would argue that all things being equal, one's particular act or behavior in general
should result not only in a greater amount of pleasure or happiness than pain or
sorrow for oneself, but also for others. Although the consequentialists have often
been accused of being hedonists for holding pleasure and happiness as the greatest
good in their moral theory, this critique is often misguided, for by pleasure or
happiness most consequentialists simply mean something like quality of life or
well-being. That these notions are rather vague is perhaps one of the fundamental
weaknesses of this theory.

One of the most important "schools" of consequentialism is utilitarianism.
The utilitarians have argued that "utility" is the highest value to be promoted. For
these philosophers "utility" simply means "usefulness" (Goodin 2000: 242). While
the early utilitarians argued that it was pleasure and happiness that had ultimate
utility, twentieth-century utilitarians have tried to move away from this so-called
hedonist utilitarianism. Preference utilitarians, for example, have argued that beyond
pleasure and happiness individuals or institutions should act so as to satisfy and
promote their preferences. These utilitarians, however, say nothing about which
preferences should be preferred over others, instead they simply maintain that no
matter the preferences, it is morally appropriate to satisfy them once they are held.
The problems of this position are obvious, for it seems to be potentially even more
hedonistic than the pleasure and happiness utilitarians, and perhaps could even lead
to rather evil results.

Welfare utilitarians, on the other hand, have tried to get away from this desire-
satisfying type of utilitarianism, and instead have tried to give a theory that will
promote the welfare of a society or group of people. The danger with this version
of utilitarianism, however, is that in attempting to move beyond the satisfaction of
individuals' desires and focus on the welfare of the group, it could potentially allow
for the imposition of unwanted or even unseemly acts against particular individuals
for the purpose of providing greater welfare to the group. As can be seen, then,
utilitarians of the twentieth century have been struggling with one of the main
questions raised by consequentialism in general, and utilitarianism in particular,
namely, the relationship between the individual and society. This question goes back
to the beginnings of utilitarianism.

In the nineteenth century utilitarianism was the predominant moral theory in the English-speaking world. This was so particularly because of the writings of Jeremy Bentham in the eighteenth century and John Stuart Mill in the nineteenth. It was Bentham who forever united utilitarianism with the concepts of pleasure and happiness. For Bentham, acts and behavior could only be judged on whether or not they resulted in an increased sum of pleasure for either the individual or the social group. For Bentham, then, utility amounted to the principle of the greatest happiness for the greatest number. MacIntyre claims that Bentham held this principle because the latter saw that there is a logical impossibility for a metaphysical theory of morals (1998[1966]: 234). In other words, there is no criterion by which acts can be judged other than their consequences. And because it is obvious to any honest observer that pleasurable results are better than painful ones, this can be the only criterion for moral acts.

It was this principle of utility that was inherited by J. S. Mill. Mill, however, tried to take this principle further. While Bentham is famous for his claim that "quantity of pleasure being equal, pushpin is as good as poetry," Mill attempted to make more subtle distinctions between kinds of activities. For Mill there are both higher and lower pleasures – poetry being a higher and pushpin being a lower pleasure. Mill also addressed the question of what should be done in those many cases when it is not clear which act would result in the more pleasurable outcome. Mill's response is that the principle of utility holds only in those cases when it is clear. This, however, is the same as saying that there is another criterion by which such actions can be judged, and renders utility a secondary principle of judgment. This is certainly not what Mill had intended.

Despite the problems with utilitarianism it was, as I have already said, the predominant moral theory of the nineteenth century and remains influential in philosophy today in its various modern forms. Perhaps one of the reasons this is so is because in many ways it is a theoretical statement of modern liberal society's most cherished assumptions. What counts as good, on the one hand, is the result and not necessarily the intention – liberalism is very practical – and on the other, the well-being of individuals. Because in the liberal view society is nothing other than the sum total of individuals, if all individuals are acting so that the outcome will satisfy their own desires or preferences, and the result is their increased happiness, then society as a whole will ultimately be happier. The utilitarian slogan of the greatest happiness for the greatest number, then, relies upon a moral invisible hand for its realization. It was just this idea that Emile Durkheim found especially troubling. As we will see in the next section, Durkheim's moral theory was particularly aimed at debunking these utilitarian assumptions.

The Roots of a Social Scientific Theory of Morality

Durkheim

Emile Durkheim dedicated his life to establishing sociology as an accepted and respected academic discipline. Although his main works were not explicitly dedicated to the topic, he considered sociology to be what he called a science of moral facts. What he meant by this, however, is a bit ambiguous. In this section we will take a look at Durkheim's theory of morality, considering how it can be understood in light of the philosophical traditions about which we just spoke, and anticipating the influences it would have on the anthropological tradition.

Durkheim's moral theory, or as he might put it, his science of moral facts, is in large part a response to two of the moral philosophical schools – those of utilitarianism and Kantianism. As a student in Paris, Durkheim became highly influenced by the Kantian philosopher Charles Renouvier. As Thompson points out, Durkheim was attracted to Renouvier's "uncompromising rationalism" and "his central concern with morality and the need to study it scientifically" (2002: 30). Durkheim was particularly interested in the question of the possibility of human freedom in a world of determining laws. As we will shortly see, this question became central to his moral theory. He also learned from Renouvier that the a priori categories of Reason by which Kant claimed the world was ordered could in fact be altered through human means. While for Renouvier these means were individual will and choice, Durkheim would eventually interpret this sociologically and claim that these categories differed between societies and were thus socially determined (Lukes 1977: 56–7). Although this interpretation was most clearly established in Durkheim's classic work *The Elementary Forms of the Religious Life*, it is also central to his views on morality.

In many ways, then, Durkheim's sociology and moral theory can be seen as a sociological interpretation of Kantianism. He is much less disposed toward utilitarianism. Indeed, his entire body of work can be read as an attempt to dethrone the then predominant sociological, economic, and political theory of utilitarianism. His primary adversary in this struggle was Herbert Spencer, the most influential sociologist of the mid nineteenth century and a utilitarian. From Durkheim's perspective, Spencer's sociology was little more than an intellectual expression of the time's prevailing ideology. Its emphasis on the individual and an evolutionary framework that posited social evolution as a coherent extension of natural evolution were for Durkheim not only expressions of ideology, but were part of an abstract sociological theory that was not adequately supported with documentation (Thompson 2002: 17). By contrast Durkheim's sociology and theory of morality place society central rather than the individual, remain evolutionary, but make a distinction between natural and social evolution, and claim to be based solely on the observation and analysis of social and moral facts. Throughout this section, then, it will become clear that Durkheim's theory of morality is primarily aimed at debunking the predominant theory of utilitarianism at the time, which as we have already seen, claims that the foundation of morality is the individual's pursuit of happiness.

The topic of morality is not a central focus in any of Durkheim's major works. It is, however, often just offstage, directing if you will, the main themes of the works. In a sense, each of them can be seen as addressing the moral problem of reconciling individual freedom and social order (Thompson 2002: 71). It was not until late in his career, however, that he turned to writing a book explicitly on the topic of morality. Unfortunately, he died after completing only the introduction. Nevertheless, while his position that morality is essentially socially determined is certainly clear throughout his major works, it is in lectures on moral education and a discussion paper delivered to an audience of philosophers that Durkheim lays out his theory of morality. It is on these two lectures that I will focus my explication.

It seems obvious that the most influential aspects of Durkheimian morality for many anthropologists have been gleaned from his occasional discussion of the topic in his major works, for example, his claim in both *The Division of Labor in Society* and *Suicide* that social solidarity is not only an essential element of morality, but indeed its very source (Miller 2002: 56). Likewise, his claim in *The Elementary Forms* that our categories of thought, including our moral beliefs, differ from society to society has served as a foundation for relativist notions of morality. Because these categories and beliefs are at their core established through religious structures, practices, and rituals, morality has its origins, so Durkheim claims, in religion. It is these features of Durkheimian morality, then, that have been most influential on anthropological views of morality. Nevertheless, it is important to see how these core features have been expanded upon and critically thought through in order to understand more deeply how Durkheim theorized morality.

It is quite likely that few anthropologists are familiar with either the series of lectures most probably written in the years 1898–9 and published posthumously as *Moral Education*, or the discussion paper given to a group of philosophers in 1906 in which Durkheim most clearly lays out his theory of morality. *Moral Education* is a series of lectures given to students of pedagogy on how to integrate moral teaching into a secular education. The posthumously published book is in two parts. The first outlines Durkheim's theory of morality; the second shows how this theory can be integrated into educative practices so as to teach children a proper and secular morality. I will focus my analysis on the first part, that is, the theory, while drawing from the discussion paper "The Determination of Moral Facts" in order to provide further insight.

Morality, so Durkheim argues, consists of three essential elements – discipline, attachment to society, and autonomy (1961[1925]). The first part of *Moral Education* is dedicated to the analysis of these three elements. While he claims that he has discovered these three elements by means of analyzing specific moral beliefs and behavior – or what he might call moral facts – most of what he presents in the first part of the book is a formal analysis of morality as such. In other words, Durkheim provides an abstract theory of morality that, so he claims, provides the formal structure of the various historical and socially differing moralities (1961[1925]: 33). Thus, while Durkheim argues that the *content* of various moralities differs both historically and socially, the *form* of all moralities remains the same.

The first element of this universal form of morality is discipline. Indeed, what Durkheim calls "the spirit of discipline" is "the fundamental element of morality" (1961[1925]: 31). It would seem, then, that without discipline neither of the other two elements nor morality itself would be possible. What is this discipline? In many respects it is similar to Aristotle's virtue ethics of the mean. In claiming that discipline does not restrict the development of one's constitution, Durkheim provides several examples of how going beyond a moderate amount of certain activities, such as eating, walking, and loving animals, can be viewed as a "disease" (1961[1925]: 38). Durkheim not only draws an analogy between these kinds of activities and morality, but in fact closely ties them together, for when individuals morally discipline themselves in such a way that they limit the range of possibilities within which they can acceptably behave, it "not only buttresses the moral life, properly speaking" but also "performs an important function in forming character and personality in general" (1961[1925]: 46). "In fact," he continues, "the most essential element of character is this capacity for restraint ... which allows us to contain our passions, our desires, our habits, and subject them to law" (1961[1925]: 46). Thus, discipline "forms about each person an imaginary wall," in the face of which the excesses of human passions are halted (1961[1925]: 42).

Morality, then, despite being in part constructive, is essentially restrictive. This is so because discipline encompasses two aspects of morality – regularity and authority. That is to say, because morality regulates behavior and holds absolute authority over the individual, these two aspects are combined in the more complex element of discipline. While in the *Moral Education* Durkheim emphasizes this more restrictive combination, in "The Determination of Moral Facts" he strikes a balance between the authoritative or obligatory nature of morality and what he calls its desirability. It is because of its desirability that one feels as though it is good to act morally. It is proper here to speak of this as a feeling, for with the notion of the desirability of morality, Durkheim attempts to bridge the gap between the rationality of following the obligatory duty of morality and the actual lived experience of performing moral acts and behavior because it is considered to be good. In "Moral Facts" Durkheim explains away the duality of obligation and desire by linking them both to the true source of morality, that is, society. In *Moral Education*, on the other hand, where he doesn't speak of desire but instead speaks of authority/obligation and regularity, this duality is linked by discipline.

This discipline, however, cannot be for purely selfish ends, as Durkheim claims the utilitarians argue. For morality can only have impersonal ends. These ends, however, cannot be for other individuals qua individuals. Rather, in order for morality to be both regulating and authoritative it must have a supra-individual source and object. Whereas, this supra-individual source was traditionally seen as God, Durkheim claims that in fact it is society itself. Thus, anticipating his conclusions of *The Elementary Forms*, Durkheim concludes that because God is nothing other than a projection of society itself, it is in fact society that is the source of morality. Therefore, even though morality was originally intimately tied to religion, it is in truth bound to the structures of society. As Durkheim puts it, "the domain of the moral begins where the domain of the social begins" (1961[1925]: 60).

But what is the social? In "Moral Facts" he defines society as "above all a composition of ideas, beliefs and sentiments of all sorts which realize themselves through individuals. Foremost of these ideas is the moral ideal which is society's principal *raison d'être*" (Durkheim 1953: 59). Setting aside the adequacy of this definition, it is clear that for Durkheim society exists for the purpose of authoritatively regulating behavior through morality. Morality, then, is equated with society. There can be no real distinction between the two. It is this claim that has been the main obstacle to anthropologists explicitly studying morality. For if anthropologists either intentionally or implicitly follow Durkheim in assuming that morality and society are somehow equated, then the question arises of just how one can anthropologically study morality as a distinct set of beliefs and practices. As will become clear throughout this book, this question has not yet been adequately answered.

But if morality is essentially equated with society, Durkheim is clear in stating that every individual in fact belongs to several societies, each of which has their own morality, for he considers such groups as the family, the nation, and even humanity as distinct societies. While individuals are certainly bound by the moralities of each of these societies, there is in fact a hierarchy among them. Thus, because the family is subordinate to the nation, and humanity has as of yet not organized itself into any one coherent group, the nation has priority in terms of being the ultimate authority and source of morality. It is here that Durkheim begins to become interesting for considering moral plurality. If a society of people can be made up of multifarious smaller "societies," for it should not be assumed that the family is the only one, then it becomes possible to envision a society of people consisting of multifarious moralities. The question that needs to be asked, then, is whether or not Durkheim was correct in positing a hierarchy of these moralities. This can only be answered through further research.

Durkheim makes clear that the two essential elements of morality so far discussed – discipline and attachment to society – are necessary elements of the form of all moralities. He is less clear about the third element of autonomy, for while to some extent he seems to associate autonomy with human nature itself (here is where Durkheim begins to conflate two versions of human nature, one a priori, the other social), he also makes it very clear that autonomy is lacking in the habituated morality of non-modern peoples. It is only in the modern context, so he claims, that moral autonomy becomes possible.

Here the question must be asked: what is this autonomy? Durkheim's Kantianism becomes clear at this point. He claims that we "do not regard an act as completely moral except when we perform it freely without coercion of any sort." He continues: we "are not free if the law by which we regulate our behavior is imposed on us, if we have not freely desired it" (Durkheim 1961[1925]: 112). Nevertheless, Durkheim argues that this is not the kind of freedom of which Kant spoke. As we have already seen, Kant posited freedom, or autonomy, as following the moral law of which oneself as a rational being is the author. Durkheim misread this as a claim that the free will stood outside of nature in order to make moral decisions. But for Kant this moral law of which all rational beings are the author is merely the form of law, the very same form by which the laws of nature are also rationally ordered. In this way, then, the moral law for Kant is of the same order as nature. This is precisely Durkheim's position. He simply replaces Reason with society, and in doing so provides the latter with the same categorical and moral legislative priority and authority as Kant gives the former. Like Kant, then, autonomy for Durkheim is the individual freely choosing to act according to that moral law which he recognizes as having ultimate authority and thus worthy of respect. For both Kant and Durkheim one is autonomous not because they could have chosen otherwise, but because they chose the only way they rightly could have without coercion.

Durkheim, however, goes even further in positing the role of a science of moral facts in the historically progressing role of autonomy to morality. Because according to Durkheim autonomy, although seemingly an essential element of the form of morality, only progressively manifests itself in moral reasoning and behavior as a society becomes more complex, a proper science of moral facts can further advance the progress of this manifestation. By rationally analyzing moral facts, science – that is, sociology – can make available the insights that allow individuals to become increasingly morally reflective. Such reflectivity will be learned by individuals by means of education and other public discourse. Thus, according to Durkheim, in a society where morality, aided by sociology, is secular and rational, individuals will no longer, as they are in non-modern societies, be constrained by the habits of morality, but instead, through their understanding of the reasons of morality, can freely choose to act accordingly because of this understanding.

What is interesting about Durkheim's notion of autonomy is that it opens a space for individual differences of morality. Indeed, he acknowledges that although there is a common morality held by all members of a society, each one of these members also holds their own particular morality. Each "individual has, to a certain extent, his own morality. Even where conformity is highest, each individual constructs, in part, his own morality. Each one of us has his own inner moral life and there is no individual conscience that exactly translates the communal moral conscience" (Durkheim 1953: 78). If this is already the case without a heightened sense of autonomy instilled in persons by a science of moral facts, then how much more could this be the case with the reflective autonomy provided by this science? Durkheim, nevertheless, rejects the possibility that morality is purely individual and holds to the position that each of these individual conceptions is a personal interpretation of the collective social morality. Whether or not this is true, of course, remains a research question.

As we have seen then, Durkheim's explicit theory of morality focuses on the form that morality as a universal phenomenon takes. This form consists of three essential elements – discipline, attachment to society, and autonomy. It is interesting to note that although Durkheim clearly considers morality a set of rules that are to be applied to specific situations (1961[1925]: 26), these three elements and the way in which he discusses them are more reminiscent of a morality of dispositional cultivation than a rule-bound morality. As he puts it, "morality is a totality of definite rules; it is like so many *molds* with limiting boundaries, into which we must pour our behavior" (1961[1925]: 26, my italics). Rules for Durkheim, then, are that which mold and shape individuals. It would seem that they are not, as Durkheim puts it, living and operating "around us" (1961[1925]: 26). Rather, they live and operate *within* us by means of the discipline and autonomy that not only society imposes on each person, but that each person imposes on herself. We will have several opportunities throughout this book to see how this occurs.

Weber

With Durkheim we see an explicit attempt to construct a sociological theory of morality. This attempt is less obvious in the work of Max Weber. A contemporary of Durkheim, Weber is the most important of the historically minded, interpretive sociologists of late nineteenth- and early twentieth-century Germany. For Weber the most important sociological question of the day was to understand the historical process by which modern European society had come about; in other words, coming to understand the origins of what he saw as the intense rationalization of not only capitalism and politics, but society in general.

For our purposes this modern, rationalized society was best characterized by Weber as resulting from the separation of fact and value. To some extent facts are equated with rationality and values with irrationality. For us, perhaps, it would be more useful to think of facts in terms of practices and values in terms of meanings. In some ways the rationality/irrationality dichotomy still holds, but with a slightly different connotation. According to Weber's scheme, then, factual practices should be thought of as rational practices, that is, as rule-bound, coherent, compatible, and consistent practices for the purpose of realizing a specific and well-defined end. Weber's most famous example of a factual, rational practice is that of rational capitalism.

On the other hand, Weber's notion of meaningful values posits these values as irrational in at least three ways. First, because for Weber all value choices are to some extent equally valid, they are necessarily irrational. The equal validity of each of these values is not, however, a moral judgment, it is only a logical judgment. This is simply to say that because value-positions are irreconcilable, they are necessarily irrational. Secondly, because each individual must choose from this array of equally valid values, this choice must necessarily be an irrational choice. Because each of the values are equally valid on their own terms, and therefore there is no objectively rational reason for choosing one over another, the choice must be at heart an irrational one. And, finally, because these meaningful values do not necessarily lead to or guarantee the realization of a specifiable end, they are irrational. Weber's most famous example of a meaningful value is that of religion. Thus the fact/value distinction made by Weber is best thought of in terms of rationality and irrationality only in terms of the practices and meanings being evaluated and not according to some objective standard of rationality.

It is not uncommon that Weber's notion of meaningful values is interpreted as morality itself. For example, Thiele claims that Weber "uses the term value as a synonym for morality, so, in his schema, morality is pitted against factuality" (1996: 98). This interpretation, however, results in an ever-widening gap between morality and factuality, or morality and practice. It is not clear that this is what Weber was getting at. While it is true that Weber did see an increasing divide between the realm of fact and value in the modern world, this did not necessitate the loss of morality in the modern world. This is so because, for Weber, values do not equal morality.

Weber, in fact, does not define morality in any explicit way. Nor does he assign it specifically to the world of values or to the world of facts. By maintaining this ambiguity Weber may actually be clearer on his notion of morality than it appears at first glance. For by not assigning morality to either the world of values or facts, he is actually placing it outside both. This is not to say that for Weber morality is a transcendent category that holds moral authority over both worlds. Instead, Weber sees morality as the interconnecting link between fact and value. Morality for Weber, then, is the everyday lived relationship between fact and values, or between practice and meaning.

Because morality is the relationship between fact and value, it can only be defined formally. Its content, on the other hand, will always change according to which values are chosen and which practices are being performed. This does not mean, however, that Weber was a defender of opportunism. In response to the self-interested person who chooses different values and different practices, and thus, different moralities, in each situation, Weber would most likely claim that this person has not really chosen at all. He lacks what Thiele has called genuineness (1996), for Weber's argument seems to be that it is only in the genuine or consistent adherence to one's values in the performance of various practices can one live a moral life (Factor and Turner 1979: 329). This genuineness is what Weber referred to as living according to one's calling. Having chosen a particular set of values, and having chosen or found oneself within a particular world of facts, one is called to act in certain specific ways. To live according to this calling, then, is to live a moral life.

This notion of living a moral life through a calling is clearly seen in one of the last lectures he gave – "Politics as a Vocation." I will not go into too much detail in my analysis of this lecture, but for our purposes will focus on the latter part of it where Weber delineates the distinction between an ethics of ultimate ends and an ethics of responsibility. The true politician, the politician, as Weber puts it, who lives "for" politics with passion, responsibility, and proportion, is the person with a calling for politics (1958: 115–17). To have a calling, one must have what Weber calls "faith." This faith is always for some idea or value that serves as motivation of one's activity in the world of facts. To have a calling, as I have already pointed out, is to live according to a faith in a certain set of values.

It would be a mistake, according to Weber, to believe that just because one has a calling her morality must always aim toward the ultimate end of her chosen values. Indeed, Weber sees this kind of ethics of ultimate ends as naïve and completely unattached to the world of facts. In other words, it is irresponsible vis-à-vis the kinds of practices one must perform, and the people with whom one must interact, as an adherent to a certain calling, in this case politics. This is so, argues Weber, because an ethics of ultimate ends rarely, if ever, brings about the actual ends hoped for, since they are so often impossibly met in the realities of everyday life. Thus, this ethics is in reality an ethics of good intentions, and the consequences be damned.

What is much more appropriate for the person of calling is an ethics of responsibility. The responsible person answers for her deeds. She too may hope for the best possible outcome, but also realizes that sometimes these outcomes are only possible through not so moral acts. By taking responsibility for all of her actions, she can consistently and coherently maintain the path of her calling. In other words, and paradoxically, the person who acts by an ethics of responsibility more closely follows her chosen values than does the person of ultimate ends. In doing so, she enacts her values in the world of facts – and indeed this is morality for Weber – no matter the consequences, for this is what one must do if they have genuinely been called to have faith in a certain set of values. Notice here the influence of deontology on Weber's thought. As Weber himself points out, though, this person is actually precariously balancing an ethics of ultimate ends with an ethics of responsibility. It is this balance that is the true character of the person who has been called to politics. For in keeping the ultimate end in sight, the true politician must sometimes use extraordinary means in the hope of reaching it. No matter the means or the consequences, the true politician, the called politician, must above all take full responsibility for her actions.

The true significance of a calling to Weber's notion of morality is undoubtedly seen, however, in his most famous work *The Protestant Ethic and the Spirit of Capitalism*. This work has long been misunderstood as a description of the religious roots of capitalism (Thiele 1996: 136–7). But throughout *The Protestant Ethic* Weber is clear that forms of capitalism far pre-dated Protestantism all around the world, and that his analysis treats "only one side of the causal chain" (Weber 1999[1930]:

27). Weber, then, is not concerned with explaining the origins of capitalism, but with understanding why a certain form of capitalism so quickly and easily became assimilated into the lives of some Europeans during a specific historical moment. In doing so, Weber is not explaining the origins of capitalism, but through describing the ascendancy of rational capitalism is in fact coming to understand the historical shift from a focus on meaningful values to rational facts. For the modern world, including capitalism, according to Weber, is characterized by the predominance of rationality.

This rationality is possible because of the calling each of us in the modern world feels. As Weber puts it, "one's duty in a calling, is what is most characteristic of the social ethic of capitalistic culture, and is in a sense the fundamental basis of it. It is an obligation which the individual is supposed to feel and does feel towards the content of his professional activity, no matter in what it consists" (1999[1930]: 54). Whether one is a capitalist entrepreneur, a proletariat factory worker, or a bourgeois intellectual, one has a relationship not only to one's work but to the world of facts as a whole by means of a calling. This calling is intimately felt and obliges one through duty to act in certain ways. This calling, then, as the bridge between the world of facts and values, is the foundation for morality.

If this calling as the moral foundation is the bridge between the world of facts and values in the modern world, what are these two worlds that are bridged? The world of facts, as already mentioned, is the world of practices. It ranges from capitalistic organized business to the factory floor, from government bureaucracies to familial relations, from intellectual institutions and work to military organization and strategy. The world of factual practices *is* the modern world in which we live and act.

The world of values is not so easy to describe. And it is this world that Weber attempts to get at in *The Protestant Ethic*. What makes it particularly difficult not only to describe, but to understand is that the values that inform the factual practices of the modern person may not be the ones they think they are. In other words, one may not be conscious of the actual values and the origins of those values that motivate one's practices. One may not be aware of the roots of the obligations and duties one feels in their calling. It is these roots that Weber attempts to uncover in his work.

While the modern world, according to Weber, feels itself as disenchanted, its core values have their foundation in religion, specifically what he calls the worldly asceticism of certain Protestant sects. Calvinism, Weber argues, took a unique approach to the question of the eternal salvation of the fallen human being. Unlike Catholicism, which teaches a never-ending cycle of sin and redemption, Calvinism teaches the doctrine of predestination. By God's grace, and by it alone, one is saved. More specifically, this grace is predestined; it is already established before one begins life in the world. Because of this, whether one spends the eternal afterlife in the paradise of heaven or the agonizing depths of hell has nothing to do with how one acts and lives in the world. For one's place in eternity has already been predetermined. Not only can one do nothing to help assure their place in paradise, neither are there any signs of who is saved and who is not.

What is one left to do in this state of inhumane loneliness (Weber 1999[1930]: 104)? Weber claims that Calvin's answer to this question is to worship God. This is done not only through formal means of worship such as church attendance, but also by means of the everyday following of God's will. This can most accurately be done by following one's calling in life, specifically, by doing one's profession well. Because Calvinists believed their lot in life was given to them by God, they believed they were worshiping him to the utmost by performing their tasks in life as best they could. Weber claims that this notion eventually led to the idea that one could prove their faith through their worldly activity (1999[1930]: 121).

Even though Calvinism's notions of predestination and calling led to intense concern for worldly activity (that is, the practices of the world of facts), it shunned any enjoyment of this world. Work was to be done for the sake of work, not for the material enjoyments it could produce. Monetary profits were not to be used for the purchase of luxury material goods, but were to be reinvested in work so as to more effectively worship God. This is the worldly asceticism of Calvinism. This asceticism is also seen in the rational method of this everyday form of worship. Weber points out that rational methods of working on the self had long been a part of Catholic monastic life, but this was a life separate, and in a sense, transcendent to the world of factual practices. Calvinism, for the first time, brought this method into everyday social life. One could most efficiently worship God through work in the world by doing it rationally. With Calvinism, then, Weber argues that we see for the first time the combination of religion and rationality in the everyday world of facts. It is in this combination found in the form of a worldly asceticism that Weber sees the roots of rational capitalism.

The spirit of capitalism, according to Weber, is this very Protestant work ethic minus God. The morality of this ethic, which has now become the morality of capitalism, remains, but it no longer has its roots in its founding values. For this world of values has been left behind in the ever-increasing importance of the world of facts in the modern world. This modern world and its facts, according to Weber, have become disenchanted. No longer understanding the meaningful values behind their morals and their practices, modern humans are now stuck in an iron cage. As Weber puts it, the "Puritan wanted to work in a calling; we are forced to do so" (1999[1930]: 181).

In sum, what can be said of Weber's notion of morality? First it cannot be equated with his notion of values. As I have suggested, morality is best thought of as the bridge between the world of facts and values, or practices and meaning. It is closely associated with the idea of a calling, for it is with a calling that a person closely binds herself to a particular set of values and facts. While Weber focused on the increasing rationality of the modern world in *The Protestant Ethic*, it is perhaps more helpful to consider the importance of his lecture on "Politics as a Vocation." For it is here that we see the plurality of the modern world. There are multifarious "choices" for the modern person to make in terms of in which meaningful values and in which factual practices she will participate. Thus, very similar to the neo-Aristotelian virtue theory of MacIntyre, Weber posits a moral theory that holds different duties and obligations, virtues and responsibilities, and ends and means according to which world of facts and which world of values one is called to live in. In this way, then, Weber delineates a theory of morality that is at one and the same time personal and social.

Foucault

Although Michel Foucault should be counted as a contemporary social theorist (in fact, he was a philosopher and historian) and not as one of the founding figures of modern social theory, there is no doubt that his writings on ethics have been central to the way in which many anthropologists have recently approached their studies of local moralities. For this reason, it is necessary to include him in this chapter and section, for in a very real way Foucault can be seen as a foundational figure in the recent anthropological study of moralities. This will become abundantly clear as we move through the book.

What is also clear is that Foucault's approach to the study of ethics is in some ways very similar to that of both Weber and the Aristotelians. Indeed, this is not surprising since most of what Foucault wrote about ethics focused on the ancient Greco-Roman writings and practices of ethics, as well as the early and medieval Christian literature and practices, much of which was influenced by the former. In addition, Foucault acknowledges Weber's part in inspiring his thinking on ethical questions, especially that concerned with what he calls technologies of the self (2000a: 224).

The first thing that is important to point out about Foucault's work on the topic is the distinction he makes between morality and ethics. Morality is the code or the rules that a society, or to be more precise, social institutions claim and attempt to impose on its members (Foucault 2000b: 263). These moral codes determine which acts and behaviors are permitted and forbidden, as well as their respective positive or negative value. Morality, then, can be seen as the publicly expressed code of proper and expected behavior and acts by such social institutions as the Church, law, or culturally endorsed social relations, e.g. proper sexual relations or medical and psychological normality.

Foucault does not give much attention to morality in his writings. Instead, he focuses his attention on what he calls ethics, which he defines as "the kind of relationship you ought to have with yourself" (2000b: 263), or as he put it a bit more provocatively elsewhere, ethics is "the conscious practice of freedom" (Foucault 2000c: 284). I will get back to this notion of freedom shortly, but for now it is important to see that for Foucault ethics is the way in which individual persons make themselves into morally appropriate persons. That is to say, ethics is the way that persons *consciously* work on themselves so as to become the kind of person who is recognized within their community as a moral person. In this way, then, Foucault, like I said of Weber above, views ethics as both a personal and a social process.

This is so because of the necessity of freedom to Foucault's idea of ethics. If ethics is the conscious practice of freedom, then there can be no ethics without freedom. But what is this freedom? Foucault is never very clear on this, but I think we can discern some possible meanings from his writings. Foucault writes that freedom "is the ontological condition of ethics" (2000c: 284). By this he means that ethics, that is, conscious working on or caring for oneself, is not possible if there is not some kind of choice available. A person must have some kind of freedom of choice – and it would seem that this choice must go beyond the simple duality of choosing to act rightly or wrongly – in order to ethically work on oneself. Therefore, if we make the assumption of some extreme relativists that each society only has one morality, then in Foucault's view there can be no ethics in that society because there is no freedom of choice. Throughout this book I will suggest that this freedom of choice takes the form of a certain limited range of possibilities available to all persons within a society, this is a notion with which I believe Foucault would have been comfortable. Because this range of possibilities provides a choice, and indeed, a choice must arise in particular situations for certain reasons, this freedom that allows ethics also allows for reflection. In fact, Foucault calls ethics "the considered form that freedom takes" because freedom, in order to be ethical, must be a consciously aware freedom that reflects on itself in order to do proper ethical work (2000c: 284). For Foucault, then, one is always consciously aware that she is doing ethical work on herself.

A second meaning of freedom in Foucault is a person's freedom from herself. What does this mean? Because so much of Foucault's ethical writings focus on ancient and early Christian ethics, it is very hard to separate his own theory of ethics from that of the sociohistorical ethics that he is describing. For instance, for the ancient Greeks it was very important for a person not to be a slave to one's own desires and passions. While Foucault does not necessarily attempt to sketch out a universal notion of ethics, he does clearly suggest that his notion of ethics – that is, conscious work on the self – is something that is likely characteristic of all societies. Therefore, it is likely that although this ethics will take various forms depending on the time and place, each will put a value on the person being free of something in order to properly do ethical work. Therefore, while for the ancient Greeks it may have been freedom from desire and passion, for people living in other societies it may be something like freedom from the influence of other persons, or freedom from material interests, or freedom from non-religious interests. It is the task of the anthropologist, I suggest, to discover just what it is each society expects their members to be free of. This will go a long way toward discovering the kind of ethics they live by and the kind of moral world they inhabit.

These two notions of freedom suggest another aspect of Foucault's ethics that is very important, namely, the fact that Foucault sees ethics as a creative process. He often refers to ethics as an aesthetics or as working on the self as a process of working on art. The artist must have freedom to choose how she will do her work, as well as freedom from particular constraints that will stop her from reaching her goal (these are the two kinds of freedoms I just discussed). The same is true for the person who is ethically working on herself. Indeed, Foucault claims that "we have to create ourselves as a work of art" (2000b: 262). This is an important aspect of his ethical theory because it entails the claim that there is no original self that must be set free or revealed in order to be morally authentic or free. The self is created by means of ethical work; it is not there already to do the work. Thus, as opposed to the majority of ethical theories, which depend upon a prior authentic self to find certain predetermined ways to be moral, Foucault claims that there is no prior self before ethical work is done. The self in its various forms (and it is important to note that he refers to the self as a form and not a substance) is the result of ethics.

How do these various forms of the self come about? Foucault argues this is done by means of what he calls technologies of the self. Again, while Foucault only considers various technologies of the self from the ancient and medieval world of Europe, he claims that there are in fact technologies of the self in all societies (2000a: 277). Technologies of the self "permit individuals to effect by their own means, or with the help of others, a certain number of operations on their own bodies and souls, thoughts, conduct, and way of being, so as to transform themselves in order to attain a certain state of happiness, purity, wisdom, perfection, or immortality" (2000a: 225). These technologies, then, are the means by which persons do ethical work on themselves, and as already said, Foucault claims some form of these technologies are found in all societies.

While this may be true, Foucault is perhaps the first to acknowledge that Western philosophical views of morality, and many anthropological views, for example, the rule-oriented relativism I discussed in the Introduction, have for several centuries disregarded or condemned as immoral any focus on the self. The self in most of these traditions is simply seen as that which must conform itself to some exterior moral expectation. Foucault tells us it was different in the ancient Greco-Roman world where the ethical priority was on caring for the self. It was in the context of this caring for, or working on, the self that technologies of the self are most obvious. However, because Foucault contends that these technologies exist in some form or another in all societies, they remain central to our everyday ethical lives even if they are no longer central to philosophical discourse on ethics.

In his research into the ethical lives of the ancients, Foucault has come up with some of what he considers to be the most significant technologies of the self from this period. In particular he focuses on Stoic technologies of writing letters to friends in which one discloses the minute details of one's everyday life activities; the close examination of the self and the conscience, and the attempt to order one's inner life in an almost administrative kind of way; remembering of the self as a meditation on who one is and what one has experienced, as well as imaginative preparation for future possible life situations; and the interpretation of dreams (2000a: 238–41). He also discusses the importance of public penance and confession in the early history of Christianity (2000a: 242–9). In each of these examples we see how individual persons work on themselves by means of these various technologies in order to become socially recognized moral persons. In each example freedom to some extent is exercised, choices are made and certain actions and behaviors and thoughts are excluded, and most importantly individual persons consciously work to create themselves in a way that they choose to be.

As will be seen, several of the anthropologists I will discuss throughout this book have been influenced by the work of Foucault. I will be upfront from the beginning and claim Foucault as a central influence on the way that I think about morality and ethics and their anthropological study. In particular I find his emphasis on freedom and conscious reflection to be especially important. It is for this reason that I will continually come back to the importance of considering ethical work as happening within a range of possibilities in each context, and that it is these possibilities that allow for such reflection.

Some Final Words

As will be seen throughout the rest of this book, both Durkheim and Weber each have had significant influence on the ways in which morality has been considered by anthropologists. While the influence of Durkheim is clearly more apparent, Weber's place remains and, indeed, is gaining ground in more recent studies. Perhaps not coincidentally, virtue theory is increasingly finding a home in the works of several recent anthropological studies of moralities. Related to this "rediscovery" of both Weber and virtue theory is the obvious importance of the work of Foucault in anthropology in general, and the anthropology of moralities in particular. As we move forward we will have an opportunity to track these influences, as well as question their usefulness. In doing so, we will not only come to a better understanding of the assumptions that guide anthropological studies of moralities, but consider other possibilities for future studies yet to be undertaken.

Part II
Religion and Law

–2–

Religion

As we have seen in the last chapter, both Durkheim and Weber gave primary significance to the realm of religion in their writings on morality. This would come to have considerable influence on the ways in which anthropologists, on the one hand, interpreted the religious beliefs and practices of the peoples they studied, and, on the other hand, went out to the field in order to explicitly study local moralities. In this chapter we will take a closer look at some of the themes around which anthropologists have considered the influence of religious beliefs and practices on the moral conceptions and practices of the peoples they study. As will be seen, these themes and the ways in which this influence is thought to occur are quite varied, and yet the basic assumption of each of the anthropologists in this chapter is that religion and morality are to some extent closely related. As Michael Lambek puts it, "religion provides objects and occasions, no less than models, 'of and for' meaningful, ethical practice" (2000: 313). Let us take a look, then, at some of the ways this relationship has been taken up by anthropologists.

Witchcraft

The practices generally referred to as witchcraft by anthropologists are often interpreted by them as expressions of local moral conceptions. This interpretation stems from one of the earliest and most influential ethnographic studies of witchcraft as part of a moral system, E. E. Evans-Pritchard's study of the Azande of Africa. Although it is true that Evans-Pritchard distinguishes witchcraft from religion, for our purposes it is best to consider witchcraft as moral practice in this chapter.

Witchcraft for the Azande, Evans-Pritchard argues, "embrace[s] a system of values which regulate human conduct" (1968[1937]: 63). It is not, therefore, synonymous with morality, but is a significant concept within Azande morality. As Evans-Pritchard puts it, "'It is witchcraft' may often be translated simply as 'It is bad'" (1968[1937]: 107). As will be seen in this section, witchcraft has been interpreted as an expression of the negative moral dispositions of individuals, which is in turn considered motivation for unjustified behavior towards others, and thus a means of assigning responsibility for particular misfortunate events.

For the Azande witchcraft explains the relationship between individual persons and misfortune. It is not a general state of affairs, but rather is enacted by an individual against another at a specific time. Bewitchment, then, is seen as situational and tied to specific misfortunate events. For example, if one's garden plot is particularly unproductive, or if a hunting expedition is unfruitful, or, as I will discuss further in Chapter 5, if one falls ill, this is the result of witchcraft perpetrated against one and can, with the help of an oracle, be traced back to the bewitching practices of one or more specific individuals.

Individuals bewitch others because of some ill-will they have towards the latter. Thus, witchcraft among the Azande and many other peoples around the world is used if one feels greed, anger, or envy toward another. Witchcraft, then, is an expression of what might be called immoral dispositions and these dispositions are often seen as motivation for the enactment of witchcraft. It is in this relationship between immoral dispositions, motivation, and enactment that witchcraft is seen by some anthropologists as a moral concept.

For example, this relationship can be seen with witches among the Etoro of Papua New Guinea. Raymond Kelly claims that one does not simply become a witch by receiving the seed of witchcraft from a witch. Rather, this seed must be "nurtured by the malice and ill-will in a person's heart. The individual thus bears the ultimate responsibility for the mutation of his soul that makes him a witch" (Kelly 2002: 268). For the Etoro, then, as with the Azande, witchcraft is passed from one generation to the next, for the former by the transmission of sexual fluids during intergenerational homosexual activities, for the latter by familial inheritance. For both, however, whether or not one actually practices witchcraft depends upon the individual and his or her moral sentiments. If one is characterized by good moral sentiments, it is unlikely he will perform witchcraft. On the other hand, if one is characterized by immoral sentiments, then he is more likely to actively pursue witchcraft. As Kelly puts it, a "witch is the epitome of maliciousness [sic] and antisocial selfishness, for he (or she) feeds on the souls and bodies of others out of spite, and with full intent to cause harm; he states his gluttony as well as his hate and grows large and vigorous at others' expense" (2002: 270). Thus, for example, a particularly despised kind of witch among the Etoro is a *sa:go*, or an individual who greedily takes the essential life force of young men, in doing so, not allowing the latter to mature naturally. This particularly disdained greed is seen not only as a transgression against society, but also against nature (2002: 272).

Evans-Pritchard claims that while not all persons are witches, nearly all Azande at one time or another have been accused of witchcraft. It is for this reason that the accusation of witchcraft does not negatively affect the long-term status of an individual within the community (1968[1937]: 114). Rather, a person is accused of bewitching another and held responsible for doing so only in the situation of the misfortune suffered; once the misfortunate event has passed, so too has the accusation lost its social effect. This is so because one of the most significant moral characteristics of witchcraft is that it functions to place responsibility for a misfortune onto a specific individual. For example, if a Zande man has a fruitless hunting expedition, it is quite likely because his expedition had been bewitched by one of his neighbors who for one reason or another has ill-will towards him. Thus, it is this neighbor who is responsible, that is, accountable for the misfortunate hunting trip. However, once the negative effects of the profitless hunting trip have passed, so too has the responsibility, that is, the status of witch, of the neighbor. In other words, once there is no longer a misfortunate event or its consequences to be responsible for, an individual is no longer held accountable as a witch. He retains his status as a socially acceptable member of the social community.

Christoph von Fürer-Haimendorf reports a different attitude among the Gonds of South Asia (1967: 126). Among the Gonds the status of witch remains with an individual beyond the particular situations of bewitchment. It is for this reason, then, that a witch may be driven out of her village. This is so because she is seen as an immediate danger to the village. Nevertheless, she is not completely excommunicated from society and retains her rights as a member of the tribe. In particular, she may still reside in the village of her kin without thereby endangering or polluting those who take her in. Thus, for the Gonds, unlike for the Azande, a witch is not one who has been marked responsible for a particular misfortunate event experienced by another, but is instead considered an individual who regularly transgresses society's rules (1967: 126).

An even more extreme response to witches is written about by Kelly, who claims that at times witches among the Etoro are executed (2002: 268). These two examples, then, show that unlike the Azande situational assignment of the status of witch to an individual, the Gonds and the Etoro see this status remaining with an individual beyond moments of bewitchment and its effects. This suggests that while witchcraft is a means of marking situational responsibility among the Azande, it is a means for the Gonds and the Etoro to identify individuals as having essentially immoral character or dispositions. In each of the cases, however, being marked with the status of a witch is to be marked as one who is responsible for an immoral act or disposition.

Evans-Pritchard suggests that ultimately witchcraft serves to provide for good social relations (1968[1937]: 117). Since one can never be sure who among their fellow Azande are in fact witches, it is best to assume that they are all witches and try to keep good relations. This tactic works because one is only bewitched by a person who already holds negative moral feelings towards you. Similarly, if a person is jealous of his neighbor he may well try to limit the public expression of this feeling so as not to be accused of witchcraft. This double effect of the fear of witchcraft, then, functions to maintain good social relations between Azande.

Lambek and Solway, in contrasting witchcraft with what they call justified anger, tease out one of the characteristics of witchcraft that seems to hold in each of these examples. While the example of anger (*dikgaba*) they give from Botswana is justified and often causes unintentional misfortune for others, witchcraft, so they suggest, is always considered unjustified and intentional (2001: 54, 57). This justified anger is not only sanctioned by the community, but by the ancestors as well. Witchcraft, on the other hand, is not. This holds true in each of the examples provided in this section. Witchcraft, then, is often interpreted by anthropologists as a form of "moral discourse" (Rasmussen 1998) because it provides a means by which a social community can express its contempt for certain kinds of behavior and dispositions. In doing so, these communities erect various explicit and implicit obstacles to the performance of these morally questioned behaviors and dispositions.

Moral Consciousness and the Ethics of Self

One of the ways in which anthropologists consider the influence of religion on morality is through the Durkheimian perspective that religious concepts play a significant role in shaping person's moral worlds. Such concepts as sin, karma, afterlife, and soul, for example, often have a central place in the ways in which people articulate their conceptions and experiences of morality. When considering morality from this perspective, however, it is important to realize that we are talking about how people speak about their morality, not how they actually act. In this sense, then, the study of moral conceptions and how they are influenced by religious conceptions is a study of reported beliefs.

Steven Parish has done research of this kind among the Newar of Nepal and claims that religious and cultural concepts "render the mind capable of the moral knowing required for persons to live a moral life" (1991: 323). He continues by very clearly stating that this rendering "does not mean that people will behave in a moral way." While it is certainly possible, and indeed often the case, that these concepts influence how people act and help guide individuals toward moral behavior, more than anything these concepts provide a way for persons to give meaning to their moral worlds and experience. Thus, one of the primary ways in which religion influences morality is by providing a conceptual framework within which moral experience makes sense.

According to Parish, one of the main religious and moral concepts of the Newar is the heart, which they consider the seat of moral conscience and consciousness. This is so not only because the heart is the locus of cognitive, mnemonic, and emotional experience, but particularly because this is where resides the "god who dwells in the heart" (1991: 319). This god, who is embodied within each Newar's heart, acts as both a moral cause and judge. Knowing that this god resides within their heart, Newar are motivated to act morally for fear of the retribution, or "curse," it will place upon them if they do not. In this sense, then, this god within the heart, as Parish puts it, encourages the "self-monitoring" of moral activity. Because Newar "know" that god dwells in their heart, they have reason to reflexively be aware of how they act in the world.

A similar notion is found among some of the Muscovites with whom I did research. Several of my interlocutors, whether they are religious or not, spoke about the necessity of having god within them in order to be moral. This was at times spoken of, as the Newar do, as god within the heart, other times as a spark of god within, and other times simply as having god in or with you. No matter how it was articulated, the conception expresses the necessity of the internalized embodiment of god for the possible enactment of morality. As one person told me, in order to be moral, "God must be inside you."

This moral conception is closely related to the Orthodox Christian image/likeness distinction. According to Orthodox theology, all humans are born with the image of God within them; it is this image that provides the potentiality for a life with God. The likeness, on the other hand, is the realization of this life, a realization not all persons can achieve. It is the image, nevertheless, that is more significant, for it is because of the image each person has within them that one has the capacity to be with God. It is this capacity that is the foundation for a moral life. It is, if you will, the well from which moral roots can be nourished. It is this religious concept, then, that has influenced the everyday moral conceptions and articulations of many of my religious and non-religious Muscovite interlocutors.

As can be seen, in these two very different cultures there seems to be some kind of shared understanding that in order for a person to be moral, she must have within her some aspect of a god. The question of motivation for acting morally has been a central question of moral philosophers for a very long time. In this cross-cultural example, however, it is quite clear that in the everyday moral lives of both the Newar and some Muscovites the question of motivation is no problem at all. It is clear to them that they are obliged to act morally because in some way their god resides within them. The problem in the everyday lives of these people, then, is not motivation, but enactment. That is to say, how does one who already knows *why* she should act morally *actually do so*? This, perhaps, is the moral question all persons face in their lives.

If persons have a particular kind of moral consciousness, then how do they acquire it? This is a question Parish has considered in much depth (1994). Based upon his research with the Newar, Parish claims that the moral consciousness and personhood of Newar individuals is closely linked to "religious forms" (1994: 188) of meaning and practice. One such form is that of the various rituals of rites of passage persons must go through in the course of their life. In other words, for the Newar moral persons are not created by nature but by ritual (1994: 237). That is, persons are born incomplete and only made morally whole through the process of ritual. Examples of such rituals are *busakha*, or the rite for young boys that establishes a social identity that marks them separate from females and members of other castes, and *kaeta puja*, or the rite for boys that marks them as full members of their social group and caste. Such rituals, among other things, establish not only a new social and personal identity, but also a new set of responsibilities and obligations.

What is particularly important about these rituals from the point of view of the anthropology of moralities is that the ritual is not the endpoint of the moral transformation, but the beginning. The rituals make available, and close off other, certain possible ways of being moral in the social world (1994: 274). In other words, the rituals make available to persons a certain range of possibilities for becoming new moral persons. As will be seen throughout this book, this notion of a range of possibilities is central for considering the ways in which persons conceive of themselves as, are socially recognized as, and form themselves into moral persons. Because rituals establish a certain range of possible moral ways of being, they mark the beginning of the process of moral transformation.

This is so because even though a ritual officially ushers a person into a new social status, identity, and world, and in so doing makes a new range of possibilities available, the person must still come to embody this new moral way of being. This is a process that takes time and work. As Parish puts it, the "rites evoke a personhood that must be developed, sculpted, and polished over time" (1994: 247). This is not only a personal project, but also a social one. For while the self-reflection and self-discipline of the one remaking their moral self is central to this process, so too is the work done on the person by those around him. Thus, for example, a young boy who after going through one of these rituals continues to act in ways that were allowed prior to the rite but not after, is continuously chastised for his behavior and reminded of his new responsibilities and obligations. Thus, the crafting of moral persons through ritual among the Newar is primarily a social process initiated by ritual and effected on the body, mind, and emotions of individual persons.

Much of the anthropology of religion that has focused on local moralities, and especially those concerned with the link between morality, personhood, and religion, has taken a Foucauldian approach. This is perhaps due to the influence of Talal Asad. Asad's work has brought about a focus on the disciplinary practices associated with religion. In arguing against Foucault that the Christian rhetoric of renouncing the self was not a sacrifice of the self, but was instead a means of constructing a "self-policing" and disciplined self, Asad suggests the importance of reorganizing the soul for Christian ascetic practices in particular, and, as it has been used by others, religious practices in general (1993). Mahmood rightly points out that such an approach to the study of moralities does not focus on the moral codes, rules, and regulations, but instead on the ways in which persons establish a relationship between various "constituent elements" of themselves, such as body, reason, and emotion, and particular moral codes and norms (2003: 846).

James Laidlaw has adopted this Foucauldian approach for his study of ascetic practices among Jain renouncers and laypersons in India. Laidlaw makes a distinction between moral codes of obligation and ethical practices chosen by individuals in order to work on and develop certain aspects of their character or self, and focuses his analysis on the latter. In doing so, he claims that rather than being a coherent metaphysical system shared and practiced by all Jains, Jainism consists of a multiplicity of conflicting values and ideals that are chosen and performed by individuals (Laidlaw 1995: 394). What is interesting for us is how Laidlaw examines various projects that Jain asceticism provides to laypersons as a "range of modes of working on, and re-forming, the self" (1995: 151). These projects can be seen, then, in light of Asad's notion of organizing the soul, as a primary tactic for constructing the kind of self one chooses to become.

One of these projects can be seen as centered on the Jain concept of *ahimsa*. *Ahimsa*, which is often translated as non-violence, is considered by many as *the* central virtue of Jainism (1995: 153). Laidlaw argues that *ahimsa* should not simply be thought of as pacifism, but instead is an ethics of quarantine that seeks to avoid bodily contact with other life-forms, in particular the innumerable microscopic life-forms living all around us. The most common way this ethics is practiced by laypersons is through diet, and it is through diet that Jains come to think of themselves as distinctively Jain. Unlike renouncers who hold to very strict dietary rules, ideally leading to a fast to death, laypersons choose from a variety of different dietary and fasting options. These include the avoidance of forbidden foods, not using seasoning, eating only once a day, setting a numerical limit on the kinds of food to be eaten, and drinking only filtered water. Each of these practices is a way for Jains to perform the ethics of quarantine that is *ahimsa*. For in doing so, they avoid the microscopic life-forms that are found on certain kinds of food and in water. Dietary practices are important ethical performances for Jains, then, because in choosing to follow certain dietary rules Jains train themselves to be more aware of the world in which they live, a world inhabited by innumerable microscopic life-forms, and the kinds of relations they should have with these life-forms. In other words, through dietary practices, lay Jains are able to practice the virtue of non-violence or *ahimsa*.

Another religious practice that has moral significance for many peoples is prayer. Prayer is more than communication with or verbal expression of reverence for the gods, it is also a means of social relationship with other persons, gods and also the self. Prayer takes many forms, and depending on how it is uttered, may have various results, intended or otherwise. For example, prayer spoken aloud with others around may in fact be said just as much for the other human listeners as it is for divine listeners. Similarly, silent prayer can have results on the speaker of the prayer beyond that of expressing faith. Prayer, then, in certain circumstances can be seen as a moral practice as well as a religious practice.

Joel Robbins has made just this point in his discussion of prayer among the Urapmin of Papua New Guinea. Since the late 1970s the Urapmin have been ardent followers of charismatic Protestantism and this shift of religion has led to interesting ways of utilizing prayer. The Urapmin traditionally do not hold the same understandings of language-use that is typically associated with Western modernity and Protestantism. In particular, they do not hold the assumption that words spoken are truthful references of the speaker's intentions. Words for the Urapmin are not necessarily trustworthy. Prayer, however, has become a kind of speech that is trusted.

This is so because for the Urapmin prayer is seen as a kind of ritual (Robbins 2001: 907).

This is important for the Urapmin because it is in ritual that committed action is thought to take place. Thus, if prayer is considered as ritual, then it too is an act of commitment. As an act of commitment, prayer is a special form of speech that allows, so Robbins contends, Urapmin individuals to constitute themselves as responsible and truthful subjects (2001: 906–7). It is thought that because God can see one's intentions, and if prayer is, at least ostensibly, directed toward God, then prayer must be truthful since one would never lie to God. This reasoning is particularly important for public prayer. For one of the ways in which prayer is utilized in public is for the purpose of apology. Traditionally, because of the distrust of the link between speech and intention, verbal forms of apology are not trusted among the Urapmin. However, when apology takes the form of prayer, it can be trusted because in prayer one's intentions are truthfully expressed.

As can be seen, prayer plays a significant moral role for the Urapmin in at least two ways. First, it constitutes a responsible and truthful subject. In doing so, it allows an Urapmin individual to not only understand himself as a moral person, but also others to see him in this way. Second, prayer allows for the mediation of social relations, such that tensions and disputes are more easily settled through public prayerful expressions of apology. The Urapmin example, then, shows how a religious practice can be intentionally and unintentionally utilized for other, in this case, moral purposes.

If Urapmin Pentecostal Christians constitute themselves as committed persons through prayer conceived as ritual, then some American Pentecostals also attempt to constitute themselves as committed persons but through the eschewing of prayer as ritual. Instead, according to Shoaps (2002), members of the Assemblies of God, an American Pentecostal organization, proclaim a discourse of personalized, or spontaneously created, prayer as the only way of "earnestly" expressing one's faith. Thus, this earnest expression of faith through spontaneous, non-ritualized, forms of prayer is central for constructing themselves as true persons of faith. For the Pentecostals studied by Shoaps, to be earnest true persons of faith is to be "touching heaven" (2002: 52–3).

The idea of earnestness as touching heaven has two connotations. First, those who do not pray the way these Pentecostals do, do not touch heaven. This is suggested in the way in which the pastors of the Assemblies of God speak about ritualized prayer and those who use it, such as Roman Catholics, in a negatively evaluative manner (2002: 51). Second, to touch heaven through personalized, earnest prayer is to engage in a personal, communicative relationship with God (2002: 54). Thus, to pray in this way is to be, or to create, the kind of person who has this kind of relationship with God. These connotations, then, show how for these American Pentecostals spontaneous, non-ritualized prayer is an ethical tactic for creating an earnest individual who is able to have a personal relationship with God.

Prayer was also described by one of my interlocutors in Moscow as a communicative relationship, or *obshchenie*. She described prayer to me as a direct petition to God in particular moments of moral dilemma. Thus unlike the more ritualized versions of prayer that are common in Russian Orthodox Church services, and the kind that are shunned by Assemblies of God pastors, this ethical tactic of petitionary prayer is informal, situational, and personal. When this Russian Orthodox woman finds herself in a moral dilemma, for example, whether or not she should pay for a train ticket she could get away without paying for, she prays to God for help in resolving the dilemma and looks to him for advice on how to act.

But this seeking of help from God through prayer is not simply asking him to tell her how to act. Rather, because the Russian notion of *obshchenie* implies a dialogical relationship between the two speakers, each of the two is in some way transformed through the process. Thus, prayer thought of as *obshchenie* results in this woman discovering for herself, through the very act of prayer, how she should act in the moment of moral dilemma. She does not claim that God told her how to act. Rather, it is because of prayer directly addressed to God that she is able to figure out for herself how to act. Prayer for this Russian Orthodox woman, then, is a process of what might be called moral reasoning by which she is able to negotiate difficult moral dilemmas. Not only is this a process of moral reasoning, but prayer is also a means for this woman to ethically improve herself. Like the Egyptian women with which Mahmood has worked (2003), prayer is a way for this Russian Orthodox woman to cultivate certain ethical dispositions that can be utilized in future moments of moral dilemma.

Clearly there are various cross-cultural ways of utilizing prayer as a moral practice and as a tactic for ethical self-improvement. Each relies on prayer as a speech-act that verbally, whether aloud or silently, performs certain moral and ethical expectations, reasonings, or practices. But as can be seen from these examples, prayer is not only spoken but it is often also heard by others. Thus, prayer as that which is heard, or listened to, is also a public sign of moral intent and motivation. Prayer, then, is often just as important morally for how it is heard and responded to by others as it is for how it is spoken.

While prayer is a verbal discipline that can have moral and ethical implications for both how it is spoken and how it is heard, there are other religious practices which have their moral significance simply in how they are heard. One such example is provided in the work of Charles Hirschkind, who has focused on the ethics of the aural discipline of listening. In studying a group of young Egyptian men who listen to cassette recordings of Muslim sermons, Hirschkind has found that these recordings provide moral training in ways that go beyond the simple communication of Muslim moral values through preaching. Instead, the process of listening is itself an ethical discipline that leads to the self-improvement of the listeners. Hirschkind's approach, echoing the distinction Mahmood makes, emphasizes the ways in which individuals train themselves through the ethical discipline of listening, and in so doing acquire certain valued ethical bodily dispositions, rather than moral rules or normative beliefs (2001: 638).

These recordings are typically listened to in many different social contexts, for example, by taxi drivers, workers in cafes, and by wives cooking in the kitchen. Nevertheless, listening to sermons can only have their intended ethical results if they are listened to under what Hirschkind calls, following Austin, their appropriate felicity conditions (2001: 633). That is, listening to these sermons can only be ethically improving if they are listened to in the proper way, that is, with attentiveness, intention, and humility. This requires that one already have embodied a certain kind of ethical disposition prior to listening. It is this already acquired disposition that allows further ethical self-improvement.

One of the most important results of this self-improvement is the strengthening of one's will so that wrongful behavior can be resisted. This strengthening of the will leaves one with a calm heart, which perhaps can be interpreted as an assurance that one is acting and behaving properly. This assurance is possible because by listening to the sermons a certain set of ethical responses are typically reported by the listeners, these are: fear, humility, regret, repentance, and tranquility (Hirschkind 2001: 627). These responses allow the listeners to discriminate between proper and improper conduct. In time and with the proper discipline of listening, these ethical responses can become embodied dispositions and may lead one to change their ways for the good. In this way, then, the kinds of ethical skills that are acquired through listening to recorded sermons can be transferred to other social contexts since they have become embodied ethical dispositions, and as such, have become part of who these listeners are.

In this section we have seen various ways in which religious conceptions and practices help shape person's moral worlds and provide disciplinary tactics for ethical self-constitution and improvement. Much of what was discussed in this section can best be viewed as examples of what, as we saw in the last chapter, Foucault called technologies of the self. That is to say, particular ways that individuals work on themselves in order to become a certain kind of moral person. Although according to many traditional moral philosophies, such practices as diet, prayer, and attentive listening would not be considered ethical practices, these anthropologists, following the theoretical lead of Foucault and Asad, have shown for various peoples around the world they are indeed central practices in their moral lives.

What needs to be recognized, however, is that the worlds in which these persons live and these religious and moral conceptions and ethical practices are lived out is, to various degrees, always changing. Because of this, these conceptions and practices also change. In the next section we will take a look at how some of these changes occur in various contexts.

Change, Religion and Moralities

In the last section we saw various ways in which religious concepts and practices influence the ways in which persons constitute and cultivate themselves. These processes can become particularly significant for some persons, and particularly obvious to anthropologists, during times of social and cultural change. While social change is closely tied to institutional change, culture change, so argues Joel Robbins, is best considered as occurring only with value change (2005: 12; 2007). In many cases, for example, in the former Soviet Union and Eastern Bloc, the two cannot be easily separated. It has been argued that it is during times of social and cultural change that local moralities and the practices with which they are constituted can most clearly be discerned and studied by anthropologists (Robbins 2005, 2007; Zigon 2006, 2007).

Social and cultural change does not simply call religious and moral practice into question through the introduction of non-native institutions, practices and values, but it also allows previously non-dominant practices and values to emerge as an option for persons to follow. Whatever the case may be, times of change become times of questioning, for these periods of everyday upheaval often force persons and social groups to consciously confront questions of who they are and who they want to be. Although this is a question of self-identity, it is also a moral question, and it is not uncommon that persons and social groups turn to religion for techniques and practices for answering these questions.

Michael Lambek has provided a portrait of one such person in the African French territory of Mayotte. Mayotte, a small island in the Indian Ocean that voted in the mid 1970s to remain a territory of France, has since been experiencing intense social and cultural change due to this continued relationship. In particular, there has been an increased shift of values away from those traditionally held in Mayotte. In order to show one person's response to this shift of values in the context of social and cultural change, Lambek provides an Aristotelian analysis of Nuriaty, a middle-aged woman and spirit medium who has recently become possessed by the spirit of the last Sultan of Mayotte prior to the French takeover in the mid nineteenth century.

Nuriaty claims that she was originally possessed by the Sultan for the purpose of imaginatively removing from the island one of the buried saints of the territory so as to protect his sanctity in the face of the increasing defilement his grave and shrine were exposed to in these changing times. As a medium of a national hero, however, Nuriaty has increasingly played a significant role in attempts to preserve the island's culture and values. Lambek tries to show, then, that by means of this possession, Nuriaty has embodied both a historical consciousness and a moral conscience.

In making this point Lambek interprets Nuriaty's actions using Aristotle's notions of *poiesis* (crafting) and *phronesis* (practical wisdom) (2002: 35–6). Lambek argues that Nuriaty's actions as a spirit medium can be viewed as a crafting of history. I would suggest, however, that it goes beyond this, for she is also crafting the present. That is, in crafting and articulating a particular kind of history, she is at the same time attempting to reshape the present in a way that is more meaningful for both herself and her Mayotte peers than that of contemporary French and consumer values. More importantly, perhaps, Nuriaty's possession is also an example of *phronesis*. Lambek describes Nuriaty's actions as *phronesis* in the following way: she "is exercising judgment over the situation; she is addressing the contingent by means of values which transcend it; she is articulating a vision of historical actions; she is acting with reason for the good" (2002: 36). In other words, by enacting practical wisdom through her possession by the Sultan, Nuriaty is skillfully acting according to the situation at hand in a way that is not only recognizable but valued by her community. It is in this sense, then, that Nuriaty is not simply resisting the power of French hegemony or enacting agency, but is in fact responding with moral will and courage to the situation of social and cultural change in Mayotte.

The postcolonial situation around the world, much like during colonial times, remains a space of confrontation between traditional religious and moral values, beliefs, and practices and foreign ones. The case of Nuriaty shows that the past is often recycled as a response to this confrontation. In her case, the past takes the form of a historical consciousness that informs and gives authority to her present moral conscience in the face of change. This consciousness can be seen as an imaginative relationship with politico-historical figures that provide such authority.

Wendy James has shown how the past conceived in another way also plays a significant role in the ways in which the Uduk people of the Sudan deal with social and cultural change in their lives. In the twentieth century the Uduk have not only had to deal with international and civil wars, forced migration and colonial rule, they have also faced the challenge of maintaining their religious and moral way of life as foreign religious missionaries, including Christian, Islamic, and Nilotic, have increasingly proselytized among them. In response to this missionary activity, the Uduk have increasingly turned to what James calls their "cultural archive" (1999: 4–6). Borrowing from Foucault's concept of archive, James claims that the Uduk have a "depository of cultural representations" that persist through history and "superficial change" and are the enduring foundation of "past reference and future validation." It is this cultural archive that James sees as remaining the "foundations of [the Uduk] moral world," despite the work of missionaries and their apparent partial success of conversion (1999: 6).

One of the most important uses of this archive by the Uduk is by certain diviners who belong to the Ebony Order. This Order centers on the consultation of an ebony oracle, which because it is always listening is knowledgeable about people's concerns, worries, and sufferings, and reveals to them the appropriate way to deal with these. Here again, as in the last section, we see the importance of listening to moral understandings and practices. Because the Ebony Order provides an authoritative moral voice and foundation based on the cultural archive, James argues, it is the main force keeping the foreign missionaries at bay, and thus stemming change.

While this may be true, the concept of a cultural archive seems misleading. For it suggests the permanence of conceptions and practices that can at times be forgotten and other times reinstituted. Indeed, James certainly gives this impression when she writes that the archive is a "lasting base ... [that] may at times rest dormant but on occasion be drawn upon" (1999: 6). But because, as James herself puts it, this archive is imagined (1999: 12), it is not so much a depository as it is a created past, which has authority because it is seen as having permanence and authenticity vis-à-vis the change brought on by foreign values and practices. Thus, while both the Uduk and Nuriaty turn to a perceived authentic past in order to constitute their moral worlds in the face of social and cultural change, this past is always imagined. Nevertheless, because all pasts are to a degree imagined, this does not take away from the authority of these moral worlds. For it must be recognized that to some extent all moral worlds are imagined worlds.

Change does not only occur due to the influence of foreign political and religious institutions. Indeed change is part and parcel of social and cultural life. For this reason it does not always draw the attention of those who are living through this change. However, when large-scale change occurs within a society, which does happen occasionally, nearly everyone within that society is in some ways affected. One such case is the former Soviet Union. Take the case of Russia. Although Russia has been going through some very obvious changes since the mid 1980s and throughout the post-Soviet period after 1991, in fact, Russia has been experiencing large-scale change to some degree almost continuously since the eighteenth century. All of this change, including the past twenty years, is due to internal reform and revolution and is not externally imposed. Orthodox Christianity, which in one form or another is considered by most Russians to be their religion, has had to adjust in various ways to this change. The moral conceptions and practices related to Orthodox Christianity have, however, not always undergone the same adjustments. Whether they have or not, depends upon which period and what moral conceptions and practices are being considered.

Douglas Rogers has taken on the daunting task of discerning these possible religious and moral shifts and variations since the mid nineteenth century in a rural Russian village predominantly made up of Old Believer Orthodox Christians. In particular, Rogers considers how changing patterns of exchange and accumulation in the post-emancipation, Soviet, and post-Soviet periods have influenced and brought about new dilemmas for properly forming relationships in this world as well as the other world (2004: 31). He focuses his analysis on the divide many of the Old Believer residents of this village make between this world and the next and the proper moral practices associated with each. Similar to the Jains studied by Laidlaw, these Old Believers must deal with the problem of how to live properly in this world of economic transactions and work and yet remain pure enough to enter the other world after death. This is a particularly difficult problem, Rogers claims, because transgression and impurity could not only endanger personal salvation, but also the salvation of those in the community.

Paradoxically, this distinction between this world and the other world remained during the Soviet period despite the Soviet states many attempts to inculcate an atheist worldview, and thus the erasure of the concept of another world. By erecting significant institutional barriers to the practice of religion among younger generations, the Soviets effectively created a divide between the non-practicing younger generation and the practicing older generation. This was the same divide between the working generation and the non-working generation. In creating this divide, then, the Soviet policies toward religion, although a significant change from the policies of the old regime, helped maintain the Old Belief distinction between this world of work and the other world of prayer. Thus, despite the vast social and, to a lesser extent, cultural change that occurred in Russia during the Soviet period, the moral practices associated with these two worlds remained, more or less, intact (2004: 205).

While this may have been the case for Old Believers living in the rural village during Soviet times, Melissa Caldwell describes how Russian Orthodox notions and practices of charity have shifted with the demands of the post-Soviet period. During the Soviet period the Russian Orthodox Church was not permitted by the state to participate in charity activities. Only the state could provide such services. In the post-Soviet period, however, the Russian state is providing less and less charity services and the Russian Orthodox Church is just one of many non-governmental institutions and organizations that are trying to fill the void.

This change in the source of charity has also led to a shift in what Caldwell calls the ethics of benevolence among charity services. One aspect of this change for the Russian Orthodox Church is only providing services to members of the Church. More interesting for our purposes, however, is their increased emphasis on an ethics of self-responsibility. In contrast to Soviet charitable services, which because of its paternalistic tendencies left many Russians feeling that they are entitled to such services, post-Soviet charitable services are trying to teach individuals to take responsibility for their own interests, well-being, and future (Caldwell 2005: 6–7). The Church has also taken this stance toward charity and benevolence and is increasingly providing self-help training and emphasizing personal responsibility, particularly fiscal and reproductive/sexual responsibility, in its charitable work.

Here we see an example of how the Russian Orthodox Church mirrors the broader social and cultural changes taking place in Russia. As Russia makes a transition out of a socialist politico-economic system towards a liberal, market-oriented system, values of individualism and personal responsibility are increasingly touted. These are values that many do not consider to be Russian or Russian Orthodox. But as Caldwell shows, the Church has increasingly taken them up. Thus, here we have an example of how religious and moral conceptions and practices can mirror and change along with broader societal-wide change.

Change does not always occur in one's homeland. Persons can also experience social and cultural change when they themselves move to different parts of the world. As members of a diasporic community, these persons must deal with the question of how to integrate into a new social and cultural setting without entirely giving up their own cultural meanings, values, and practices. Often, integrating into a new community entails shifting one's moral understandings and practices.

Anne Vallely has documented this struggle among diasporic Jains living in Canada (2002). As discussed earlier in this chapter, the central virtue of Jainism is *ahimsa* or non-violence. *Ahimsa* can be seen as an ethic of quarantine that seeks to avoid contact with other living beings. Among Jains, both ascetics and lay, living in India this ethic is for the purpose of self-realization and purifying the soul. It is, as Vallely puts it, liberation-centric (2002: 556). Jains living in Canada are still concerned with the central virtue of *ahimsa*, but for them it has come to have a different interpretation and is thus practiced differently.

As both Vallely and Laidlaw point out, the Indian ascetic practices associated with *ahimsa* are not for the purpose of relieving the suffering of other living beings, but instead are aimed at realizing the practitioner's liberation from *samsara*, or the cycle of death and rebirth. For Canadian Jains, however, *ahimsa* has taken on an Other-oriented focus in its concern for the suffering of other living beings, in particular animals. This shift from a personal to an Other-oriented ethics has led many Canadian Jains to take up environmentalism and animal rights as ethical projects. Despite both Indian and Canadian Jains sharing vegetarianism as a central aspect of *ahimsa* practice, their respective reasons are clearly different. For the former, it remains a way to avoid the killing of other living beings and in doing so to avoid the accumulation of karma that will continue the cycle of death and rebirth, while for the latter it is a way of not being responsible for the unnecessary suffering of animals and the destruction of other living beings in nature. Both interpretations maintain nature as the "moral theatre, within which one's ethical being is established, cultivated, and judged" (2002: 560), yet the way in which this occurs has clearly shifted.

In this example, then, it is clear that religio-moral practices can undergo shifts of interpretation and, indeed even change, when persons move to different social and cultural worlds. Many virtues and practices of the "old world" may remain central to the diasporic community, but they will often receive different interpretations inspired by the new social and cultural context. As can be seen in this section, then, various forms of social and cultural change can affect moral beliefs and practices. From the emergence of market and consumer economies in postcolonial and post-socialist contexts, to the introduction of different religions, to the movement of diasporic communities, moralities shift with the winds of change.

Some Final Words

As this chapter makes clear, religion and morality are seen by many anthropologists as related and intertwined in important ways. Perhaps more than anything else, this reveals the influence of both Durkheim and Weber on anthropological approaches to studying local moralities. This influence is even more obvious when it is noted that several of the studies discussed in this chapter are not explicit studies of local moralities. Rather, morality or ethics is used by the anthropologist in these studies as an analytic tool for trying to understand the religious practices they studied. It is likely that these concepts seemed particularly apt as analytic tools because of the assumption of the close relationship between morality and religion.

While to some degree it is clear that religion and morality are in fact closely related for some societies, social groups, and individual persons, it would be a mistake to assume that this is always and everywhere the case. Indeed, it would seem to be the role of the anthropologist to investigate precisely for whom, when, and how religious conceptions and practice count as moral ones. It seems likely that the outcome of such investigations would reveal that while religious conceptions and practices can at times and for some have particular moral importance, moral conceptions and practices are in fact much broader than their religious influences. This should become obvious as we move further through this book.

–3–

Law

The social theorist Zygmunt Bauman argues that in the gap between actually existing personal inclinations and the assumed way these persons should act if they properly understood their own self-interests, ethical codes can be utilized for purposes of social domination. In modern Western countries these ethical codes take the form of ethical theory for philosophers and law for legislators (Bauman 1993: 16–36). It is this gap, or some version thereof, that anthropologists of law often attempt to study. Their focus of study, however, goes well beyond Western notions of law, legislation, and jurisprudence. Take, for instance, one of the earliest examples of a modern anthropology of law and its relation to morality, Malinowski's study of law, crime, and custom among the Trobriand Islanders (1926). In his study Malinowski shows how there is sometimes a significant distinction between principles of law and what might be called moral sentiments, a distinction which he claims is "tolerated by custom." As will become clear in this chapter, then, law and morality have various relations to one another. It will be our task to consider just some of these relations.

Very broadly speaking, it can be said that anthropological approaches to law investigate "enforceable norms" and encompass "law-like activities and processes of establishing order in many other social domains, formal and informal, official and unofficial, in our own society and in others" (Moore 2005: 1). While many anthropologists of law do not directly study morality, it has traditionally been argued that laws and law-like activities when understood within local logic are morally justified and make moral sense to local peoples (Moore 2005: 2). So too has it been argued that moral judgments, understandings, and ontology underlie legal structures and decisions (Just 2001: 17; Pirie 2006: 173). But as Pardo has pointed out, "what is legal is not always broadly regarded in society as moral and legitimate and what is illegal as immoral and illegitimate" (2004: 5). Thus, just as jurists and philosophers of law do not agree about the relationship between law and morality (e.g. Hart 1961; Fuller 1969), so too anthropologists of law do not agree on this relationship. It will be our task in this chapter to tease out this relationship from various anthropological works.

Nevertheless, there does seem to be a general agreement that law is an example of what Geertz calls local knowledge. As such law is "not a bounded set of norms, rules, principles" or values (Geertz 1989: 173), but instead it changes as does society and culture. But it too is part of the dialectic of change. Because law is constructive and interpretive, it not only regulates behavior, as Bauman seems to suggest, it also creates new possibilities for acting and reinterpreting these acts. Perhaps, then, it is too simple to say that law merely regulates morals – law is more than the oral or textual codification of moral norms – it also allows the possibility for moral imagination and creativity. So too, as will be seen, are new moral worlds unintentionally created by means of the reforms of existing or the implementation of entirely new legal systems.

One thing that is clear is that each society is characterized to some extent by a plurality of legal structures or law-like processes (von Benda-Beckmann 2002). While this is perhaps most clear in many of the postcolonial countries around the world (Galanter 2005: 49), it is certainly just as true in the former colonial powers. Take for example official laws and unofficial law-like processes concerning sexuality in the United States. At various levels of the government structure, from the federal level to the city level, there are oftentimes different, and sometimes contradictory, laws concerning specific sexual practices, for example, sodomy. Similarly, there are other institutions, such as churches, schools, and youth clubs, that may proclaim law-like positions on these practices. Oftentimes these unofficial law-like positions have more influence over what people actually say they believe and what they do than the official laws. Further, if it is true that law helps create the possibility for moral creativity, then each of these legal and law-like positions does not simply reflect a preexisting morality, nor do they serve simply as restriction, but they also allow for a variety of moral positions on the topic of sexuality within one society. Perhaps it can be said, then, that all societies are not only characterized by legal pluralism, but also by moral pluralism, and that each helps create the other anew.

In this chapter we will consider various ways in which anthropologists have undertaken the study of law and law-like processes in different societies. As I have already said, anthropologists of law do not regularly take up their studies as an explicit study of moralities. Thus, in this chapter I will need to put on my interpreter's cap a bit more tightly in order to tease out the implications of some of these studies for an anthropology of moralities. In what follows I will take up three explicit foci of the anthropology of law – the state, property, and human rights – that I see as having particular moral import. In doing so, I hope to inspire anthropologists of law to approach their work in new ways that will contribute to a better understanding of local moralities and how they are related to the various layers of law within each society.

State and Law

The secular nation-state has become the predominant form of governing land and population in the modern world. For Weber the modern state is characterized by its rational bureaucracy. One aspect of this bureaucracy that makes it so rational, and by this Weber intends the primacy of the means–end relationship, is law. Indeed, it has been argued that the modern state and law are inseparable. And to some extent this is true, but it only tells us the "what" of this relationship and leaves out the "how." It is in addressing the "how" of the relationship between the modern state and law that anthropologists can best consider the relationship between law and morality in the context of the modern state. For by looking at the "how" of law, it is possible to see how states create the context not only for governing the behavior of populations, but also carve out a space for morality, conceived here as outside the direct purview of law, and help shape responsible persons vis-à-vis both the law and morality.

What I am trying to suggest is that in modern secular societies there is an integral relationship between law and morality. What is perhaps most important to consider in this relationship is what might be called the negative constitution of morality by means of law; that is to say, those instances when morality becomes defined as that which lies outside the official legal structure. Talal Asad provides an example of this when he describes this process by showing how legal reforms in late nineteenth-century colonial Egypt led to the construction of the family as the central sphere of moral training (2003: 205–56). This is not to say that the family was left completely outside of law-like processes by the secularizing state, far from it. Rather, by assigning the category of family to the jurisdiction of *sharī'a*, or traditional Islamic religious law, Egyptian legal reformers at one and the same time rendered *sharī'a* a kind of moral code rather than authoritative law, and in so doing constituted the family as a moral sphere. Asad argues that this is merely one example of how secular states use law to separate both religion and morality into the realm of private belief.

If secular states legally create conceptual spaces that differentiate between law and morality, increasingly they also create real spaces that differentiate between populations that can morally govern themselves and those that cannot. Borrowing from Foucault's concept of governmentality, these spaces of self-governance, such as gated communities, no smoking areas, and shopping malls, have been said to work according to the logic of spatial governmentality (Perry 2000). For Foucault, governmentality consists of the strategies and practices implemented by modern states in order to shape, change, and affect the conduct of persons. What makes governmentality so successful is that these strategies and practices are designed to be enacted by persons on themselves. In other words, through governmentality modern states create self-governing persons. Foucault's notion of governmentality, then, is very similar to what he called, and what we discussed in Chapter 1 as, technologies of the self.

These new spaces of spatial governmentality have a different logic of governing than law. Unlike law, spatial governmentality focuses on managing space rather than correcting the behavior of persons, it manages risk rather than enforces moral norms, and it puts increasing emphasis on the self-governance of persons within these spaces (Merry 2001: 16–17). There is, then, more concern with what might be called security and risk control than discipline, for spatial governmentality relies more on persons being able to act morally than the state enforcing law. This necessarily divides the population into those who can and those who cannot govern themselves. It should be noted, however, that what counts as moral and what counts as self-governing in these spaces may often rely more on class, gender, or race than anything else. Those who do not appear to "fit in" to the space, for example, young black men walking near a gated community or a homeless person sitting in Times Square, may be perceived by those managing the space as acting in a morally inappropriate or even potentially dangerous manner. Here it is possible to see that notions of what counts as appropriate moral or legal behavior is always founded on relations of power.

If the state manages certain spaces by means of strategies and practices of governmentality, then so too are there other spaces that by choice or otherwise are not controlled by the state, its laws, or governmentality. These spaces are often on borders and frontiers, but can also be found blocks away from the securely controlled urban spaces of spatial governmentality. Consider, for example, the very close proximity of different neighborhoods in New York or other such cities. Nevertheless, while these spaces may appear from the view of liberal secularism to be lawless and chaotic, they are often "administered" by a strict local morality of networks, kinship, and local solidarity. One such example are the various vigilante groups of Africa and North America discussed by Abrahams (1996) and the way in which they, although holding an ambiguous legal standing within the state and at times slipping into illegality, claim not only to uphold the law when the state is unable or unwilling to do so, but also to uphold local notions of morality. In upholding local morality and not simply the law, these groups are often supported by locals because they "are seen to represent ideas of [moral] justice in contrast to those of strict legality" (Abrahams 1996: 52).

In times of radical societal change much of a state's territory can become a space of, if not lawlessness, then certainly of legal uncertainty. This time of change is also often interpreted by locals and others as a time lacking morality. This is certainly how many of the post-Soviet states have been viewed by locals and non-locals alike. Often, and just as I have described for spaces of "lawlessness" within a state, local notions of morality fill in where the state's law is impotent. What seems clear in the post-Soviet case, however, is that local notions of morality are radically pluralized such that what counts as moral for one person or group does not count for another. Consider, for example, the array of local notions of morality that fill the impotent void of the post-socialist Ukrainian legal system. Catherine Wanner (2005) provides several case studies showing how personally or group held moral values provide both the motivation and the reasoning for perpetrating various acts of corruption concerning property rights, loan sharking, and embezzlement. What is most interesting about these cases is that morality is not interpreted in terms of absolute good and bad or right and wrong as it so often can be. Rather, it is a kind of Weberian investment in a certain social, status, or even situational position that if properly adhered to, leads to particular kinds of acts and behavior that is only justified in terms of what might be called the propositional position. In other words, morality as Wanner describes it are those acts and behaviors that maintain or follow from the multifarious social, political, and economic contingents that make up the person or group's position within a certain given situation. Morality, here, is not judged in terms of good and bad or right and wrong, but in terms of how well it follows from the propositional position. In this way, the legal system in the Ukraine is used, abused, or avoided as one's interests dictate.

Just as the lawlessness of the Ukraine allows for this kind of Weberian investment, so too has a similar situation arisen in Russia. It seems, nevertheless, that in Russia a locally controlled order has been imposed on this state of lawlessness. While the police in the mid 1990s were generally unable to uphold laws and provide security to the population, local gangs and mafia stepped in to provide these services for a price. Nancy Ries (2002: 278) writes that while the mafia is generally seen as one of the primary causes of the destruction of the legal order in post-Soviet Russia, they are also locally considered as the only ones able to provide any kind of justice and order. This is done by providing *kryshi* or roofs to local businesses and sellers who need protection against other gangs or support in guaranteeing that money they have lent out will be repaid. Not only do they provide the order and security that the police and state cannot, but they also describe themselves as morally disciplined persons who provide an honest service to the community and who hold good family and personal values (Ries 2002: 281). These two post-Soviet cases are particularly interesting for our purposes because they bring to attention the flexibility of the concept of morality in everyday use. Morality need not be associated with notions of good, bad, right, or wrong, nor need it be performed by persons or groups the majority of people believe to be "moral" or "lawful." Indeed, these two cases show very clearly that often what counts as morality at the local level is contingent on the socio-politico-economic context in which acts are performed. In large part this context greatly depends on how well the state manages to, on the one hand, discursively define this context as controlled by law, and on the other hand, legitimately uphold this discourse through various means of discipline, surveillance, and the use of violence.

One of the central foundations of this legal-moral context in the modern nation-state is the morally disciplined and legally responsible person. Indeed, according to Mauss (1997), the very notion of the person came into being by means of Roman legal classification. Eventually the modern state came to rely on this notion of a person, which by the nineteenth century had taken the form of a subjectivized person armed with the moral skills of free will, autonomy, intention, and discipline, as the foundation for its legal structure. This subjectivized person is the responsible person; the person responsible to herself, to morality, to the law, and to the state (see Dupret 2004: 16–29). But this subjective-responsible person was not already there ready to be taken in by the modern state. Rather, this new kind of person had to be constituted in the very process of forming the modern, secular nation-state (Asad 2003). In fact, just as this new form of person could not exist without this new form of state, so too this new state could not exist without this kind of person. The two were mutually constituted in their respective and intimately connected processes of coming to be. Modern secular law played a significant role in creating both.

Earlier I described how Talal Asad shows that in late nineteenth- and early twentieth-century Egypt the family became the central realm of moral training as it was put under the jurisdiction of *sharī'a*, which was rendered akin to a moral code by its relationship with the new secular state law. This is just one example of what Salvatore calls the implosion of *sharī'a*, by which he means its redefinition in the face of secular law and Islamic reformers as a so-called "permanent source of norm-ative disciplining and anticipation of behaviour demanded to the [morally] faithful" (2004: 126). But as Salvatore points out, this idea of *sharī'a* as the foundational kernel for moral order relies on the notion of a responsible, disciplined and self-governing person, that is, a subjectivized person, which is essential to the secular notion of law. This example shows that in the modern state it is very difficult, if not misleading, to make clear-cut distinctions between morality, law, and the state. For in constituting itself as the legitimate institution of power, the modern state must simultaneously constitute its citizens, that is subjectivized, responsible persons, by means of, on the one hand, state law, and on the other, public and private realms of morality, each of which help define and maintain the other.

Moral Economies, Inequality, and Property

In the last section we saw how the modern state has played a central role in the con-stitution of what counts as morality in the contemporary world. This has been done by means of establishing new legal systems, which simultaneously establish realms of morality outside the law or in conjunction with the law, by controlling certain spaces of priority within the greater territory, and in doing both of these, creating moral subjective persons of responsibility who are characterized by self-governance. What is also anthropologically interesting about the modern state and its relationship with morality is that it is a space of vast inequality of wealth and resources. This inequality often revolves around property relations. To speak of property relations is to go beyond the legalistic notion of property rights and to emphasize the ways in which persons and communities are patterned, networked, and differentiated by means of their relationship with property (see Hann and the Property Relations Group 2003). In this section, we will take a look at how these relations, which are often characterized by inequality, have been analyzed from a moral perspective by some anthropologists.

One of the ways in which the notion of morality has crept into anthropological studies is through the idea of a moral economy. The moral economy has become a central academic notion since it was first introduced in the writings of the social historian E. P. Thompson. For Thompson the moral economy is grounded in a "consistent traditional view of social norms and obligations" that includes rights that are "supported by the wider consensus of the community," which in turn help define legitimate and illegitimate economic and production practices (1991: 188). It was this moral economy, so Thompson argues, and its confrontation with the new political economy of the so-called free market that provided both legitimation and motivation for various peasant food riots in late eighteenth-century England. Because the new market economy practices that were introduced at this time were during times of dearth and famine considered unjust and immoral compared to the subsistence security many of the peasants believed moral economic practices provided, food riots were conceived of as morally appropriate responses.

James Scott, the political scientist-cum-anthropologist, picked up the notion of the moral economy from Thompson and showed how it is helpful for understanding how peasants in another historical context – that of nineteenth- and twentieth-century Southeast Asia – accept, resist, and rebel against political and economic inequality (Scott 1976). This inequality, for the most part, is accepted because of a more or less tacit agreement that the condition of inequality will, nonetheless, lead to a state of relative subsistence security for all. Inequality, then, is considered legitimate by peasants because it is seen as that which guarantees subsistence. Over the long durée, these relations of inequality are fused with a kind of moral authority that ground their existence. Much like with Thompson's eighteenth-century English peasants, however, when subsistence for these Southeast Asian peasants is threatened by a change in politico-economic relations and/or production practices, resistance and rebellion become viable options for not only maintaining their subsistence level, but what is one and the same thing, maintaining one aspect of their moral order.

What should be clear from the work of both Thompson and Scott is that the idea of the moral economy is a very limited way of conceiving of local moralities. It is limited, that is, because moral economy is concerned simply with economic and production relations and the ways in which these relations acquire moral significance over time. The moral economy, then, is contrasted with the political economy of the market system, which seeks to depersonalize, and thus, demoralize economic and production relations. Simply put, the idea of the moral economy is an alternative way of imagining economic and production relations, a way that because it has the subsistent well-being of the community as its starting point is infused with moral import.

Both Thompson and Scott spoke of the moral economy of local communities facing radical political, economic, and social change, all of which are significant aspects of a societal-wide moral breakdown, radiating from national centers of power to local villages. For this reason the idea of moral economy has been utilized by many anthropologists to discuss local resistance to the nation-state. It is also a useful notion for considering local resistance to the increasingly evident global and transnational processes with which peasants the world over are now confronted. The changes and difficulties brought on by these processes are increasingly resisted in various ways by peasants. From the recent indigenous and leftist democratic victories in such places as Bolivia and Venezuela, to peasant-led global activists for the human right to food, to the language of rights and justice, and demands for moral and ethical trade relations, all are reminiscent of the moral economy language of peasants of yesteryear. As Edelman puts it, "the discourse of 'rights' and justice, of a 'reliable subsistence,' and of a 'moral economy' reembedded in society – albeit global society – are clearly their central pillars" (2005: 341).

While the moral economy is a limited idea of local moralities vis-à-vis economic and production relations, which can also be interestingly used to analyze peasant resistance to global processes, it is not a way of conceiving of local moralities *in toto*. For the moral economy should be understood as always existing within the bounds of more encompassing moral understandings and legal structures (Sivaramakrishnan 2005). Unfortunately, moral economy does not always seem to be understood in this way. In discussing changes of property relations in the post-socialist context of Eurasia, for example, Hann utilizes the idea of moral economy as a way of understanding the nexus of "'objective' changes in the realm of political economy and people's 'subjective' experience of these changes" (2003: 4). While this is certainly true to the intentions of Thompson and Scott, if I understand Hann correctly, it at times seems as though he speaks of moral economy as a set of values that go beyond morally imbued economic and production relations. Thus, when he speaks of "institutions and organisations potentially capable of articulating and representing the moral economy" or decisions made by "the local community" as "an expression of the moral economy" (2003: 34–5), it seems as if he speaking of community-shared moral values and understandings which encompass more than a specific historical tradition of economic and production relations. Indeed, Hann further gives this impression by only defining moral economy by referencing Thompson's description of it as the "tissue of customs and usages" (2003: 6). But as Thompson himself makes clear in the context of this phrase, this "tissue" only regards "economic" relations and is only made apparent through the breakdown of these relations in their confrontation with the market of a political economy (Thompson 1991: 340). Thus, it appears that moral economy as used by Hann is equated with what might be called a local notion of morality. And while this claim might be tenable if it were explicitly argued, it is not the moral economy of which Thompson and Scott wrote.

One of Hann's colleagues in the Property Relations Group at the Max Planck Institute for Social Anthropology utilizes the notion of moral economy in a way reminiscent of Thompson and Scott, but yet takes it in a different and interesting direction. Speaking of the reemergence of traditional kin and property relations in China after the breakdown of centralized control over these realms, Brandtstädter (2003: 433–7) speaks of the acceptance by local Chinese of the inequalities and "wasting" of property inherent to these traditional relations and the rituals associated with them as due to the moral need for integration and stability. This integration and stability is possible because kinship and property in Southern China, so it is argued, should not be thought of simply in terms of the mode of production, but more importantly as a mode of integration by means of gift exchange and sharing in ancestral property. This is what Brandtstädter calls the moral economy of kinship and property.

Property relations and their moral significance for locals have been interpreted in ways other than through the idea of moral economy. Again, if the notion of moral economy in its original intent is a way to understand the moral sensibilities of locals who accept, and at times resist, inequality, for example, in property, wealth, or food distribution, then property relations can certainly have moral significance for locals in other ways. For property relations are also a way for persons to cultivate and maintain interpersonal relations of various sorts or to mark identity in ways imbued with moral authority. These relationships and identities become particularly clear during times of change or societal breakdown, not only for the anthropologists but also for local peoples.

For example, Torsello (2003) shows how villagers in Southern Slovakia have had shifting feelings of trust toward the institution of their agricultural cooperative and the managers who run it. Since its establishment in 1949 the cooperative has gone through various phases of change, including the post-socialist decollectiviza-tion phase. These changes have each led to a shift in relationships of trust between it, its managers, and local villagers. Nevertheless, Torsello argues, because many individual villagers have personal contacts within the cooperative, contacts that are founded on a moral relationship of trust, these villagers are able to overcome potential mistrust for the institution and continue to cooperate and work with the local post-socialist version of the agricultural cooperative. As can be seen, then, as property relations change over time, so too do moral feelings and relationships. Indeed, it is the moral feeling of trust that underpins certain relationships that allows many of these villagers to survive the often chaotic phase of decollectivization and privatization by maintaining, at least a tenuous, relationship with the cooperative.

In discussing the various phases of change this Slovakian cooperative has gone through since its inception, Torsello shows that various times during the socialist period the cooperative grew to include more and more land and farms in the surrounding area until eventually it grew to include a large part of the local region. This growth led to an increased distance between the local farmers and the administrative, that is, controlling, centers of the land. In a sense, there was an increased distancing of the property relations. As this distance grew, so too did the mistrust. Thus, it is possible to say that, at least in this case, trust decreases as the property relations and those who control it are further and further removed from one's hands. It would seem, then, that a certain set of property relations are conceived by locals as more moral when they are closer at hand. They need not be owned or controlled directly by the trusting person, but this person must feel a certain kind of closeness to how property relations are maintained and ordered.

Property and distance can have a moral relationship that goes beyond the control of property relations. For ownership of local land and who owns that land can also go a long way in defining local notions of identity and morality. For example, Rapport argues that ownership of land is central in defining local notions of moral identity in a small English village. For these villagers, it is not so important that one actually owns the land, but who else owns it, for outsiders are not welcome. Increasingly outsiders are beginning to move to this small countryside village, and in doing so disrupting traditional patterns of life. Thus, local ownership of the land holds moral weight. Indeed, as Rapport puts it, outsiders who seek to own land in this village are often met with the moral response of righteous indignation (1997: 93). Distance and property relations works in two ways here. First, outsiders, that is, those born-at-a-distance, are morally inappropriate owners of local land. Second, if an outsider does buy land, even if she lives right next door, she remains at a moral distance from oneself.

Similarly, Svašek (2006) shows that local responses in a Czech village to an outsider owning land can be morally responded to in a multitude of ways. Indeed, it should be obvious that outsiders buying land will have a different moral interpretation of their ownership than locals, but locals themselves often have differing moral responses. While some see it as harmful to local identity or a struggle over competing moral justifications of land usage, others welcome outsiders and the potential benefits they may bring to the community. There is, then, a local pluralism vis-à-vis the moral understanding of property relations. This should come as no surprise, however, as anthropologists today should expect such local pluralism in their studies of local moralities. For as can be seen, property relations, ownership and a sense of distance can be interpreted in various ways and imbued with differing moral significance by local peoples. This moral significance often goes well beyond notions of land rights, but includes such things as identity, conflicting moral conceptions and practices, and moral relations between persons.

Property, it must be added, goes well beyond land ownership. For any object, material or otherwise, can be possessed and controlled exclusively by an individual or a collective of some kind. And this possession and control is not only maintained through particular moral assumptions, but is also often responded to by others with moral expectations. One of the ways in which these assumptions and expectations come together is through sharing. As Widlok argues, sharing need not be performed for the calculated reason of reciprocity. In fact, sharing might be better thought of as a virtue, which Widlock defines as an action done for its own sake (2004: 64). In other words, sharing of property, such as food or the intellectual property rights of medicine, could be better thought of as a virtue not because it leads to certain consequences, but because it is good in itself to share and provide access to that which is needed and others may not have. Of course this depends on the agreement of all involved that providing access to those who do not have but need is in fact a good in itself. Such an agreement, unfortunately, is rarely made outside of very small-scale contexts.

From moral economies, to moral identities, to virtues, property relations of all sorts have been analyzed by anthropologists as having moral significance for local persons. Because property relations are almost always encoded in legal structures or enforced through law-like processes, it has been a primary way for anthropologists to consider the relationship between law and morality. What is perhaps most interesting about looking at property relations from the perspective of the anthropology of moralities is that it often reveals the deep-seated moral pluralism to be found within any society or social context. For the disagreements that arise around property relations are often founded on the conflicting moral assumptions that various actors bring to the table.

Human Rights

In 1948 the newly formed United Nations promulgated what has become, if not its most influential, then one of its best-known documents – the Universal Declaration of Human Rights. There had already been similar such documents, for example the American Declaration of Independence and Bill of Rights, and the French Declaration of the Rights of Man, but this was the first endorsed by an international body claiming to represent and speak for all the peoples of the world. Expecting an endorsement of the document as an "expression of certain basic and universal moral facts," UNESCO turned to Melville Herskovits, one of the leading anthropologists of the day (Goodale 2006a: 1). Such an endorsement was not forthcoming. Instead, Herskovits published what was called the American Anthropological Association's "Statement on Human Rights" in late 1947.

Goodale argues that Herskovits could not endorse a possible universal declaration of rights on three grounds: empirical, epistemological, and ethical (2006a: 1–2). Herskovits claimed that because anthropology had shown that moral systems differ both culturally and historically, any universal claims could only be prescriptive. Secondly, he argued that it was not the place of anthropology to make judgments about particular cultural practices vis-à-vis so-called universal rights. And lastly, Herskovits warned against what has since become called "moral imperialism" (see Hernández-Truyol 2002). That is to say, if the declaration of universal rights prescribes certain moral values to some peoples who do not already hold them, then by this very fact it is denying them their freedom to live by their own culture's moral system. On these three grounds, then, Herskovits firmly rooted anthropology on the side of relativism in the universal-relativism debates that have plagued human rights discourse ever since.

After the 1947 statement written by Herskovits, the subject of human rights was little addressed by anthropologists until the 1980s. When it finally was taken up again, many anthropologists at the time again sided with the relativism end of the debate, which by the 1990s had also come to be associated with defending the local against the global. To some extent, these anthropologists were very similar to the so-called salvage anthropologists of the beginning of the century, as both sought to save as much local culture and its practices as possible from the ever-approaching homogeneity of modernity, globalization, and the universality of human rights.

Even if this response to universal human rights does not take the more active form it can take in the hands of some applied anthropologists, it remains in the writings of many anthropologists today. For example, in discussing the local impact of the international community's imposition of human rights trials in postwar Sierra Leone, the existential anthropologist Michael Jackson (2005) asks the provocative question: whose human rights? His answer: not those of the Sierra Leoneans. Instead, Jackson sees human rights discourse as the privilege of the powerful. As a modern day form of a civilizing mission, human rights discourse, so argues Jackson, is the attempt of the privileged powerful to take "moral ownership" of the suffering powerless (2005: 166–7). Indeed, what is most interesting about Jackson's critique is that human rights discourse rarely takes notice of the social and global conditions that give rise to much of the suffering these rights are meant to alleviate. Rather, because human rights are conceived in terms of the moral individualism that defines much of the moral discourse of modernity, those who attempt to uphold the human rights of suffering others tend to ignore these social conditions and instead seek responsible agents in the form of individuals or groups of individuals. Thus, as Jackson, among many others, points out, the very notion of universal human rights is founded on the individualistic moral assumptions of what is often referred to as the West.

In particular, human rights are closely tied to the natural law tradition, which we discussed in the first chapter. As we saw, the idea of natural law depends on an assumed universal and essential human nature, which is naturally endowed with certain rights. To make this assumption entails the necessity of denying any incompatible differences between cultures, societies, and historical moments. That is to say, it necessitates the denial of pluralism. Difference can exist within the framework of natural law, but the differences must remain relatively superficial, in a sense, only covering over what is essentially shared. Natural law as a moral theory was worked out in the forms in which we mostly know it today by medieval philosophers, lawyers, and theologians, and had its heyday in the Enlightenment. Once Kant got a hold of natural law theory and turned it into a theory of duties, natural law slipped out of the mainstream of, at least, philosophical thinking. It was not until after the tragedies of World War II that natural law once again found itself in favor. This, of course, is not surprising, for natural law is a particularly attractive idea after times of war, revolution, and international destruction. Indeed, the theory was originally worked out in medieval times during a period of great international war and chaos, and the three great natural rights documents of the late eighteenth century were the result of two revolutions. So what better way to respond to the devastation of the war and Holocaust than proclaiming the universal rights of all persons based on their shared nature as human beings?

The problem, of course, is: who counts as human and who is in charge of guaranteeing their rights? Talal Asad (2003) attempts to answer just these questions. In doing so, he points out the irony of the fact that it is the recognition by states of its citizens that can both guarantee these citizens their human rights and deny them these rights. This is so because one only has human rights by first having national rights. Thus, it is not as a human *qua* human that one is endowed with human rights in the post-1948 world, but as a recognized citizen of a particular nation-state. Even refugees depend upon *other* states for their so-called human rights. So too do NGOs and international institutions, for these organizations and institutions have no power to act in the interest of others' rights without the approval of the states within which they hope to work.

States, then, and not some abstract definition of a shared humanity guarantee human rights. In this sense, furthermore, it can also be said that states define that which counts as human, for in a very real way, if one does not have a certain status based on the legal framework of one's own state, then one may also not have the opportunity to have their human rights recognized. In a world dominated by human rights discourse, this is the same as saying that they do not have the opportunity to have their humanity recognized. And yet, according to the UN's Declaration on Human Rights, it is the law of each state that is to guarantee these rights. Asad points out that this conflation of law with rights results in the usurpation of moral discourse (2003: 138), for it leaves no other recourse for those whose rights are not protected by their state's law. Their choices are limited to either the law, which does not guarantee their human rights, or human rights discourse. When law, rights, and morality become one, no other moral alternatives remain available.

Some anthropologists, however, take a different perspective on how human rights discourse influences moralities. While Asad suggests that the conflation of law and rights usurps or leaves little space for alternative moralities, Richard Wilson, for example, argues that human rights discourse must be understood as pluralistic. This is so because it "includes a vast array of different [and incompatible] kinds of moral and political projects" (Wilson 2006: 77). From liberal individualism to communitarian multiculturalism, human rights discourse has grown well beyond its original natural law foundation. Or has it? Perhaps it is more accurate to say that the natural law foundation has expanded. In other words, a communitarian multiculturalist – a position seemingly unlikely to assume an essentialist view of humanity – might very well defend his claim for the basic human right of cultural self-determination based on the assumption that all humans, *by their nature*, have the right to do so. That is to say, the claim would be that it is a basic human right to choose a culture. But as Jane Cowan astutely points out, cultures and societies are not chosen, they are born into, and thus it is very difficult to defend a position that claims one has a human right to choose to remain in or leave a culture (2006: 14). Therefore, while it may be true that various incompatible, that is pluralistic, moral and political projects have taken up the banner of human rights, the very notion of these rights still rests on natural law assumptions.

While it is true that human rights discourse is based on natural law theory, it is not equivalent to it. Nor does it on its own provide a basis for a complete moral philosophy (Wilson 2006: 78). Rather, it is more realistic to say that in today's world human rights discourse provides what Wilson calls a Habermasian precondition for "rational, meaningful dialogue" on the most important political and moral issues (2006: 82). In other words, it is nearly impossible to enter a conversation anywhere in the world today about a moral or political issue without the notion of human rights somehow informing the dialogue. It has become, as Mark Goodale puts it, the "dominant transnational moral discourse" (2006b: 25). This does not mean, however, that it is the dominant moral understanding in any specific locale. Rather, it simply means that it stands as a background understanding, and thus informs and influences local notions of morality in ways that no other abstract moral discourse does today. Thus, although hegemonic, human rights discourse is yet just one of many aspects of what Goodale calls local "ethical theor[ies] as social practice."

It plays this role not simply because it is the "dominant transnational moral discourse," but also because, and related to this, sometimes persons or groups of persons strategically utilize human rights discourse for their own local purposes (Merry 2006: 44). One example of this is how the Zapatista Army of National Liberation (EZLN) in Mexico switched their revolutionary focus from a national and class perspective to that of local indigenous rights (Gledhill 1998: 94). This happened not only because these rights better represented the interests of their local supportive base, but also because in the post-Cold War years the discourse of rights, both human and indigenous, has more local, national, and international appeal than that of class struggle. This switch of revolutionary focus entails a switch of moral focus and *telos* as well. Whereas class struggle seeks to overturn the injustices of social and economic inequality and exploitation, struggles over identity, or indigenous rights, seek such moral goals as self-determination, social dignity, and respect. Here we see what is perhaps most interesting, and paradoxical, about claims for indigenous rights. That is, while calling for rights to be granted to the collective (the community, the ethnic group, the indigenous group, etc.), the rights demanded are an extension of the very human rights assumed to be inherent for individual human persons. Thus, an appeal for group or indigenous rights relies on the very same moral and epistemological assumptions of individualism that are also at the heart of the national and global ideologies *from* which these groups hope to gain rights. What is clear, then, is that the notion of indigenous rights is not at all revolutionary, and indeed much like the "revolutionary" ideologies that preceded it, runs the risk of creating other forms of domination and exploitation because of its very co-option of these assumptions. Indeed, this is the very strength, and danger, of hegemonic discourse, of which, as we have already seen, human rights discourse most certainly is an example.

Another potentially risky paradox of indigenous rights discourse is that it relies on yet another construction of Western power. That is, the very concept of "indigenous" is itself a construct of colonialism (Gledhill 1998: 104), and, as Povinelli (2002) shows for the case of Aborigines in Australia, is still being constructed by means of "nonindigenous" Australian legal structures and moral sensibilities. This happens, for example, in legal cases when Aborigines attempt to gain certain land rights based on their status as "indigenous" persons. In these cases the Aborigines need to walk a fine line between proving themselves as authentic Aborigines, and thus deserving of certain indigenous and cultural rights, and, in doing so, not to morally offend the "nonindigenous" Australians with any potentially morally repugnant practices, particularly certain sexual practices, or beliefs. Thus, what becomes discursively recognized by the Australian legal structure as "indigenous," and thus what formally counts as Aboriginal for both the "indigenous" and "nonindigenous" Australians alike, is more a result of the legal structures and moral sensibilities of the latter than of the actual practices and beliefs of Aboriginal persons.

As we have seen, then, human rights and morality are intimately connected in several ways. Not only does human rights discourse have its origins in the natural law theory of morality, but so too does it stand as background understanding that influences and helps shape various kinds of local moralities. So too do these local moralities sometimes feed back and influence what counts as human rights. In this way, then, it is too simple to say that human rights discourse is a hegemonic moral discourse that colonizes local moral worlds. For colonization implies control. But as we have seen, human rights discourse is often used locally in strategic ways that further local causes. Thus, while this discourse certainly is hegemonic, it is not totalizing. Instead, it remains available for local persons and groups to utilize, within limits, in their own way for their own moral projects.

Some Final Words

At the begin of this chapter it was pointed out that for quite some time anthropologists, philosophers, and jurists have been unable to agree about the relationship between law and morality. What I think has become clear in this chapter is that possibly the question has been misleading. Perhaps the question should not be whether law and law-like processes are moral or reflect local moral understandings, but instead should ask how law and law-like processes help constitute what counts as the moral. In other words, it seems that one of the lines of inquiry open to the anthropologist of moralities interested in law is to consider how law, and its processes, practices, and discourses, creates a space for what can justifiably be considered moral. As we have seen in this chapter, the state, property and inequality, and human rights are just some of the possibilities for such research. Although not covered in this chapter, I suspect inquiries into legal definitions of the person (this seems especially fruitful in light of our earlier discussion of the dialectical relationship between the subjectivized person and modern, secular law), contractual law, and dispute resolution at all social levels would also provide fertile ground for an anthropology of moralities. Whatever the topic, it seems clear that anthropological investigations of law and law-like processes provide ripe material for those interested in local notions of moralities.

Case Study 1

Moral Torment in Papua New Guinea

In his book *Becoming Sinners: Christianity and Moral Torment in a Papua New Guinea Society,* Joel Robbins looks at how radical cultural change has led many Urapmin to a state of intense moral torment. The Urapmin are a small society of people numbering nearly 400 living in the western highlands of Papua New Guinea. Contemporary Urapmins have found themselves experiencing a societal-wide moral breakdown (Robbins 2004). This is so because they are caught living with two cultures – a newly adopted Pentecostal Christian culture and their traditional Urapmin one. Robbins argues that in adopting a new Pentecostal Christian culture in whole, it was not gradually assimilated into the traditional Urapmin culture (2004: 3). Thus, many aspects of the traditional Urapmin culture were left intact, leaving the Urapmin people caught between two significantly different cultural and moral systems. Having been caught in this betwixt state, Robbins argues, morality is a constant issue for them.

> This is so because the moral domain – as a domain of conscious choice – is a place where change comes to consciousness. For those caught living between a traditional cultural system and one they have newly adopted, morality is likely to provide the window through which they can see the contradictions with which they have to live. This is why ... the Urapmin conception of their situation so single-mindedly understands and explains it in terms of moral difficulty. (2004: 14).

The Urapmin, then, are living through a societal-wide moral breakdown. While individual Urapmin certainly experience their own moral breakdowns in the course of living their usual everyday human lives, they also have the extra burden of what Robbins describes as nearly a constant state of moral questioning due to this societal-wide breakdown. How has Robbins studied this situation and how do the Urapmin live through this state of constant moral questioning?

Robbins defines the moral sphere as a sphere of conscious choice. As he puts it:

> Having defined the moral domain as one in which actors are culturally constructed as being aware both of the directive force of values and of the choices left open to them in responding to that force, we have to recognize that it is fundamentally a domain that consists of actions undertaken consciously ... Consciousness of the issues involved is thus a criterion of moral choice. (2004: 315–16)

It is for this reason, then, that Robbins centers his analytic attention on specific realms and practices of ethical choice such as the will, law, and technologies of the self. In doing so, he focuses on the ways in which each of these can only be understood as ethical choices in the context of the moral breakdown the Urapmin experience due to the tensions and contradictions of the two conflicting cultural and moral worldviews they are currently living through.

Because the Urapmin are stuck between two contradictory moral systems, they are also stuck between two contradictory conceptions of will. The traditional Urapmin moral system "values the will when it is deployed to create or positively transform social relationships" (2004: 289). Considered in this way, the will coincides with the law, a set of fundamental prohibitions that are at the core of the traditional moral system (2004: 184–5). While the will is valued when it coincides with the law, it is considered immoral if the will acts to disrupt social relations or eschew certain social obligations. However, when the law and will "are brought into a mutually conditioning dialectic with each other in people's hearts," (2004: 195) then they are the foundation for the traditional Urapmin moral system. The will, then, if properly managed can have positive moral qualities according to this traditional system.

Christian morality, on the other hand, condemns the will as an expression of one's own desire and emotions, and therefore, an obstacle to following God's will. Thus, for the Christian morality adopted by the Urapmin, the will is always sinful (2004: 225). Many Urapmin, then, are stuck between a notion of the will that can have positive moral qualities and another notion that only views the will as immoral. It would seem that in the present there is no possibility of reconciling these two views. It is for this reason, Robbins suggests, that this contradiction is responded to in terms of millennialism.

What, then, do the Urapmin do in the present of their perpetual moral torment? Robbins' answer is that they work on themselves so that they can be prepared for the salvational moment of the millennium. Because Christian salvation is only possible through a renunciation of the will, this is the ultimate goal of the Urapmin technologies of the self utilized to work on themselves. Thus, it would seem, the ethical demand being responded to by the Urapmin is to move beyond the traditional Urapmin notion of will and renounce it completely. Robbins focuses on two technologies of the self meant for this purpose: moral self-reflection and confession.

Robbins claims that all Urapmin of at least the age twelve "reflect on their feelings and actions in order to identify their sins" (2004: 232). By maintaining an accurate list of sins committed since one's last confession, the Urapmin are not only better prepared for the next confession, but more importantly keep a close watch on their acts, inner emotions, and the will that motivates both of these. In this way, moral self-reflection is one tactic utilized by Urapmin to respond to the ethical demand of their societal-wide moral breakdown. Another tactic utilized is confession. As a way of washing away one's sins, the "new life that confession initiates also points toward the new life to come in heaven" (2004: 277). Thus, as a central technology of the self for Urapmin Christians, confession works on the will in two ways. First, it trains the will to renounce its independence from the will of God, and in so doing, confession, secondly, prepares one for the millennium.

These two technologies of the self work together to move Urapmin individuals toward salvation. By constantly maintaining vigilance and moral self-reflection, the Urapmin are better prepared to participate in an efficacious confession. Having done so, the Urapmin individual is better prepared for the judgment of the millennium. It should be noted, of course, that both of these technologies are focused on individual salvation, and are therefore at odds with the traditional communal, or what Robbins calls relational, moral values of the Urapmin system. Thus, in practicing these very technologies of the self as a way to respond to the demand of the moral breakdown, the Urapmin are likely at the same time furthering the contradictions. The torment continues.

Robbins' study of the Urapmin and their moral torment provides an excellent example of the way in which an anthropology of moralities is interestingly and precisely done when focused on an explicit example of a moral breakdown or questioning. In doing so, Robbins makes a very clear distinction between Urapmin concerns and questions about morality, on the one hand, and what might be called culture or social structure, on the other hand. In this way, Robbins avoids the Durkheimian assumption that morality is synonymous with society or social structure, and instead shows the active process of reflection, questioning, and acting that constitutes the moral realm.

Part III
Sexuality, Gender, and Health

–4–

Gender and Sexuality

For years it seemed as though anthropologists ignored the existence of women in societies around the world. Apart from a few exceptions, for years men, their activities, and their words were the focus of anthropological monographs. This slowly began to change in the late 1960s and early 1970s with the feminist critique of anthropological research and its writings. From this point on women, and what has eventually come to be called the study of gender, that is, culturally constructed differences between men and women, became central to many anthropological studies. One result of this critique and the shift it brought about has been the questioning of the subordination of women in societies around the world and how, if at all, women are able to act against such subordination. Such questioning is clearly related to the study of local moralities and will be a primary concern in this chapter.

As will be seen, however, the feminist critique did more than bring about the study of the place of women in society. It also opened possibilities for research into local notions of sexuality and a shift in the way kinship studies are conceived. For this reason these two topics will also be considered in this chapter. What becomes clear throughout is that while the feminist critique was important for opening these new spaces of research and anthropological writing, it at times does not go far enough in recognizing the complexities and contradictions, the fragmentary relationships, and the negotiations that occur in the everyday life relations between men and women. It is this and its relationship to local moralities that I will try to show in this chapter.

Gender and Moralities

Perhaps one of the most central topics of concern for anthropologists of gender, and particularly feminist anthropologists, is that of agency. The concept of agency indicates an individual's relationship to potentially deterministic structures. These individuals can be groups of peoples and institutions, but are also often individual persons. The structures are historical, political, economic, or what is often generally called social structures. The commonest way of conceiving of the relationship of agency is that these individuals, in some way, exercise freedom of action, speech, or thought in resistance against the usually determining structure. The exercise of this freedom, so it is argued, depends upon the autonomous subject. That is to say, the agent is a subject who is autonomous, that is, free from determination or even significant influence, from any other structure, entity, or person than herself. The notion of the autonomous agent, then, is clearly a byproduct of the Kantian notion of the autonomous moral person.

In terms of gender, anthropologists have focused on the ways in which women, or groups of women, enact agency by resisting patriarchal structural orders. In other words, many feminist anthropologists have interpreted local structures as repressing women and benefiting men, and thus see attempts by women to act against this repression as agentive resistance to the patriarchal order. The assumption by many of these anthropologists is that women the world over should recognize their repressed state and, if and when they do, should want to resist, act against, and ultimately change this order. What is clear here is that these anthropologists universalize a particular local political ideal by assuming that it holds for all women in all times and places. This Western, secular-liberal ideal, which goes hand-in-hand with the notion of the autonomously acting subject, assumes that the individual person can and should be able to recognize her domination by a repressive order, and having thus recognized this has a duty to resist and change this order. This notion of agency, then, can be seen as the academic version of the Western ideological principle of freedom.

One example of such an approach that also touches on a topic relevant to an anthropology of moralities is Sarah Uhl's (1991) work on female friendship in Andalusia. For Uhl true friendship is a lasting and emotionally deep relationship between persons based upon trust and loyalty, and bonded through shared experience. This notion of friendship, however, is said, by anthropologists and locals alike, to exist only between men. Uhl points out that the ethnographic literature on southern Europe neglects the question of why locals, and anthropologists for that matter, often say that friendship is something that men have and that women do not. Indeed, in neglecting to critically examine this, Uhl argues, the ethnographic literature perpetuates a local ideology of male dominance. Uhl further claims that the concept of friendship has become "genderized" both within the literature and within the local social milieu of southern Europe (1991: 91). This is so because it is often claimed that women have "moral restrictions" placed upon them so that they have certain obligations to the home and the domestic group that exclude possibilities of friendship (1991: 90). Nevertheless, Uhl contends that women in Andalusia do in fact have friends and the difficulty of seeing this fact in everyday life is not because of its rarity, but because of the tactics of resistance exercised by these women.

Uhl proposes that in southern European societies female friendship is hidden from public appearance by what she calls "a message hidden within other messages" (1991: 92). The use of such hidden messages is a tactic that allows women to present a certain "impression and manages a situation." As Uhl goes on to argue, "adult female friendship constitutes a hidden message in that it is subsumed into women's public expressions of domesticity and is thus practically imperceptible in public contexts" (1991: 92). Indeed, such usage of hidden messages may not always be consciously used and may even at times include the role of an outsider, such as an anthropologist, in keeping these messages hidden. For example, one of the ways that women can keep friendships hidden is by using a different term for friends than men do. Thus, women rarely use the word *amiga* in talking about friendship, but instead use kin terms or proper names. In doing so, they use the male-oriented hegemonic language in order to transmit the hidden messages of female friendship.

While it is quite likely that Andalusian women do in fact have friends, what is important for our purposes is to consider the way in which Uhl analyzes her ethnographic data in order to show this likelihood. While Uhl does not use the analytic language of agency and resistance, it is quite clear that these concepts are behind her analysis. Consider the idea of hidden messages. To speak of hidden messages is to speak of communication that runs counter to the dominant discourse. It is what one uses in order to communicate that which cannot be said but yet one *wants* to say. In order to transmit a hidden message, one must be aware of, one must know and understand, the dominant discourse. Not only must one know the dominant discourse, so too must one know how to get around it, that is, how to speak with hidden messages. Indeed, to take Uhl's analysis to its logical conclusion, the Andalusian women know and understand the dominant discourse so well that they can even undermine it with hidden messages nonconsciously and with the help of outsiders. Uhl's portrayal of these southern European women, then, is certainly an example of the knowing-autonomous subject resisting dominating structures of society, and in so doing, participating in the moral relationship of trusting and true friendship (1991: 95–9).

As I have already said, I do not doubt the existence of female friendship in southern Europe. What I critique is Uhl's analysis of the phenomenon. In her desire to show that these women do in fact have friendships, she must propose the use of hidden messages by women who are portrayed as resisting agents. Unfortunately this argument is not very convincing, so much more so because it seems to take its starting point as the assumption that women must have friends. As she argues, female friendship should be investigated because others have shown it to be an important phenomenon in community integration and "it has been noted for women in some communities" (1991: 92). Indeed, it can be argued that one of the biggest shortcomings of the agency and resistance line of analysis is that it starts with assumptions, most commonly that of the necessity of autonomous subjects who are ready to resist dominance, and then proceeds to "show" how such agentive resistance can be found the world over. This approach clearly runs counter to the spirit of anthropological analysis.

A completely different approach, and one critical of the autonomous agent, is that of Saba Mahmood (2005). Influenced by the work of Foucault, Mahmood critiques the notion of the autonomous subject and those feminist anthropologists who use it as reflecting a secular-liberal ideology. This does not mean, however, that she does not see the anthropological investigation of agency, and particularly its relevance to questions of morality and ethics, as important. Rather, Mahmood contends that anthropologists must move beyond agency as simply that of an autonomous subject. Contrasting with this approach, Mahmood views subjects as those persons who find themselves within historically particular discursive traditions, and as such, work on themselves in certain ways in order to become the kinds of persons these traditions ideally value.

The question may be raised at this point: how could such a notion be conceived of as agency? But this very question assumes that agency can only be performed by an autonomous subject who stands over and against repressive, dominating, or determining structures, and as such can act independently and counter to these structures. It is just such an assumption that Mahmood is trying to get away from and as such the question misses her point. This can be more clearly seen if we remember that earlier in this section I described agency as a relationship between individuals and structures. Viewed in this way, the autonomous subject, if possible at all, is only one possible relationship between these two entities.

Another possible relationship is that of power. In such a relationship the structure, or what Mahmood calls the discursive tradition, provides what might be called a range of possibilities for being and acting. It is within this range of possibilities that individuals work on themselves in certain ways in order to become certain kinds of persons. Agency in this way is conceived not as how individuals free themselves from the restraints and dominance of structures, but as how individuals make themselves into the kinds of persons who fit into certain structures. That is, how they make themselves into socially and morally appropriate persons.

Consider an example from Mahmood's work. Shyness and modesty are two of the most important virtues in Islam. Like all virtues in Islam, these virtues are gendered, that is, the extent to which one must exhibit shyness and modesty differs between men and women. One of the primary ways in which the Muslim women in the piety movement with which Mahmood did her research seek to achieve the appropriate level of shyness and modesty is through wearing a veil. They also learn to act shy and modest even when they do not feel so. In time, by wearing the veil even if at first it seems strange and unfeminine, and by acting shy and modest even if one does not feel it, these women come to embody the Islamic virtues of shyness and modesty and as such have accomplished a certain level of ethical and virtuous achievement.

From the perspective of a feminist anthropology concerned with finding resisting agents, these women would be viewed as giving into, or as dominated by, a patriarchal structure intent on repressing women. From the point of view of Mahmood, who sees agency as the relationship between historically and culturally particular individuals and structures, these women are ethically training themselves to be virtuous women within a particular socio-historic-cultural context. Agency for Mahmood, then, is not resistance to structures, but the active embodiment of these structures so that one can better become the kind of person recognized as a virtuous member of the community, tradition, or what have you. Such a notion of agency has much in common with the Aristotelian virtue ethics and Foucauldian technologies of the self that we discussed in Chapter 1. For what is significantly important for Mahmood, Aristotle, and Foucault is the ways in which persons work on their total selves, that is, their minds, bodies, emotions, feelings, and even souls, in order to be the kind of person deemed ethically appropriate within a particular socio-historic-cultural tradition.

A similar approach can be seen in the work of Usha Menon and her study of *śakti*, or female energy/power, among Hindu women (2002). Very similar to Mahmood, Menon argues that Hindu women perform their moral agency not through resistance to patriarchal ideologies and structures, but through the self-refinement necessary to achieve the ideal female self, that is, a self endowed with *śakti*. This is done by developing within themselves the primary Hindu female virtues of duty, self-control, and service to others (2002: 142). Thus, far from resisting the patriarchal order of Hindu society, the moral agency of these women seeks to reconfirm this order.

Again, calling such behavior and goals moral agency only seems strange if one assumes it as a concept that only holds for autonomous subjects who should in some way resist determining and dominating structures. But if instead one is concerned, as are both Menon and Mahmood, with understanding how persons ethically work on themselves and attempt to develop themselves into socially recognizable moral persons, then such a notion is extremely helpful.

However, it should be noted that by coming to embody *śakti* within themselves, Menon argues, Hindu women gain a particular kind of power status. Thus, what is particularly important about Menon's work is to show that Hindu women can still achieve a significant amount of power and moral authority without resisting the unequal societal structures. For in developing themselves into the proper kind of Hindu woman, these women gain the power to procreate and nurture, and thus a level of moral authority unattainable by men. Further, they are said to be able to "transform the undoable into the doable, and the impossible into the possible" (2002: 145–6). Unfortunately, Menon only gives examples from Hindu canonical stories to illustrate such powers. Nevertheless, it is clear that for the Hindu women with whom she worked, these stories provide moral guidance and exemplars for the kinds of lives they hope to live.

What is perhaps most interesting about Menon's argument is that it is the very inequality of gender relations that allows for such a notion of moral agency. That is to say, according to Menon, in Hindu societies this moral order, which can ultimately give women such overwhelming powers, is only possible because of this gender inequality. This inequality is based on the culturally perceived relative purity of men and the impurity of women, and it is just this difference that allows for the development of *śakti*. For in coming to embody the moral virtues of duty, self-control, and service to others, all of which necessitates the giving up of the ego, women have more potential to ethically develop themselves than do men. In doing so, then, they gain a moral authority within the family and community that provides them with a good deal of power despite their continued subordinate gender position.

Each of these are not only examples of how different anthropologists have utilized the concept of agency in discussing the morality of gender, but they also ultimately rest on the distinction between men and women and how this distinction assumes different moralities for each gender. Indeed, in their own way, each of these examples relies on the by now often critiqued association of, on the one hand, women with nature and the domestic sphere and, on the other, men with culture/society and the public/political sphere (Ortner 1974). This distinction and the double standards that go along with it, although heavily critiqued and questioned, has been the basis for much gender studies in the last quarter century or so. The most basic critique leveled against this is that local realities are more complex than this relatively straightforward and simple distinction.

It is this critique that informs Marilyn Strathern's (1997) analysis of Hagen gender moralities in Papua New Guinea. According to Strathern the morality of gender among the Hagen is not simply a matter of the difference between men and women, but depends greatly on who is interacting with whom. Thus, the distinction is not between men and women, but as Strathern calls it, the distinction between same-sex and cross-sex relations. That is to say, for example, a Hagen woman has different moral obligations and expectations when interacting with a man than she does with a woman. And while Strathern does not make this point explicitly, it seems clear from her analysis that these obligations and expectations also differ according to which clan the other man or woman belong. But this doubling of double standards is not all, for among the Hagen there is not only the usual distinction between the moral and the immoral, but so too are there acts which fall outside of this duality. There are, then, amoral acts as well. According to Strathern, then, the gendered morality of the Hagen is not based on the simple male/female, culture(society)/nature, public(political)/domestic distinction upon which so much feminist and anthropology of gender work relies, but is instead a complex web of integrated and contextually shifting relations that goes well beyond double standards.

Strathern also calls into question another prominent distinction made famous by the work of Carol Gilligan and often used by feminist commentators of gendered morality. Based on research among American men and women, Gilligan (1982) argues that while men hold an ethics of justice founded on abstract notions of human nature and universality, women hold an ethics of care founded on the experience of relationships with other persons. Gilligan further argues that although these are two very different moral positions, they can ultimately be reconciled because at their base each shares some basic assumptions about the need to respect and not harm other persons. For Gilligan, then, the abstract gets subsumed by relations, and in this sense it can be said that she is arguing for the actual predominance of the ethics of care over that of justice. In other words, she can be seen as arguing for the inversion of the dominant Euro-American moral ideology.

Strathern too sees a distinction between male and female moralities in Hagen, but as already said, they are more complex than this simple divide. Further, Strathern critiques Gilligan's argument by showing that among the Hagen both men and women's morality is based in contextual relationships. Because these moralities are based on relationships, they are, unlike with Gilligan, *irreconcilable*. Thus, when a Hagen person finds herself in a contextual situation where more than one moral alternative is possible, she must choose between them (Strathern 1997: 136–7).

What makes for such a situation? As discussed above, gendered morality among the Hagen differs primarily not between men and women, but based on the kind of relationship in which one is engaged, that is, either same-sex or cross-sex relations. Ultimately, however, men's moral obligations are for their clan, while women's moral obligations are split between their clan of origin and their clan of marriage. Thus, this adds another web of complexity to Hagen gendered morality. But because Hagens are aware of each of these differences, and according to Strathern weigh heavily the significance of the relations within which they are engaged and the various obligations and expectations the relationships carry, Hagen persons can with relative ease recognize the alternative moralities possible in each situation and choose accordingly. Strathern, then, makes an important contribution to the anthropology of moralities because she shows the complexity with which moral reasoning and decision-making takes place, and in doing so, shows that gendered morality goes well beyond a simple male/female divide.

While the majority of work on gender relations focuses on women, there is a significant amount of work that concentrates on men. One of the primary topics of the study of men is that of masculinity. The idea of masculinity encompasses not only a sense of identity, but perhaps more importantly for our purposes the values that are socially recognized as expressing this identity. In this sense, masculinity can be seen as a performance, that is to say, a public expression of enacted values. These enacted values often also have moral significance, and it is for this reason that masculinity can also be seen as a moral performance.

Michael Herzfeld (1985) has taken just this approach to the study of masculinity in a mountain village on the Greek island of Crete. Herzfeld is one of those anthropologists about whom I wrote in the introduction that uses the concept of morality without having actually done explicit ethnographic research on the topic of morality. Therefore, morality for Herzfeld is an analytic concept and not necessarily a local concept. While this poses problems for the reader, specifically in terms of not knowing if locals would interpret their own words and actions as morally imbued, as does the anthropologist, nevertheless, such studies, and particularly Herzfeld's, can be interestingly read from the perspective of the anthropology of moralities.

For the Glendiots, the Cretan villagers with whom Herzfeld did his research, masculinity or manhood can often be equated with a certain kind of morality. Just what kind of morality is this? It is a kind of performative morality that is not only the enactment of a certain kind of action, but an enactment done in such a way that it is recognized as beyond the norm. All Glendiot men may dance well, work hard, or be able to steel another's sheep. But to do each of these in such a way that others immediately recognize the excellence of their performance, this is what counts as masculinity among the Glendiot. Because this moral performance of Glendiot masculinity depends upon the social recognition of the meaning of the act as having significance beyond the normal enactment of the very same act, Herzfeld calls these enactments semiotic. Herzfeld focuses on the semiotic because the Glendiots, so he tells us, are overly concerned with meaning.

But meaning need not only refer to the realm of representation and significance, which is what Herzfeld seems to mean when he speaks of semiotics and the meaning of acts. And it is here that I question Herzfeld's interpretation. For meaning can also be recognized in non-representational actions and need not have significance in the sense of signifying anything beyond the act; in this sense we can speak of the moral meaning of actions as virtues. In other words, an act can have meaning simply because it is recognized by others as a virtuous act. To speak of a virtuous act in this sense is to speak of performing a valued act well. It is this, I suggest, that has meaning for the Glendiots and for this reason it is perhaps more precise to speak of the Glendiots having a virtue theory of masculinity and not a semiotic theory. Thus, as Herzfeld himself writes, among the Glendiot "there is less focus on 'being a good man' than on 'being *good at* being a man'" (1985: 16).

How do Glendiot men be good at being men? One example of how this is done shows precisely how local notions of virtue and morality can go against many of our own moral assumptions. For one of the primary ways in which Glendiot men can perform their manhood virtuously is by resisting the state, its ideology and law, and doing so with flare. Such resistance can take the form of stealing another's sheep, seeking revenge outside the law, or resisting efforts by the police to maintain their authority.

All of this sounds paradoxical when considered in light of the feminist claim that the state, indeed power itself, is an expression of masculine and patriarchal dominance, a claim echoed by the social theorist Bourdieu when he writes that modern states have "ratified and underscored the prescriptions and proscriptions of private patriarchy with those of a *public patriarchy*," and in so doing, have established an "androcentric vision" of moral order (2001: 87). And yet this moral order as established in the form of the Greek state does not seem to express the Glendiot notion of masculinity. This clearly calls into question the long-held feminist critique of the state and power and begs the question: just what kind of, or better yet, whose masculinity and patriarchy does the state and power represent if it does at all? If masculinity and patriarchy cannot be established as universally viable terms, as the Glendiot case clearly seems to suggest, then does this critique hold? And if it does hold, then perhaps one of the more interesting anthropological questions to be asked would be how local masculinities, and not only women, resist, are dominated by, or work on themselves to live within these power structures.

Even if dominant masculine moralities are not openly resisted by men within a society, this does not mean that these men are always comfortable with the principles of this kind of morality. Take, for example, the men of the Gisu of Uganda. For Gisu men violence is the mark of masculinity. That is, to be a man is to confront and find oneself regularly in the context of violence with other men. But as Suzette Heald claims, in a society lacking any central authority or a strong sense of law, morality must play the role of maintaining social order. This is particularly important for men and their relationship with violence. Thus, Heald argues, self-control and responsibility are important moral counterbalances to the masculine ideological expectations of violence (1999: 4, 71–2).

This precarious moral negotiation between self-control and responsibility, on the one hand, and masculine violence, on the other, are performatively symbolized in the circumcision rituals all Gisu young men must endure. This is so because circumcision is an inherently violent and painful act, and yet, the young men undergoing this ritual must not react to the violent pain. In this non-reaction, the young men are able to publicly perform their ability to exercise self-control and, in so doing, show that they have the responsibility necessary to be a Gisu man. The primary responsibility of Gisu men, so argues Heald, is to properly negotiate the moral dilemmas within contexts of violence and do so with self-control. Therefore, the way in which young Gisu men react to the circumcision ritual is a sign of their future moral character.

Here we see that much like the Glendiots, Gisu men also negotiate a certain relationship with their respective society's concept of masculinity and the moral expectations of this concept. Thus, both Glendiot and Gisu men can be seen as enacting moral agency in the sense spoken of above as a relationship between individuals and structures. Much like the women discussed at the beginning of this section, here we see that men also have a relationship to dominant moral ideologies and structures that are not exactly congruent. As already suggested, this non-congruency calls into question one of feminism's main critiques, that is, that morality and power are expressions of masculinity and patriarchy. This section, then, from Mahmood's important work on women in an Islamist piety movement in Egypt to Herzfeld's insightful analysis of manhood in mountainous Crete, has sought to offer counterexamples to the often overly straightforward, not to mention particularly secular-liberal, assumptions of some feminist anthropologists. In so doing, it has attempted to show how a more complex analysis of local gendered moralities can not only contribute to the anthropological study of moralities, but also make studies of agency and gender more interestingly subtle.

Sexuality

In an insightful paper presented at the workshop on Rethinking Moralities at the Max Planck Institute for Social Anthropology, Marian Burchardt argues that too often academic studies of sexuality do not address its moral aspects (2005: 1). Part of the reason this is so, Burchardt goes on to claim, is because feminism, which is one of the intellectual and political forces behind the increased study of sexuality since the 1970s, tends to consider morality a repressive discourse that upholds the structures of gender and sexual inequalities. Whether Burchardt or the feminists he claims to be describing are right about this or not, it is clear, as Foucault has shown, that sexuality is a locus of moral order within the discursive formation of modernity. In this section I will attempt to show how various anthropological studies of sexuality have been, or can be, interpreted in light of an anthropology of moralities.

An important contribution to the study of sexuality as the study of morality is an article by Ann Stoler on the ways in which Europeans, from the early years of colonization until its end, attempted to control sex in the colonies, and how this control was intimately tied to notions of race, gender, and indeed the very categories of colonizer and colonized (Stoler 1989). Although Stoler is quick to point out that this process differed according to local contexts, which colonial power was involved and the historic time period, it is clear, she argues, that sex as a particular kind of moral order was central not only for controlling, but also for defining the colonial context.

It seems that the central issue concerning sex in the colonies during this entire period was how to provide medically, psychologically, and morally safe women for European male colonizers. While there was hardly ever any doubt among colonial powers that prostitution and homosexuality did not provide this kind of safety, other options were hotly debated and changed over time. The vast majority of the colonial period, right up to the twentieth century, was characterized by tight restrictions on European women going to colonies. In fact, many colonial institutions went as far as only hiring single European men to go to the colonies. There they were expected to find a local woman as quickly as possible to become his concubine. Thus concubinage, with its non-European woman playing the role of house servant, local guide, emotional caretaker, and sexual partner, provided European colonizing men with a pseudo-family lifestyle in the colonies. This lifestyle was thought to provide the kind of medical, psychological, and moral safety that prostitution and homosexuality could not, while its clear hierarchical order helped create and maintain the greater racial, gender, and colonial hierarchy so important to the colonial endeavor.

By the twentieth century, however, this concubinage system was increasingly critiqued back in the colonial centers as immoral. It was at this point that European married and unmarried women were increasingly allowed and encouraged to move to the colonies. Once there, European women were positioned as the bearers of colonial morality and expected to support their husbands (and if single to find a husband in due time), keep the home, maintain a healthy diet for their family, and above all to exhibit sexual restraint. The importance of the expected sexual restraint of these women is something Stoler underplays, for here we see a mirroring of the increasingly important Victorian sexual-moral expectations making their way to the colonies from the colonial center. What would be interesting is to see how these expectations were similar or different than those back in the European centers, and an account for these similarities and differences.

This shift from a concubinage system to one reflecting Victorian bourgeois family values is not simply a matter of reproducing a moral system from the homeland. Instead, it is perhaps more indicative, Stoler tells us, of the increased questioning of the moral superiority of the colonizers. At the beginning of the twentieth century when colonial independence and nationalistic movements were on the rise, anything that suggested the moral, physical, or intellectual inferiority of the European colonizers required immediate attention. Thus, for example, British colonial administrators were required to retire at the age of fifty-five so that no non-Europeans could ever see a European age and degenerate (Stoler 1989: 645). So too did the concubinage system suggest the moral inferiority of the European colonizers. As such, it was deemed that only a proper family and the kind of sexual restraint it necessitates should be the kind of sexual and intimate unions condoned in the colonies. Thus, Stoler argues that sex and its moral interpretations were a central aspect of the continuous renegotiations of meaning and order during the colonial period.

If sex as a locus of moral order was vital to the colonial project, so too has it been and remains a central aspect of the moral order of postcolonial modernity. From gender relations to birth control, sexuality continues as one of the most significant aspects of moral debates and order in the contemporary world. Indeed, just as Stoler points out how sexuality was a focus point for moral debates concerning the proper kind of relations between genders in the colonial world, so too does this continue today. Take, for example, gender relations in the small northeastern Brazilian city of Caruaru (Rebhun 2004). While international images of Brazil are that of a sexually liberated country where men and women are free to express their sexuality, Rebhun shows that this is not the case in the conservative city of Caruaru. Indeed, one must wonder just how true it is of the rest of the country, for images and imaginations fueled by tourist dollars may not represent the realities of Brazilian sexual relations. Whatever the case may be for the rest of Brazil, this image certainly becomes less and less appropriate as one travels from the centers of the tourist industry.

In Caruaru one's moral worth is highly dependent upon one's sexual reputation. This is particularly true for women. Thus counter to the tourist images, the women of Caruaru are not free to express and enact their sexuality. Rebhun argues that in Caruaru there are discrete moral categories into which women are placed based upon their sexual relations with men. These categories, in a sense, rank the moral worth of women and include, in descending moral worth, everyone from the legal wife of a man, to his mistress, to the servants with whom he is free to have sexual relations, to prostitutes. Therefore, while men in Caruaru may in fact be free to engage in a variety of sexual relations, and in so doing acquire if not increased moral worth, then at least a certain level of masculine prestige, the women of Caruaru have no option other than to remain a virgin until marriage in order to maintain their moral worth as women. Indeed, if a woman loses her virginity prior to marriage "many men treat her as if she were a prostitute, a thing you can use and throw away" (Rebhun 2004: 186). Sexuality in this context, then, is a sign of one's moral worth.

It is interesting to note that quite another schema of categorization takes place in the Mexican context of the research of Marit Melhuus (1997). Here women are considered good or bad based on whether they are virgin brides who become loyal wives and nurturing mothers (good) or are not virgins and thus questionable wives and mothers (bad). Men, on the other hand, are categorized on a sliding scale of morality that entails more ambiguity than it does clarity, for there is no morally bad man on this scale. Thus, Melhuus contends, the category of bad woman is needed in order for there to be a link between sexuality and morality, for it is the bad woman that defines both the good man and good woman. The notion of the sexual categorization of women and its importance to local notions of moral worth, then, is clearly seen in these two different local contexts.

If sexuality is related to one's moral worth in Caruaru, so too is it related to other social categories that give it further weight in local moral interpretations. For similar to Stoler's contention that sexuality in the colonial context was a moral locus for defining other categories of race, gender, and colonialism itself, Rebhun argues that one's sexual reputation, and thus one's moral worth, in Caruaru is intimately related to questions of race. Just as there are discrete categorizations of women's moral worth based on their sexual relations, so too are there discrete racial categories that describe the perceived racial traits of a person. These traits range from skin color (in Brazil skin color is conceived as a range of lightness and darkness) to character attributes. According to Rebhun a woman's sexual reputation is intimately connected to her perceived racial category. For women who are perceived as darker are also often thought to be more sexually promiscuous. I write "perceived" here because Rebhun also claims that a woman is considered to be darker if she is known to be sexually promiscuous. Thus in Caruaru there is a line of moral reasoning that can be read as something like the following: dark women are sexually promiscuous and thus morally inferior. But because darkness and sexuality are socially interpretable categories, it is never clear which of the two is the primary determinant in this reasoning. Indeed, it can be said that in Caruaru darkness and sexuality are interconnected to such a degree that, in fact, they may be one and the same moral category.

Sexuality, and particularly female sexuality, is not only at the center of moral orders in the postcolonial world, but it also holds a significant place in moral debates in the United States. Indeed, debates over abortion and contraception go well beyond questions of right to life versus right to choice, for these debates have at their very core the moralization and control of female bodies and their sexuality. That these debates are often rhetorically expressed in the discourse of science, medicine, or even sexual abuse, only serves to cover over the moral basis of these debates.

Take, for example, the Federal Drug Administration (FDA) hearings over the proposed shift of Plan B, one of the oral contraceptives often referred to as the morning after pill, from a prescription to an over the counter contraceptive. Wynn and Trussell (2006) give an interesting analysis of this hearing in which they contend that what at the surface level appears to be an attempt to control the pharmaceutical industry is in fact a way of disciplining the sexuality of women and young people. For once the medical and pharmaceutical industry experts gave way to public testimonies, the hearings shifted from an emphasis on biomedical and scientific argumentation to moral arguments that centered on the control of women and teen's bodies, and through this their sexuality. But as Wynn and Trussell contend, even the medical arguments often had a latent moral basis, oftentimes focusing on issues of responsibility and bodily control, and thus, they suggest that in this hearing we see the impossibility of separating medical and scientific debates from those of politics and morality.

It should be noted that the same kind of moral debate did not accompany the introduction of Viagra and other erectile dysfunction pills, and therefore discloses the double standards concerning male and female sexuality in the United States. As already noted, the moral debate surrounding Plan B focused on the control of female sexuality and who was ultimately responsible for it. Those in favor of making Plan B available over the counter argued that in making this oral contraceptive more easily available women could take responsibility for their own sexual actions and its consequences without first consulting a doctor for a prescription. In cutting out the doctor as the middleman, women would be able to take control of their own sexuality. On the other hand, those against making Plan B available over the counter spoke of the dangers of cutting the doctor out of the process. If Plan B became available over the counter then anyone could buy it for any reason – rapists, sexual molesters to give to their victims, teenage boys who could convince their young partners not to use other forms of birth control, or any woman who wanted to give themselves an "abortion." Each of these arguments against the availability of Plan B focuses on the dangers of female sexuality, the need to protect women from it and its consequences and the need to keep in place an "expert" who can help control both female desire and supposed sexual predators. Whether one was for or against the over the counter availability of Plan B, questions of female sexual control and responsibility were at the center of the moral arguments.

Not only were these issues focused upon in the debates, but so too was the question of whether or not the use of these pills constitutes an abortion. While the vast majority of the medical and pharmaceutical experts testified that Plan B is not an abortifacient, many of those against the pills over the counter availability claimed that in fact this pill is an abortifacient. The disagreement over whether the use of Plan B is contraceptive or abortive is the result of the medical and legal ambiguity over definitions of pregnancy. This ambiguity leads directly to the moral ambiguity at the heart of not only the Plan B debate, but also the abortion debate. For when there is no agreement by medical and legal authorities of precisely when pregnancy occurs, the space for moral contention is opened. Here, then, it is possible to see the intimate interconnections between science, law, and moral discourse, and how in this case the interconnection is manifest in questions of female and young persons' sexuality.

The morality of female and young persons' sexuality and its relationship to reproduction is not only expressed in debates before formal committees, but more importantly is expressed all the time in everyday life. Consider, for example, the American media's censorship of nudity while scenes of extreme violence are regular occurrences on television; or the reputations single women endure for their sexual activity while men are encouraged to get all they can; or the various forms of social pressure one receives to marry and have children; or the continued stigmatization and prejudice against homosexuals despite progress made in the last thirty years. Each of these is an example of how everyday moral discourses and practices find expression in the sexual realm.

So too does the question of what a single pregnant woman should do and the decision she makes reveal the moral concerns, pressures and expectations felt by these women. According to Marcia Ellison (2003), 48 percent of American women have had unintended pregnancies. The fact that this large percentage is unknown and unrecognized only attests to the kind of social pressures and moral expectations put on women and couples to engage responsibly in sexual activity and reproduce. While this number includes more than just single women, these women perhaps feel the pressures and dilemmas, as well as the stigma, that come along with an unintended pregnancy even more so. For while American society is becoming more tolerant of single motherhood, the single mother who has become so through an unintended pregnancy is more likely to face stigmatization.

Indeed, as Ellison has shown, the choices these women make are highly influenced, on the one hand, by the fear of stigmatization and moral disrepute, and on the other, the kinds of options available to them by law. Having done research with women who became pregnant unintentionally either prior to or after the *Roe vs. Wade* Supreme Court decision that legalized abortion, Ellison found that abortion became a much more viable option for these women after this decision. Prior to the decision, adopting away the unintended child was far and away the commonest response. Only a very few of the women interviewed decided to keep their child, and these women tended to reference their religious beliefs or a sense of moral obligation for doing so. No matter which option was chosen, the majority of the women spoke of the stigmatization they felt from friends, family, and others. For many the response of their parents was most troubling, as it was not uncommon that mothers spoke of their overwhelming disappointment and shame, and fathers referred to their own daughters as whores. Because of this, many of these women took upon themselves a virtue of silence in order to avoid such responses. Even many of those who decided to keep their children still today only reveal to their most trusted and closest friends the circumstances of their child's birth. Here, then, is just one example of how moral expectations continue to be played out within and through the bodies of women and their sexuality in the contemporary United States, and, as Ellison is apt in pointing out, how the notion of shame is a moral concept that is just as applicable in this context as it is in the Mediterranean.

Moral attention to sexuality is not only characteristic of a modern project, for it can also be a response to this very project. While such responses may claim to be anti-modern, this very claim stands within a relationship that is mutually defining. In this sense, the modern and anti-modern define one another. For what counts as modernity relies on the unmodern Others as does the unmodern rely upon the modern for its very existence. Nor should it be thought that sexuality as a moral focus is only that of females. For the male body and its sexuality is also a locus of moral attention.

Take for example Hindu celibate men in India. According to Alter (1997), *brahmacharya*, or male celibacy, is a response to the immoral lifestyle of modernity. In particular, it is a concern over the tendency of young men to give in to the passions and pleasures of modernity, a concern which is given intensified anxiety over a fear of female sexuality. In this sense, *brahmacharya* is an attempt to reassert male power in a world in which it is thought lack of control is the predominant way of life.

Control is attempted to be brought back into the world through men's celibacy, and in particular, the control of their semen. For the focus is not so much on sexual acts, that is, according to the ideology of *brahmacharya* sexual acts are not bad in themselves, but it is the loss of semen that is seen as bad. This is so because semen is the source of power, of health, and indeed even truth. Such a fluid cannot be simply released; it must be treated with care and retained for one's own vitality. In this way one seeks to gain total control over the flow of one's semen, for example, through abstinence from sex, masturbation, and even nocturnal emissions, and thus gain total control over one's own being. This, then, is an embodied morality that begins with the control of semen and ends with the control of the person.

But Alter argues that such control is about more than morality, it is also about truth, and that it is through the simplified lifestyle of *brahmacharya* and its seminal and bodily control that the truth of being is realized. It is through this duality of the minute and the universal, control and truth, that the men who practice *brahmacharya* see their celibacy as leading to socio-moral reform. By practicing the art of controlling the flow of their own semen, they are able to learn, embody, and live truth, and through this example enact change in the world. For the truth of semen control is not the satisfaction of one's desires, but happiness through one's own and others' health and helping others attain this truth for themselves.

One thing that becomes particularly clear in the examples of this section is that sexuality as a moral category is often discussed by anthropologists in a way that suggests it is utilized in a crudely functionalist way to control persons and populations. As I have been trying to point out throughout this book, this is one of the dangers we have inherited from the Durkheimian tradition. While I think it is clear that sexuality may at times stand in a more obviously public position as a moral category, and because of this seemingly take on a more "determining" and "controlling" character in local moral worlds, I would urge caution in making such conclusions. For even in this most public of moral categories, there remains a range of possibilities within which moral negotiation, debate, and interpretation takes place. It is by focusing on these ranges of possibilities and the differences and similarities of moral interpretations they provoke, that we anthropologists of moralities can best contribute to understanding how certain social categories and institutions influence moral lives.

Family, Children, and Morality

Perhaps one of the reasons gender and sexuality are so intimately connected with local moralities is due to their relationship with the upbringing of children. For the socialization of children is not simply a matter of passing on social know-how to the next generation, it is primarily a process of the moral training of children. Indeed, social knowledge is useless without the moral ability to get along properly with various persons in different situations, and it is this foundational ability that must be passed on to children. Yet this ability is not a simple acquisition of one set of social rules for morally being in a social world, but instead, as Briggs (1998) convincingly shows, a process of individuals learning and choosing from a range of possibilities available as morally acceptable within any given society. While this process is formative in the early years of childhood, it continues throughout a lifetime.

Psychologists, following the lead of Piaget (1965) and Kohlberg (Munsey 1980), have tended to focus much of their research on the moral development of children and young adults in the hopes of discovering the various moral stages through which all persons develop into moral maturity. Anthropologists tend to reject this approach for two reasons. First, because this approach assumes that *all* humans regardless of time and place develop through the same basic stages toward moral maturity, it is a fundamental denial of the significant influence of cultural interpretations and social institutions for making social and moral persons. In particular, it misses the kind of individual choice and negotiations that occur within the range of possibilities available to all social persons that Briggs (1998) argues are essential to the process of making moral persons. Second, anthropologists tend to reject this approach because it conceives of the moral education of children as a one-way process of adults teaching children, rather than as a socially significant dialogical process. In contrast, anthropologists have found that the upbringing of children is not only a moral project for the training of children, it is also a moral project for the parents, and especially so for mothers, for in many societies having children puts a woman into another social category. While this social category is certainly more prestigious than that of a childless woman, it also comes with the burden of greater responsibility, primarily the proper moral upbringing of their children. It is possible to say that for many women around the world, as well as fathers in many societies, it is a moral responsibility to raise children properly. In doing so, these parents also achieve a different moral status.

Consider for example Heather Paxson's (2004) work on the ethics of motherhood in contemporary Greece. During her fieldwork Paxson was initially perplexed by statements by childless women who said that motherhood completes a woman. This paradox was further complicated by some of their claims that in not having children they were acting responsibly. How is it, Paxson asked, that a woman could act responsibly by not having a child and yet say that only a mother is a complete woman? This paradox is a result, Paxson claims, of the modernization project of Greece and its relationship with its own past and the future as an EU member. A good modern woman is supposed to exercise rationality, choice, and responsibility, while a good woman as such is supposed to be a mother: thus the paradox. But Paxson claims the paradox may not be as clear as it seems. For motherhood does not necessarily complete a woman in the sense that it is her purpose – as if without a child her life has been "meaningless" – but rather it completes her in the sense that motherhood is a virtuous goal.

Here it is possible to see what might be called the ethics of motherhood. Paxson takes an Aristotelian approach to ethics in her analysis and posits social norms as moral virtues. I would disagree slightly with Paxson and say that for Aristotle virtue was not a matter of the proper performance of social norms and expectations, but the excellent performance of certain social *virtues*. Virtues are not social norms, but are certain highly regarded social and ethical sensibilities that must be performed with excellence and skill in very particular social contexts and situations. Motherhood, then, is not a virtuous good because it fulfills a social norm, as Paxson would seemingly have it, but instead because it requires certain kinds of ethical sensibilities properly attuned to one's social world, child, and self. Thus, very similar to how Herzfeld described Glendiot men, the mother is not necessarily a "good woman," but is in fact "good at being a woman." But because motherhood is only one natural potentiality of women, it is not the only way of being "good at being a woman," and it is for this reason that Paxson avoids the characterization of mothers as "good women."

Paxson includes in her research women who have children by means of in vitro fertilization (IVF). Unlike many of the bioethical debates that surround IVF in the Anglo-speaking world, in Greece, Paxson argues, IVF is seen as a natural means of reproduction. This is so because it is seen as a morally responsible act in which a free choice is made to fulfill the social virtue of motherhood. Here it is possible to see once again the coming together of "nature," the social, and biotechnology in the moral realm, and as such reveals the multidimensional nature of local moralities.

Signe Howell (2003) makes a similar argument regarding transnational adoption in Norway. Just as the women with whom Paxson worked who were unable to have children utilized IVF in order to become mothers, so too is transnational adoption becoming a popular way in Norway for couples to become parents. Howell interprets this as a process of kinning, by which she means "the process by which a foetus or new-born child (or a previously unconnected person) is brought into a significant and permanent relationship with a group of people that is expressed in a kin idiom" (2003: 465). Kinning, however, is not simply a matter of bringing a person into a family unit from "outside," but is rather a process of subjectivation, that is, a process of socially becoming a particular kind of person. In using this Foucauldian term Howell is borrowing from Faubion's work on the ethics of kinship (2001b), in which he argues that kinship itself is a system of subjectivation, by which he means the processes by which individuals are made into, categorized as, and make themselves into subjects or particular kinds of persons.

Howell further argues – again, similar to Paxson – that this process of kinning and subjectivation is not simply a one-way path of changing adopted outsiders into proper Norwegian persons. Rather, these are *intersubjective* processes through which both the child and the parents are re-created into new kinds of persons and, as such, acquire new kinds of moral values. Thus, what is clear from the work of both Paxson and Howell is that the relationship between parents and children is not simply a matter of parents teaching moral values to children. Instead it is perhaps more appropriate to consider this a mutual process of subjectivation by which each come to acquire new social positions in life, and through this become new kinds of moral persons.

And yet it cannot be entirely discounted that the moral socialization of children is a deeply important part of kin relations. This becomes clearly obvious in those situations, which unfortunately have become more and more common in the contemporary world, where children miss out on the moral socialization provided by their parents, relatives, and communities. One such situation is when children the world over find themselves actively taking part in wars. According to Dickson-Gómez (2003) some 300,000 children are taking part in 36 conflicts in the world today. In her research with adults who participated in the war in El Salvador during their youth, Dickson-Gómez found that by missing out on the kind of moral socialization children need, these adults today have difficulty with issues of trust and peaceful relations with others, and lack the ability to have a meaningful life. Although such situations are tragic, thankfully they are relatively limited in the world, for the vast majority of children find themselves in mostly peaceful life situations, although such socially violent forces as poverty and inequality characterize the lives of many.

A significant contribution to the anthropology of moralities has been made by Helle Rydstrøm (2003) with her description of the ways in which Vietnamese children embody local moralities through just the kind of moral socialization missed out on by the children of war. According to Rydstrøm, learning morality in the Vietnamese commune where she did her research is intimately tied to its patrilineal kin organization. This is so because the fact that men and their family line have social and kinship priority allows for a distinction between the ways in which boys and girls are conceived of as learning how to be moral persons. Thus, boys are thought to have inherited the morality that is natural to, or inherent in, the patrilineal line of decent; because the boy is thought to be closer to his father's family, so too is he closer morally by birth.

The girl, on the other hand, is conceived to be a kind of blank slate onto which proper morality must be carefully written. This is doubly important for understanding local notions of morality and how it is tied to kinship. First, because the girl is considered to be distant from the father's line she holds a morally ambiguous position and must not only be trained as a moral (female) person, but perhaps more importantly, must be trained to be a moral (female) person within a particular family. Secondly, and related to this, because she will one day leave the family to be married and become part of her husband's family, she still represents the moral and social standing of her father's family. Thus, while it may at first glance appear that the males stand as the moral centerpiece of this commune, in fact women as being born with moral blank slates work as the primary medium by which not only morality, but also kin relations, are shared and passed along.

This is also seen in the primary importance that mothers have in morally socializing both young girls and boys. Rydstrøm argues that this moral socializing does not occur through cognitive learning, but is instead a kind of bodily practice that children acquire primarily through being with, imitating, doing with, and being scolded by their mothers. In this way, so Rydstrøm claims, children come to embody a moral habitus, a term borrowed from the social theorist Bourdieu which refers to a person or group's bodily dispositions that reflect external social structures but at the same time allow for certain possibilities of choice. While this is not the place to critique Bourdieu's notion of habitus, suffice it to say I question its usefulness in terms of understanding how choice, change, and indeed even conscious attempts at morally working on oneself occur. Nevertheless, the point Rydstrøm makes by utilizing this concept is to suggest that morality is embodied through the practice of local ways of doing everyday activities and being with others, and not learned, for the most part, through intentional cognitive training.

Indeed, in each of their own ways this has been the central point of the three anthropologists I primarily considered in this section. That is to say, that through kin relations of various kinds, people, whether they be parents or children, engage in a kind of intersubjective, often unintentional but sometimes very intentional, relationship that leads to the shifting of moral status of all those involved. While parents gain a new way of moral being, understanding, and status within their communities, children come to embody a moral way of being that is recognized as appropriate by their community. Neither of these could happen without the other. Kinship, family, and childrearing, then, can be seen as a vital moral process in any community.

Some Final Words

In this chapter I have tried to show the complexities, disjunctures, and contradictions of the relationship between local moralities and notions of gender, sexuality, and kinship. As should be clear, the old feminist critique of the moral subordination of women, while still pertinent and important, is perhaps too simple. The moral reality of peoples' everyday lives is much more complicated than this model would suggest. To further complicate the matter, local moralities and their relationship to the various spheres of life I have covered in this chapter are also intimately connected to realms of politics, global and local economics, as well as religion and the like. It is this complex world of interconnections that makes the relationship between moralities, gender, sexuality, and kinship infinitely fertile for study by anthropologists.

–5–

Illness, Health, and Medicine

Since the mid 1980s medical anthropology has been one of the leading and most influential subdisciplines of anthropology. In addressing such issues as the body, personhood, narrative, and power, they have made contributions to ethnographic and theoretical approaches that have helped shift the ways in which anthropologists conceive of their work. Although to a much lesser extent, namely because the concept of morality is only now becoming more commonly utilized among anthropologists, medical anthropologists have also contributed greatly to anthropological approaches to the study of local moralities.

In this chapter we will consider some of the ways in which medical anthropology has played a significant role in the formation of what we now call an anthropology of moralities. In particular we will consider four of the central themes medical anthropologists have considered from a moral perspective. Thus we will see how their critiques of biomedicine and bioethics, a deep concern with the HIV/AIDS pandemic, and an openness to narrative research and analysis have led them to emphasize the moral realm of everyday life and discourse as a vital aspect for under-standing these issues. What is of primary importance, I suggest, is how much of their research discloses the differences – sometimes great and sometimes very subtle – between persons' moral conceptions. Let us turn, then, to the first theme of the critique of biomedicine to see how this is done.

The Morality of Biomedicine

Biomedicine is the term generally used to describe the kind of medical knowledge and practice that has come to be dominant in the Western world. From the perspective of the practitioners and most of the consumers of biomedicine, it is considered to be objectively based on a naturalistic view of the human body, and honed over years of rational and scientifically based research, discovery, and training. Because of this perspective, biomedicine is widely considered an objective and universally true stock of knowledge and practices that offers the best possible means of treating illness and disease and relieving suffering worldwide. It is just this perspective and the many assumptions that go along with it that medical anthropologists have sought to challenge. One of the ways they have done so is by showing how biomedicine itself is a contested realm of concepts, categories, and practices, and that one of the ways in which it is contested is on moral grounds. Thus, just as we saw in the last chapter that the public hearings over the availability of the morning after pill went way beyond medical concerns, so too has much of biomedical knowledge and practice undergone similar kinds of moral and political debates.

Therefore, what today might look as if it is a necessary and integral truth of biomedicine is in fact a result of a history of contested relationships, understandings, and practices. Take, for example, medical authority. For most medical personnel and biomedical consumers it is assumed that the former are the possessors of authority and power, and thus responsible for the majority of decision-making. To many of us who have been in hospitals or even doctors' offices, this seems natural. However, such an unequal relationship between doctors and patients has not always been the case. Indeed, as Judith Walzer Leavitt (1987) shows, such a relationship is historically quite recent and a result of much contested debates between patients and doctors, doctors and the Church, and among doctors themselves.

According to Leavitt, at the beginning of the twentieth century medical authority was still hotly contested. In fact, at that time medical decisions were still mainly negotiated between the doctor, the patient, the patient's family and friends, and sometimes even the patient's priest or pastor. This was particularly so for birthing, the majority of which at this time were still done at home. If complications arose, decisions had to be made. These decisions could be extremely difficult, since sometimes it required deciding between the life and death of either the mother or the fetus. The two most common alternatives were either a Cesarean section or a craniotomy. The former, which is the opening of the mother's abdomen, although at the time very risky for the mother, offered a good chance of survival for the child. The latter, which is the surgical mutilation of the fetal head to permit vaginal extraction, on the other hand, was much safer for the mother, but necessitated the termination of the fetus. While most mothers and family members tended to prefer craniotomies, priests were entirely against this procedure. Doctors also tended to prefer Cesarean sections.

However, doctors were reliant upon the others present to help make this decision. Needless to say, most doctors found this troubling because they believed the patients and their family members, as well as priests, made their decisions based upon moral, religious, and traditional forms of reasoning, while he, the doctor, considered his judgment to be based on strictly medical information and knowledge. This, of course, is what the doctors thought. Leavitt, on the other hand, shows that this was not exactly the case. By reviewing debates among doctors at the time, Leavitt shows that because they preferred the Cesarean section, which put the mother at greater risk, over craniotomy, the doctors had to find ways to defend the priority of the fetus's life over that of the mother. "This could not be accomplished using a medical argument alone. Thus, at the same moment in history when [doctors] tried to make objective science paramount ... [they] were forced to couch their own arguments in social and moral terms" (Leavitt 1987: 246). Ironically, then, in their attempts to gain full authority in medical decisions, they often relied on the same kinds of moral arguments and reasoning that they reproached patients, family members, and clergy for using. Ultimately it was most likely the increased reliance on technology in birthing that eventually led to doctors as the sole possessors of medical authority. Thus, it is interesting to note that it was not medical knowledge or practice in itself that inherently provided doctors with authority, but rather their practical skill of technology use. It is for this reason, then, that doctors also relied heavily on moral argumentation and reasoning in order to help secure their authority.

A similar situation is seen in post-Soviet Russia. According to Michele Rivkin-Fish, post-Soviet medical practice is characterized by a struggle over medical authority (2005; see also Case Study 2). Unlike during the Soviet period when all medical services were funded and managed by the state, and thus no options of choice were available, increasingly in the post-Soviet years options have become available. This has allowed for the increased contestation of medical authority. If a person does not like the service with which they are provided, they have the option, if they can afford it, to go to another hospital or clinic. Despite the possible options of state-run public medical services or private pay-for-service, which have allowed for some resistance to established medical authority, medical personnel continue to use such moral tactics as shaming and allocation of personal responsibility onto patients in order to maintain their position of authority. Thus, medical authority in post-Soviet Russia, much like in the turn of the century United States, is contested and maintained by moral, social, and political means.

It is not only medical authority that is debated on moral grounds, but so too are the practices of biomedicine. While biomedical discourse attempts to give the impression that its knowledge and practice is universally valid and adhered to by all its practitioners, ethnographic research shows that this is not the case. Take, for example, Margaret Lock's research on cross-cultural responses to irreversible loss of consciousness, or brain death, by doctors in Japan, Canada, and the United States. While neurologists in these countries "undertake essentially the same tests and measurements, use the same logical arguments, and draw the same inferences to make a diagnosis," different culturally informed moral values influence these doctors' responses to the diagnosis (Lock 2001a: 487–8). Thus, Japanese doctors are extremely reluctant to consider people with an irreversible loss of consciousness as no longer alive and with no individual rights or interests, while American and Canadian doctors, on the other hand, generally consider these "persons" no longer alive despite the fact that their bodies continue to function as fully alive (2001a: 488). Because of these different moral responses, there is a significant difference in how doctors treat these persons in terms of the procurement of organs from them. It is clear, then, that the purely medical diagnosis of brain death is intimately interconnected with local moral ideas of what constitutes life and death, personhood, and how doctors and society should relate to these moral categories as they become manifest in medical treatment.

While it is evident that medical knowledge and practice is often contested on moral grounds, a contestation which brings into question the assumption that biomedicine is universally and rationally true and applicable, it is also clear that the results of biomedical practices can also have moral interpretations. As Brodwin (1996) has shown in his study of medicine and morality in Haiti, the moral status of a sick person is at stake in the kind of diagnosis they receive. This is so because for the Haitians Brodwin studied, and indeed for many people around the world, illness, disease, and suffering are understood in terms of local moralities.

The moral status of a sick person in Haiti particularly comes into question if biomedical attempts to heal the person fail, for while most Haitians accept the benefits of biomedicine and have integrated it into their everyday lives, it is not the only available treatment for the sick. If biomedical treatment fails, this is a sign that the sickness is not a natural one, but instead is what is locally known as a *sent* sickness. That is, it is a sickness sent onto a person by another person. This is usually done out of reasons of jealousy or revenge. Thus, if one is "diagnosed" as having a sent sickness, the next step is to figure out why this sickness was sent onto the person. This is a process of interpreting one's moral character and the moral character of the person who sent the sickness. Has one harmed another? Insulted another? Or is someone else simply jealous of the person? In discovering the answers to these morally imbued questions, a proper treatment can be taken up.

Interestingly this treatment is most commonly offered by a *houngan*, or a person who serves the spirits and practices what is commonly known as Vodoun. The *houngan* is a marginal figure who, according to the moral discourse of most of the Haitians with which Brodwin worked, is morally suspect because of his or her dealings with potentially evil spirits. This marginal status is further solidified since it is to the *houngan* that a person generally comes in order to send a sickness onto another. Thus, it is the *houngan* who both sends a sickness and relieves people of sent sickness, or what is also called a *maladi Satan*. Because of this position as both the sender and reliever of sent sickness, the *houngan* holds a morally ambiguous position in Haitian society. And yet, despite this ambiguity it is the *houngan* who is sought when one is "diagnosed" with a sent sickness. Thus, notwithstanding how the *houngan* is characterized in typical moral discourse, in everyday practice he is widely considered the only possible relief and treatment of sent sickness. In the figure of the *houngan*, then, we see the embodiment of a local distinction between "official" moral discourse and what people actually do in everyday life. Additionally, and in Brodwin's work in general, we see an interesting case of how biomedical diagnoses and failure of treatment open up alternative moral worlds and moral implications for both sick persons and those others who become available to offer help.

A critical anthropological study of biomedicine, then, has revealed the intimate connection between biomedicine's discourse and practice and moral interpretations and understandings. Unlike the authoritative, universal, and rationalistic discipline that biomedicine has portrayed itself as, anthropological inquiry has shown that it has a history of contestation and negotiation that has often taken place on moral grounds. In addition, anthropologists have shown that biomedicine often exists in a world of medical pluralism, where different medical traditions and practices may be invoked by the sick and suffering. Which one of these traditions and practices is invoked often depends on the moral interpretations of those people choosing.

HIV/AIDS and Morality

As we have just seen, illness and suffering, as well as biomedicine and its failure to always alleviate the former, often have various moral interpretations. This is particularly so for the HIV/AIDS epidemic. This worldwide epidemic, which has taken the lives of tens of millions of people since the early 1980s, has proven a particularly difficult task for biomedicine. At the time of writing there is no guaranteed prevention or cure for HIV/AIDS. In addition to the failure of biomedicine vis-à-vis HIV/AIDS, the disease is generally passed from one person to another by means of activity and behavior that is cross-culturally often open to moral interpretation, i.e. both heterosexual and homosexual sex and injecting drug use. The combination of biomedicine's failure and the means by which it is transmitted from person to person have led to the fact that HIV/AIDS is interpreted in moral terms nearly everywhere the epidemic has hit. Added to this local interpretation is the fact that anthropologists have pointed out, rightly I believe, that the HIV/AIDS epidemic is not simply a result of individual behavior, but more importantly is closely linked to social and gender inequality, an interpretation which itself is often intimately entwined with the moral assumptions of the anthropologist. For these reasons it is clear that HIV/AIDS is one of the most morally imbued topics of anthropological research.

One of the most important anthropological works on the HIV/AIDS epidemic has been done by Paul Farmer (1992), who combines a political economic and interpretive approach to show that the HIV/AIDS crisis in Haiti can be characterized as a geography of blame. By interpreting the crisis in this manner, Farmer means to show that the epidemic cannot be thought of as simply a local matter, but is best understood as intimately connected with the North American/Caribbean political economic system. Thus, part of the geography of blame is the fact that in the early years of the epidemic in the United States, Haitian immigrants were widely blamed in the media and by biomedical researchers and doctors as the cause and the carriers of HIV/AIDS to the country. While this in itself may have interesting moral implications, for our purposes the significance of blame in relation to the epidemic is much more salient in Haiti itself.

Farmer does not intend his study of HIV/AIDS in Haiti to be an anthropological study of local moralities, nevertheless, his work does significantly contribute to our understanding of how local moral understandings play a role in how illness, suffering, biomedicine, and its alternatives can be interpreted and acted upon.

Similar to Brodwin's claim that in Haiti the failure of biomedical treatment leads to both a moral interpretation of the sick person and those around them, as well as the opening of alternative moral worlds for possible treatment, so too does Farmer show that the failure of biomedicine to prevent and treat HIV/AIDS has led to local moral interpretations of the disease, those who have it, and those around them.

According to Farmer, HIV/AIDS is known locally as a jealousy sickness. That is to say, it is a sent sickness intentionally sent from one person onto another, and which can only be treated by a *houngan*. Once it is realized that one is infected with this sent sickness, a "moral calculus" (Farmer 1992: 109) ensues in order to try to, on the one hand, discover who it is that sent the sickness and why, for with this discovery a cure may be more easily found, and on the other hand, a decision must be made whether the sick person and her family wants to seek retribution by sending a sickness back. This decision in itself becomes a moral question, for it entails deciding whether one wants to continue the cycle of blame, accusation, and retribution that characterizes the HIV/AIDS epidemic in Haiti.

Thus, from a certain perspective, HIV/AIDS in Haiti is not simply a biomedical problem, but rather is also a moral problem, for it opens up questions of relations between persons and families, as well as the community in general. Additionally, it should be noted, the main response to HIV/AIDS in Haiti, according to the work of Farmer, is not so much about finding a way to treat it, although that is certainly important as well, but in finding answers to such moral questions as: Who sent this sickness onto me and why? What did I do to deserve this sent sickness? Should I or my family retaliate and in so doing cause the sickness and possible death of another?

It would be very easy for someone from the United States or Europe to read about Haitian moral interpretations of sickness and HIV/AIDS and think something like the following: well they only believe in sent sickness and interpret it morally because they don't understand the biological and biomedical aspects of the disease. In other words, it would be very easy to see this as an opposition between "their" beliefs as superstitious or traditional and "our" knowledge of scientific and medical truth (Good 1994: 7–8). This distinction, however, does not adequately describe the situation. For both Brodwin and Farmer are clear that in most cases the people involved in the sent sickness are totally aware and, especially in Brodwin's case, very accepting of biomedical explanations and processes. This, however, does not get in the way of accepting alternative or additional explanations and understandings. For a disease can be understood both as a naturalistic and biomedical process, as well as a morally imbued sent sickness. One does not exclude the other.

Nor does a complete acceptance and general understanding of biomedical explanations of HIV/AIDS necessarily discount moral interpretations of the disease and the people who may have or in fact do have it. Consider for example Dilger's research on the moral understandings of sexuality and HIV/AIDS by young people in rural Tanzania (2003). According to Dilger the young people with whom he did research in Tanzania have a very strong understanding of biomedical explanations of the causes of HIV/AIDS, how it is transmitted, and the kinds of risks associated with certain sexual activities. Despite this understanding, the majority of these young people continue to engage in risky behavior. Most significantly many of them do not use condoms.

According to Dilger this is not because they do not know or understand that condoms help prevent the transmission of HIV, but rather it is because they believe they can rely on the moral capacity of trust between themselves and their sexual partners. This is especially true for men, who consider themselves able to judge the moral character of their female partners and thus their HIV status. Because of this, Dilger interprets his research subjects as reflexive moral subjects. That is, as persons who negotiate and choose between different possible moral acts and interpretations. For example, many of the young women he interviewed are stuck between traditional gender expectations and roles, and the contingencies, ambiguities, and risks that come along with modernity. Thus, while they continue to try to remain "morally accepted persons" who have sexual intercourse with their partners without condoms (for it is often assumed that they themselves are prostitutes if they demand that their partner use a condom), they at the same time need to make difficult decisions about the amount of trust they can have for their partners and the level of risk they are able to take on in their sexual relations (Dilger 2003: 43–5).

It should also be noted that many of these young Tanzanians interpret HIV/AIDS as a result of the moral breakdown of their own society, a breakdown that has occurred because of the increased influence of modernity in their country. In other words, modernity has brought with it a change in gender relations and expectations, media images and ideas foreign to Tanzania, and an emphasis on consumerism, all of which is seen to have negatively affected morality in such a way that it has led to an increase in the kinds of immoral behavior associated with the spread of HIV/AIDS. Thus, among these young Tanzanians there is not only a clear understanding of the biomedical explanations of the HIV/AIDS epidemic, but also of the social and moral explanations of the epidemic.

The same can be seen in Russia, which now has the fastest growth rate of HIV/AIDS in the world, and where I have been conducting research on the moral interpretations of the epidemic and how this interpretation influences the kinds of prevention and treatment programs offered (Zigon 2008). Thus, for example, the Russian Orthodox Church (ROC) recognizes the biomedical explanations of HIV/AIDS, but emphasizes the significance of the breakdown of morality in post-Soviet Russia as the primary cause of the epidemic. Most specifically, the ROC sees the lack of Orthodox Christian morality as the cause of HIV/AIDS. Because of this, the Church emphasizes the teaching of Orthodox Christian morality in its HIV prevention and treatment programs, and fully opposes such secular programs as needle exchange and condom distribution, also known as harm reduction programs, and sees such programs as the legalization and legitimation of sin.

These responses to the post-Soviet transition of Russia and the modernizing period in Tanzania can be seen as a moral panic. Moral panic has been described as a period of time during which a "condition, episode, person or group of persons emerges to become defined as a threat to societal values and interests" (quoted in Fordham 2001: 287). Moral panic is quite common during times of societal change, such as that in post-Soviet Russia, modernizing Tanzania, or, as Fordham argues concerning the moral panic around HIV/AIDS in Thailand, the increasing influence of globalization in that country. I have argued elsewhere that these periods of social change are often characterized as a period of general moral breakdown (Zigon 2007), and it is for this reason that moral panic is often focused on particular acts, conditions, or groups of people.

Graham Fordham (2001) has argued that Thai ways of understanding HIV/AIDS has been constructed by means of a moral panic in Thailand. The epidemic hit Thailand in the midst of massive societal change due to the influence of globalization. One of the results of globalization was the increased commodification of sex, and therefore, the increased number of prostitutes. This condition, along with the mainstream and biomedical discourse of the danger of risk groups and risk behavior, easily allowed for a reaction of moral panic against prostitutes not only as the primary cause of the HIV/AIDS epidemic in Thailand, but as a metaphor for the breakdown of traditional Thai society and morality. Thus, prostitutes were viewed not only as immoral, but also as witches. It is significant that prostitutes are labeled as witches and not merely as immoral. For while to be immoral certainly implies that one has done wrongly vis-à-vis other persons, it is not entirely clear how far reaching the consequences extend. However, to be labeled a witch is to be labeled as one who not only is immoral, but who is also dangerous to others and society in general. Labeled as witches, then, prostitutes come to embody not only the immorality of the kinds of activity viewed as the cause of the HIV/AIDS epidemic in Thailand, but also metaphorically stand in for a perceived societal-wide moral breakdown.

If prostitutes as witches are the metaphorical image used to conceptualize the moral panic centered on HIV/AIDS in Thailand, then the same can be said for condoms in Mozambique. Pfeiffer (2004) has shown how social marketing (SM), or advertising campaigns used to promote certain biomedically conceived healthy practices, such as condom use or the importance of hydration, can often backfire if not done with an awareness of how local communities might respond.

While condom social marketing (CSM) has become the centerpiece of AIDS education and prevention in sub-Saharan Africa (Pfeiffer 2004: 77), its results may not be as positive as they appear at first glance. It is certainly true that since its inception, condom purchases have risen dramatically in Mozambique, but it is also true that CSM has led to widespread rumors and belief among the population that condoms themselves are the cause of HIV. This is so because the HIV/AIDS epidemic was just beginning to be accepted by the local population as a serious problem at the time of the inception of a new CSM campaign centered on the brand name Jeito. It did not help that the campaign promoting Jeito brand condoms used images and metaphors intended to evoke sexual intercourse. Thus, many came to associate the epidemic with Jeito itself. In this sense, then, the social marketing that was intended to help prevent the spread of HIV/AIDS resulted in the inception of a moral panic that sees the very consumer product intended to stop the epidemic – Jeito brand condoms – as its cause.

So far in this section we have seen that HIV/AIDS often brings about a moral response at several different levels. Not only do local people and institutions make moral interpretations of the epidemic, but so too do the moral understandings of anthropologists influence the way they research and analyze the topic. Before we end this section it is important to consider one last way in which HIV/AIDS brings about a moral response, that is, in terms of human rights.

In my own research on institutional responses to the HIV/AIDS crisis in Russia it has become clear that the concept of human rights is central to the way in which both international and Russian NGOs attempt to discursively construct a proper response to the crisis. These rights are seen as a way of empowering, on the one hand, people living with HIV/AIDS to participate in fighting the epidemic, and on the other hand, the general population by avoiding the propagation of the epidemic. Additionally, these rights are meant to help guarantee the equal treatment of and opportunities for people living with HIV/AIDS and their families. This is particularly important, so many of the NGOs working in Russia and elsewhere claim, because of the stigma many infected and at-risk people experience from governments, medical personnel, employers or potential employers, and many others with whom they interact in their everyday lives.

Examples of such rights include the right to the best attainable standard of physical and mental health, the right to privacy, and the right to access to information and education. While it is often claimed that the notion of human rights is founded on a natural law theory, which at its most basic asserts that morality and governmental/institutional law are based on a shared human nature, Talal Asad (2003) has argued that human rights are better understood as the expression of a particular socio-politico-historical order. In other words, human rights are the expression of a certain kind of power. Asad's point seems to ring particularly true when considering the list of human rights listed above. For while each of these rights may certainly contribute to a better sense of well-being, there is no necessary connection between any of them and so-called human nature, if such a thing can truly be said to exist.

This point becomes particularly obvious when these and similar rights, all of which may seem perfectly obvious and natural to many Euro-Americans, are attempted to be implemented by NGOs and other institutions in countries where these rights are completely foreign. Take, for example, the case of NGOs in India attempting to implement the rights of privacy and confidentiality for HIV infected persons in that country's medical institutions. According to Kavita Misra (2006), although the various HIV and AIDS related NGOs express a united and coherent front in terms of supporting these rights, there are in fact deep and divided differences, debates and negotiations going on behind the scenes. Indeed, the most contentious aspect of agreeing on and implementing these rights of privacy and confidentiality in India is that traditionally there is no Indian concept, value, or even word for these rights. Thus, unless NGO activists, medical personnel, state employees and politicians, and anyone else involved in questions of privacy and confidentiality unquestioningly accept these rights as universal, then they are ripe for being questioned for their appropriateness to the cultural context.

Despite the debates aroused both within NGOs and between NGOs and other institutions regarding the rights of privacy and confidentiality for infected and at-risk peoples in India, Misra claims the notion of rights is the unifying ideal toward which AIDS activists work in India. Indeed, the same can be said for AIDS activists in South Africa as well, but as Robins (2006) points out, participation in such activism can go beyond the working for the implementation of rights and reach a level of what he calls ritual. By emphasizing this process of activism as a ritual, Robins focuses on the experience of personal transformation many of these activists undergo in the realization of their HIV status, their acceptance of this status, and their eventual turn toward activism. Thus, for Robins what is important in the experience of these activists as people who work for the rights of themselves and others is the centrality of their self-transformation, or what might be called their ability to ethically work on themselves to become new kinds of persons.

But it is not only the activists who Robins contends are undergoing a transformation, for the activists themselves are attempting, through the implementation of a rights-based approach to HIV/AIDS prevention and treatment, to construct new "responsibilized" subjects. By this it is meant "responsible citizens" who demonstrate drug treatment adherence, disclosure of HIV status, condom use, and maintenance of healthy lifestyles. In turn, these "responsible citizens" would enjoy the benefits of (or perhaps the activists would prefer to say enjoy the rights to) free health care and ARV drug therapy.

It should be noted, however, and Robins seems to miss this point, this rights-based approach seems to depend on the ethical, that is to say, the self-transformation of HIV positive and at-risk persons. Thus, similar to how much moral discourse around HIV/AIDS focuses on the so-called immoral behavior of these persons and the necessity of these persons to change their behavior to "normal" and "moral" behavior, so too does this approach in South Africa necessitate the responsibilization of these persons. In other words, in order for them to acquire their supposed rights to free health care and ARV therapy, they must first transform the kinds of persons they are. In the end, then, this rights-based approach appears to have the same, for a lack of a better phrase, grammatical structure that underlies many of the more conservative moral approaches to the HIV/AIDS epidemic.

And indeed it is important to consider the assumptions that underlie many of these rights-based and moral interpretations of not only HIV/AIDS, but many other illnesses, diseases, and suffering, and the biomedicine that claims to be the only true source of relief from them. It is to these assumptions and, most importantly, how they are narratively articulated and covered over in both everyday and official forms of speech that we will turn to in the next section.

Narrative and Medical Encounters

Medical anthropologists have been in the forefront of the narrative turn in anthropological research and analysis. Narratives allow for the articulation of the interconnection between subjective experience and the socio-politico-historical structures that help shape this experience. Medical anthropologists have thus used the narrative approach as a way to highlight, for example, the social meaning of personal suffering, the difference in the way illness and suffering is conceived between medical personnel and the sick, and as a way of showing the varying views of medical personnel toward their own clinical practices. Narratives also offer an important insight into the moral world of medical encounters, illness, and suffering. These are just some of the uses of narrative research and analysis that I will focus on in this section.

Cheryl Mattingly has consistently argued for the importance and significance of narrative research and analysis in anthropology. She has also contributed significantly to the anthropology of morality with some of her work on narratives in medical settings. In Mattingly's view, narratives tell stories "featuring human adventures and suffering" and which connect "motives, acts and consequences in causal chains" (1998: 275). While to a great extent I agree with this definition of narrative, it is important to recognize that all narratives need not, and I would even claim that most do not, articulate these causal chains in any kind of straightforward, linear, or "logical" manner. Indeed, a good part of narrative analysis often entails interpretively connecting the reasoning throughout the narratives so as to come to an understanding of what the causal chains may be. Nevertheless, Mattingly is correct to point out that narratives are ripe with potential for understanding agency and the emotions closely tied to human acts.

One of the ways in which Mattingly has closely tied narratives to morality is by positing the notion of narrative reasoning and contrasting it with clinical reasoning (1998: 284). While clinical reasoning is characterized by what she calls biomedical rationality and generally agent-free language, narrative reasoning can be characterized in three ways. First, in narrative reasoning there is an emphasis on motives as causes. This is to say that in narrative reasoning there is concern with the human subject as agent and the inner motives and desires that have led this person to act in this particular way. Thus, a clear connection is seen between the acting agent and her inner world and events that take place in the social world. Second, narrative reasoning makes a connection between individual motives and social and cultural worlds. In other words, narratives place these acting human agents within a social and historical world with other acting agents. Narrative reasoning, then, as opposed to clinical reasoning, recognizes the social nature of human suffering, illness, and disease, and the social consequences of a person experiencing them. Third, and perhaps most important for our purposes, narrative reasoning explores or asserts what Mattingly calls "the good" in a particular situation. Because narrative reasoning recognizes both the subjective and the social nature of all situations – in this context the medical situation – it allows for conclusions to be drawn about the best course of action considering the particular subjective and social context of any particular situation. In these three ways, Mattingly contrasts narrative reasoning with the kind of clinical reasoning so often emphasized in biomedical contexts.

One of the most significant benefits of focusing on narratives is that it allows for an understanding of the differences between how individuals conceptualize and experience suffering, illness, and disease. Paul Farmer (1988) uses narratives to evoke his informants' explanatory models for understanding the causes and consequences of a Haitian illness called *move san*, an illness contracted by some new mothers, which starts in the blood and spreads to other parts of the body, often infecting the breast milk rendering it dangerous to the newborn. Focusing on one case study, Farmer shows how different informants' explanatory models suggest different explanations for the illness.

Farmer suggests several different analyses of these narratives, but finally concludes that one analysis best fits the various narratives he collected. Because *move san* only affects pregnant women or new mothers and is said to be brought on by deep emotional disturbances, often as a result of verbal or physical abuse by a male, Farmer interprets it as "a warning against the abuse of women" (1988: 80). Thus, *move san* is the making public through illness of the likely private transgression against pregnant or nursing women. This making public of transgression becomes even more powerful in that it is realized in what Farmer calls the moral barometer of the metaphor of two of the body's most vital fluids, blood and milk, becoming poison. In this way, the individually different narrative accounts of *move san* reveal to Farmer the moral interpretations hidden within the everyday discourse of this illness.

If the moral meaning of *move san* is often covered over in everyday discourse on the illness, so too can the moral implications of much of what medical personnel talk to with their patients be hidden. Take, for example, medical encounters between British community nurses who make home visits with first-time mothers (Heritage and Lindström 1998). In these encounters, as is often the case in medical encounters in general, "a systematic subordination of moral issues to more instrumental or technical medical considerations" occurs. Yet, Heritage and Lindström continue, "these medical encounters are drenched with implicit moral judgments, claims, and obligations" (1998: 398).

The encounters between community nurses and first-time mothers are characterized by this same subordination of morality to biomedical instrumentality and technicality. Or perhaps it is more correct to say that this is what the nurses are trying to do. While the nurses rarely explicitly talk about moral issues, the mothers (and sometimes fathers when they are present) often hear the implicit moral judgments, evaluations, and prescriptions in the nurses' inquiries and topics of discussion. Indeed, there seems to be an ongoing negotiation between the nurses and the mothers about just what kind of discourse – medical/instrumental or moral – is actually taking place.

In fact, for our purposes, this may be the most significant aspect of Heritage and Lindström's article, that is, the clarity with which we are able to see how one person's non-moral talk is another person's moral talk. This is not to say, of course, that the nurses may not recognize the moral underpinnings of what they are saying, rather it is to say that the context of the conversation – a medical encounter between nurse and first-time mother – does not allow for the nurse to explicitly articulate the moral aspect of what she is saying. In other words, the context of conversation and the roles that persons assume in these conversations have tremendous influence over how talk is interpreted and has meaning for the persons involved. It is not enough simply to say, as Heritage and Lindström do, that the moral aspects are subordinated in medical encounters, as if they are hidden backstage until their part of the performance. Rather, a moral interpretation is just one aspect of most everyday talk (this is so because everyday talk is social), as in this case an instrumental/ technical aspect is another, and depending upon the context and the persons involved different aspects are highlighted, focused upon, and made primary. In the following chapter we will consider further the ways in which context and subjective interpretation play a significant role in how everyday talk is negotiated and made meaningful.

Heritage and Lindström, however, do provide an excellent example of how the moral aspect becomes focused upon in these medical encounters. While the majority of the nurses' talk takes on the instrumental/technical aspect of biomedical discourse, it quickly shifts to a moral aspect when a mother raises a question or a problem concerning how best to interact with her child. Indeed, this is an example of what I have called a moral breakdown or an ethical dilemma, where the nonconscious and unreflective given of the context is suddenly brought into awareness and questioned by means of a problem or dilemma (Zigon 2007). Thus, when a mother raises a problem about her interaction with her child – for example, that she does not feel love for the child and worries about her ability to take care of it – suddenly the medical encounter shifts into what we might call a moral encounter. In these instances, Heritage and Lindström point out, the nurses easily shift into an emphasis on the moral aspect of the conversation – shifting from the "how" of taking care of a baby to the "why" and the "good" of taking care of a baby, as well as an emphasis on the personal benefits a mother will gain from the mother–child relationship. It is interesting also to note that this shift is often marked by the nurses shifting attention to their own personal experience as a mother, which is an important mark of the moral aspect contrasted with the non-personal instrumental/technical character of the medical aspect.

We have just seen how context plays a significant role in whether the moral or the biomedical aspect of talk becomes primary in medical encounters between community nurses and first-time mothers. Mattingly (1998) also offers an interesting case of the shift between biomedical and moral talk, only she focuses her research on how this shift occurs within the talk of medical professionals themselves. In looking at the daily clinical practices and talk of occupational therapists, Mattingly draws attention to the ways in which they shift between what she calls chart talk and the narrative stories they tell one another. I have already discussed above the differences between these two forms of talk, the chart talk being a form of biomedical rationality and clinical reasoning and narrative stories a form of narrative reasoning.

What I would like to point out here, though, is the important point Mattingly makes about how these narrative stories play an important role in the clinical decisions and practices of these therapists. While biomedical discourse and personnel claim to be strict adherents to objective and rational reasoning communicated through chart talk, Mattingly shows that the narrative stories these therapists tell each other about their patients often play a more significant role in how they proceed with their treatment. Thus, Mattingly contends, narrative reasoning plays just as important a role in the daily clinical practices of these therapists as does clinical reasoning, if not more.

Keeping in mind what was said above about the three characteristics of narrative reasoning – its emphasis on motives, the connection between motives and the social world, and a concern with the good – it seems clear that this brings a distinctly moral form of reasoning into the clinical setting. This is so because these narrative stories draw attention to the personal and social histories of patients (as well as the therapists), emphasize the emotional and social motives of patients' (and therapists') actions, and necessitate deliberation based on the particulars of the situation rather than universal and objective criteria. Thus, this form of moral or practical reasoning is a version of the kind of Aristotelian ethics we discussed in the first chapter and, so Mattingly claims, offers a more nuanced and useful form of reasoning for the clinical setting than the so-called objective rationality biomedicine currently emphasizes in its discourse.

If narratives play an important role in clinical decision-making, so too do they play an important role, as we saw above with the work of Paul Farmer, for persons, both patients and medical personnel, in articulating their own interpretations of illness. Although biomedical rationality and explanations are increasingly becoming hegemonic around the world, narratives continue to be the primary means by which persons communicate their own experiences and interpretations. This becomes particularly clear in the work of Linda Hunt on the meaning of cancer in southern Mexico. Hunt (1998) shows how patients and medical personnel offer different explanations for the causes of cancer in their narratives, and while these explanations differ, they all carry with them a significant moral aspect.

Focusing her attention on women diagnosed with breast cancer, Hunt shows that for these women the cause of the cancer is often linked with, in their narrative accounts of the illness, their own or their partners' transgressions against local moral expectations. In fact, it is even more closely tied to local gendered moral expectations. Thus, many of these women claimed to believe that their cancer was caused by such transgressions as the failure to reproduce, having too much sex, or their husbands' infidelity. Similarly, the doctors also gave highly moral accounts of the cause of these women's cancer, but in addition to the gendered aspects of their accounts there is also a distinctly class aspect as well. This is particularly significant since the majority of these doctors' cancer patients are among the urban and rural poor. Thus, for example, the doctors frequently cited in their narrative explanations such so-called lower class morally questionable habits as hesitancy to seek out biomedical treatment and reliance on "traditional" forms of treatment, bad hygiene, and echoing the narratives of the women themselves, the infidelity of the women's husbands. Thus, Hunt makes it clear that while in official biomedical accounts of the causes of cancer, accounts emphasized by medical personnel and generally accepted by patients, such moral judgments are rarely articulated, in narrative accounts of the same phenomenon both patients and doctors speak in highly moral accents.

In this section I have tried to highlight the ways in which narrative and everyday forms of talk can either shift into or reveal the moral aspects of medical encounters. Narrative research and analysis have contributed greatly to medical anthropology, particularly in providing subjective accounts of suffering, illness, and disease, on the one hand, and disclosing the moral aspects of biomedical discourse and talk, on the other. In the next chapter we will attend more closely to the ways in which narrative, talk, and discourse all provide ways for anthropologists of moralities to come to a better understanding of personal and local moralities.

Bioethics

Bioethics is a subdiscipline and topic in which anthropologists have just recently taken interest. Actually, bioethics itself is a relatively recent concern in the biomedical world, first attracting interest in the late 1960s and early 1970s. Bioethics can be defined as the "inquiry into moral dilemmas created by the theoretical and practical application of technological developments associated with the Western biomedical sciences" (Marshall 1992: 50). More specifically, bioethics is concerned with the problems associated with confidentiality, informed consent, the lengthening of life, and the transplantation of body parts and genetic materials (1992: 50).

Like biomedical discourse, and highly influenced by the philosophers who have dominated the field since its inception, bioethics can be characterized as rationally oriented, seeking objectivity, universalistic and generalizing, as well as specifically focused on the implementation of a priori moral principles in particular circumstances. This rationalist and principle-oriented bioethics also tends to give priority to the rights of individuals, as opposed to considering the social relations within which all persons are embedded, and the autonomy of the individual, rather than considering the obligations, duties, and relationships persons may have with others that significantly influence their decisions as well as who ultimately may make decisions for them. It is these foci of bioethics that social scientists, and anthropologists in particular, have increasingly begun to critique.

The most significant contribution that anthropologists are attempting to make to the field is to show the contextualization and particularity of bioethical problems and responses. That is to say, rather than conceiving of bioethics as a rationalistic and universal science of moral principles, anthropologists are showing how bioethics can better serve individuals suffering from disease and illness by being acutely aware of the social nature of their suffering, as well as the cultural context in which this suffering takes on meaning (Hoffmaster 2001).

One of the ways in which this has been done, and very similar to some of the examples from the last section, is by focusing on narratives. Sharon Kaufman has collected narrative accounts of American doctors of various specialties who work with older persons in order to discern the tensions and ambiguities in geriatric medical practice that concern these doctors, as well as to explore the relationship between these tensions and ambiguities, culture, and ethics (2001: 15). In doing so, Kaufman provides an alternative description of what a bioethics might look like that was more focused on the particular practices and concerns of actual doctors.

Kaufman (2001: 20–33) found that within the narratives she collected from these doctors, the three biggest bioethical concerns revolve around:

1. balancing patient autonomy to choose the treatment he or she receives with the doctors' knowledge and feelings of duty to intervene without permission in order to do what they can to help;
2. the question of whether or not to use invasive diagnostic tests or aggressive treatment;
3. negotiating the line between life and death and knowing when and how much treatment to offer a person in this situation.

Thus, again, it is clear from the use of narrative analysis that these bioethical concerns of doctors are radically particularistic. This is so not only because of the concreteness of the problems, but because these problems differ and take on unique nuances with each patient. These narrative accounts, then, suggest that a principle-based, universalistic bioethics cannot adequately address most of the moral concerns of biomedical practice.

Kaufman concludes that bioethics must take the shape of a more grounded ethics. In other words, it must become much more sensitive to the uniqueness and particularity of the moral dilemmas faced by medical personnel. She draws three conclusions from her work that might help provide a framework for what an alternative bioethics could look like (2001: 33–5). First, bioethical dilemmas emerge within the flow of everyday experiences that are embedded within both structural and cultural contexts. Because of this, these dilemmas cannot be isolated from these contexts and they must be taken into account when decisions are made. Second, clinical knowledge is intimately tied to knowledge of the patient and her social and cultural history. Thus, decisions, as Mattingly points out and we discussed above, must be made for the good of the patient, and that this good is always connected to her social and cultural history goes without saying. And third, a recognition of the murky relationship between particular dilemmas and the response best suited to the case and the ultimate goals of biomedicine. Because of this murky relationship decisions may conflict with, for example, the biomedical system's commitment to technology and its emphasis on the need always to do something. Thus, a bioethics that takes the particular as its starting point may in fact have a difficult relationship with a biomedicine that continues to be rationalistically and universally based.

Indeed, this itself may be one of the most significant consequences of an anthropological approach to bioethics. As we have seen earlier in this chapter, the assumed rationalistic and universal foundations of biomedicine can be seriously questioned, and therefore a bioethics that calls this assumption into question may help alter biomedical approaches. One of the ways in which an anthropology of moralities can contribute to this is by showing how particular ethical dilemmas are interpreted in different cultural contexts, and in so doing, provide a background to better ease the current process of the global spreading of biomedical discourse and practice (Marshall 1992: 62; Muller 1994: 459).

But as Lock (2001b) has pointed out, we need to be very careful about the ease with which we throw about the concept of culture and use it to argue against such totalizing ideologies as biomedicine and bioethics. This is so because although anthropologists have, for the most part, honed this concept to an accepted and workable form, it has increasingly been utilized by persons and organizations outside of anthropology and academia for less than benevolent purposes. Thus, for example, the concept of culture is widely used in nationalistic discourse, some of which can be overtly racist and xenophobic. In terms of bioethics, culture can also be used in questionable ways. For example, in my own research on drug rehabilitation and HIV prevention in Russia I have been told several times that rehabilitation programs offered by Western and non-Russian Orthodox religions do not work because they are not "ours," that is to say, they are foreign to Russian culture and therefore will not work for Russian people. Indeed, such a view excludes some rehabilitation programs as potential resources for treating an increasingly high level of heroin addiction and HIV infection. Here, then, we see the potential dangers of using the concept of culture in an unsophisticated manner to define bioethical issues and delineate the limits of appropriate medical care and resources. Because of this Lock argues that culture itself needs to be very carefully contextualized and must not be used as an unexamined given (2001b: 64).

Unfortunately it seems that this is precisely what was done in the analysis of potentially interesting data collected about end of life decisions among four different ethnic groups in the United States (Frank, Blackhall, Michel, Murphy, Azen, and Park 1998). Focusing their analysis on a narrative account of one elderly Korean woman and extrapolating from data collected from a quantitative survey of 200 other elderly Koreans, the authors make an interesting case against the usual bioethical emphasis on individual autonomy in decision-making and the right of patients to have full knowledge of diagnoses. Indeed, the data seems quite clear that for the Korean persons involved in this research, the preference would be that family members such as adult children would be the ones to receive this information and make decisions concerning treatment and end of life strategies. Thus, these Koreans clearly prefer a course that is just about diametrically opposed to what most Western bioethicists imagine persons in their situation would want, that is, autonomy and knowledge/information.

Unfortunately, the authors do little more than ascribe the preferences of these Korean elderly people to Korean culture. As the authors put it, Korean American "attitudes about end-of-life decision making center on the importance of relationships and the responsibilities of family members rather than on patient autonomy" because such "beliefs and practices derive from the traditional culture of Korea, which has much in common with the cultures of neighboring East Asian countries" (Frank et al. 1998: 414). While the authors briefly acknowledge the influence of adapting to life in the United States, economic pressures, and the difficulties of transnational families, they do not provide any kind of in-depth or nuanced explication of why relationships and familial obligations are so significant to Korean culture or how it might be embedded within larger socio-historic power relations. Indeed, it seems that culture here is merely accepted as a fact and as a "given reality for which no further explanation is necessary" (Lock 2001b: 42). Thus, simply to say that certain bioethical preferences "derive from the traditional culture of Korea" does little to further our understanding of how local moral understandings influence these preferences, to say nothing of the potential dangers of such an unnuanced position.

A more nuanced evocation of culture and tradition in an anthropological approach to bioethics has been done by Simpson (2004) on body part and fluid donation in Sri Lanka. Since the mid 1960s Sri Lanka has been among the world leaders in eye donations, which are distributed to people in need of eyes around the world. Far and away the leading group of Sri Lankan eye donors is made up of Theravāda Buddhists. Simpson argues that this is so because of a very long tradition of body part donation among Buddhists, a practice that is also solidly represented in Buddhist stories of the Bodhisattvas.

Simpson, however, does not stop there with his discussion of bodily donations in Sri Lanka. While Theravāda Buddhists have been willingly, and perhaps even eagerly, donating their eyes for over forty years, they are much more reluctant when it comes to sperm donation. Clearly this is where a simple reference to Buddhist traditions of charity and the accumulation of merit for the next life breaks down. For here questions of manhood are involved. Gender expectations, then, trump religious duties. This is even clearer when Simpson shows that the donation of women's eggs, contrasted with the donation of sperm, is generally more acceptable.

It is not only gender that calls into question a straightforward appeal to Buddhist tradition and culture as an explanation for body part and fluid donation. For Sri Lanka is also mired in an ethnically and religiously based civil war, and Buddhists are beginning to wonder, so Simpson tells us, why they should donate their blood and body parts to the Muslims and Hindus who are violently clashing with one another. In addition to this, there is the world market of body part and fluid transactions. Theravāda Buddhists are beginning to recognize that they may be becoming a kind of Third World "natural resource" center for the more developed world. This too raises questions about whether or not they should continue to donate at the pace that they have.

Here then we see a much more nuanced approach to a bioethical decision. This approach recognizes the importance of Theravāda Buddhist tradition and culture in motivating body part and fluid donation, but it goes further in addressing other aspects of Sri Lankan culture, such as gender issues, as well as national and global socio-politico-economic issues. Thus, Simpson provides us with a picture of how one of the most important bioethical concerns in the world today, body part and fluid donation and transplantation, is negotiated at a very local level. That this negotiation takes place not by means of rational deductions, the implementation of a priori principles, rights or individual autonomy, but instead through the lens of religious and gendered culture and national and global socio-politico-economics, should open our eyes to the ways in which an anthropological approach to bioethics can provide more sophisticated and empirically-based ways of considering bioethical issues.

Some Final Words

In this chapter we have seen the various ways in which anthropologists have considered medical issues and encounters from a moral perspective. From critiques of biomedicine and bioethics to a concern with the global epidemic of HIV/AIDS and the recognition that narrative research and analysis offer insightful ways of looking at the lives of the people we study, medical anthropologists have been at the forefront of an anthropological approach to local moralities.

Nevertheless, as with much of what we have considered in this book, one is left with some dissatisfaction about the way many of these anthropologists have utilized the concept of morality. As with so many of the anthropologists throughout this book, one often wonders just whose morality we are reading about. Are we in fact reading what the local persons would consider to be their own morality or their own moral or bioethical issue? Or are we reading the anthropologists' interpretation of what the local persons might be thinking? Or are we reading the anthropologists' assumptions about what counts as morality in the local setting or perhaps even in any setting?

This is a question that is relevant for the vast majority of what we have covered in this book. But it seems appropriate to remind ourselves of it here, at the end of this chapter, since medical anthropologists have been so keen on considering the moral perspective of many of the issues they study. As anthropologists of moralities we welcome this perspective, we only urge caution, as so many others have urged caution with the concepts of culture, society, and power, in the use of the concept of morality. While this concept is ripe for potential understanding of everyday ways of being in the world, it has also become one of the most contested and closely held concepts in the world today. Therefore, if we are not careful in the ways in which we utilize the concept of morality in our own research and analysis, we run the very real risk not only of confusing our own personal assumptions of morality with those of the peoples we study, but also of having our work misunderstood by others. Only close attention to our methodological and analytical processes will guarantee that these dangers are avoided.

Case Study 2

Morality and Women's Health in Post-Soviet Russia

Similar to Joel Robbins's look at how cultural change in Papua New Guinea resulted in moral torment among the Urapmin, Michele Rivkin-Fish in her *Women's Health In Post-Soviet Russia* (2005) considers how women's health and reproductivity in post-socialist Russia is viewed as a moral issue. According to Rivkin-Fish the so-called post-Soviet transition is viewed as a moral process. As I have argued elsewhere, post-Soviet Russia can be viewed as a place of intense moral questioning and conflict over competing moral conceptions, or what I call a moral breakdown (Zigon 2006).

One social arena in which this has taken form is the medical sphere. This is especially so in regards to women's health and reproduction. As Rivkin-Fish points out, this is a particularly central sphere for moral debates in light of the so-called demographic crisis that Russia has been experiencing. Since the late 1960s Russia's population has increasingly been unable to maintain itself, and in the post-Soviet period the population has begun to drop to such an extent that increasingly the public discourse expresses a concern over the potential loss of the nation. Thus, more and more, women are considered to have a moral duty to maintain their health and reproduce.

How are women expected to do this? Since the mid 1990s this has been a pressing question, especially considering the structural obstacles to such a goal. For example, increased economic stratification, decreased governmental support for medical care, lack of supplies and hot water in maternity hospitals, and an intense questioning as to the proper ways of providing medical attention, all played a role in how women and medical personnel responded to this question. According to Rivkin-Fish, one of the ways in which this question was addressed was by putting an increased emphasis on women taking responsibility for the maintenance of their own reproductive health.

One of the central ways that this increased emphasis on women's responsibility took place in 1990s' Russia, according to Rivkin-Fish, was a reliance on Soviet moral discourse and assumptions of medical authority. In particular, she argues that the concepts of *kul'turnost'* (culturedness) and *lichnost'* (individuality/person) were utilized as disciplinary tropes in the Soviet era and suggests that their use has continued in the post-Soviet sphere of public health and women's reproduction. Thus, for example, medical personnel use these tropes for the purpose of disciplining their patients to live healthier lifestyles, practice safe sex, eschew abortions, and listen to medical personnel's instructions. In doing so they make it clear to their patients that cultured individuals ought to exhibit traits of civility, modernity, and self-dignity, and only in so doing will they effectively live healthy lives and have healthy babies. In this way, Rivkin-Fish claims, while such person-centered moral discourse takes on the appearance of being separate from state power and interest, it actually establishes medical personnel as a source of authority for moral discipline and practice.

One of the topics around which this moral discourse focused was abortion. During most of the Soviet period abortion was the main source of birth control. Because of a lack of other forms of contraception, and especially quality condoms, as well as the ease with which an abortion could be done, abortions were quite common. In the post-Soviet period, however, this changed not only in Russia but throughout most of Eastern Europe. As Rivkin-Fish puts it, the increased control over and obstacles to easy access to abortions throughout post-socialist Eastern Europe was seen as a sign of the moral superiority of these times over that of the socialist period. In Russia, it seemed that everyone from the government, to the Russian Orthodox Church, to one's doctor, to sex education specialists were deriding abortion as an immoral act. For some, abortion amounted to murder of the individual fetus, but for many of those who propagated an anti-abortion stance it amounted to the murder of the Russian nation. By selfishly giving up one's child, so it was said, a woman having an abortion was not living up to her moral duty to stem the demographic crisis and to revive the Russian nation.

Morality also became a question in reproductive medicine during this time because of the increased role of money in medical care in post-Soviet Russia. During Soviet times medical treatment was provided free of charge by the state. While to some extent this system was maintained in the 1990s, increasingly the quality of care deteriorated with a lack of funding and as some hospitals and clinics began to shift towards being a fee for service provider. During this period bribery and favors increasingly began to take a role in reproductive care. Indeed, increasingly bribery became what might be called the moral norm, for both pregnant women and medical personnel saw it as appropriate to pay doctors and staff for good quality care. This was so because, on the one hand, medical personnel in Russia receive one of the lowest salaries in the country despite their skills and importance to society, and thus increasingly both they and their patients thought it morally correct to rectify this by means of unofficial payments. On the other hand, bribery was seen as morally appropriate because in a structural situation where quality care was increasingly lacking due to shortages of supplies and funding, bribery was one of the only ways one could hope to secure such care, although it should be pointed out that this was not always the result.

While Rivkin-Fish provides a deeply interesting description of Russia's post-Soviet reproductive health situation, and shows the centrality that morality plays in both the medical and gendered aspects of this situation, it is obvious that her own moral perspective often colors her analysis. As a feminist anthropologist Rivkin-Fish is quite clear about her desire to have an emancipatory effect (2005: 94, 212–20), and to help Russian women achieve more equality in their reproductive health care. While this is certainly laudable, it requires her to make certain assumptions that certainly affect how her material is presented. Thus, for example, it is clear that Rivkin-Fish takes what Mahmood calls the secular-liberalist view of agency, that is to say, the assumption that a person, in this case women, should be able to recognize their own subordination and having done so are free to effect change politically and socially for the better. On several occasions, Rivkin-Fish bemoans the fact that Russian women and medical personnel are unable to do this, and thus, somehow, exhibit a lack. Indeed, she goes as far as to provide a "moral framework" for how these women and personnel should think about and strive to establish their reproductive health programs (2005: 208). While she certainly acknowledges that such a framework needs to adjust to local traditions and conditions, nevertheless, her focus is on providing information to moral free agents who can enact the kind of change she as the author sees appropriate for making "pragmatic" steps toward the moral ideal she envisions. In doing so, Rivkin-Fish's own moral perspective takes the spotlight away from the ways in which local and personal notions of morality are played out in this important post-Soviet context.

Part IV
Language, Narrative, and Discourse

–6–

Language, Discourse, and Narrative

Anthropologists, particularly in the American tradition, have recognized the centrality of language to belief and practice since the beginnings of the discipline (see Boas 1911; Sapir 1921; Whorf 1956). In the last twenty years or so, however, it is possible to say that anthropology has experienced a kind of linguistic turn in that there has been renewed interest outside of the subdiscipline of linguistic anthropology in the importance of language-use in everyday social life. This interest can be seen in the increased use of such analytic concepts as discourse, performance, and genre as ways to understand social practices.

This chapter will consider some of the ways in which everyday language-use is central not only to how moralities are communicated between persons and institutions, but more importantly, to how they are negotiated, created, and enacted within the give and take of communicative interactions. By looking at the ways persons speak about moral issues, dilemmas, and concerns, anthropologists have begun to consider that language-use is vital for the very concept of morality. We have begun to see that it is often through language that morality comes into being in particular contexts, and that perhaps without language there would be no morality as such. As we will see in this chapter, this process of bringing morality into being takes place on several different communicative levels and by means of different communicative practices. Let us then see how this occurs.

Discourse, Performativity, and Moral Communication

It has been argued that humans constitute themselves as moral beings through the use of language (Linell and Rommetveit 1998; Luckmann 2002). It is possible to speak of language and its uses at different levels. The two commonest levels of analysis of language can be referred to as the level of *langue*, or the abstract system of language outside of any particular language being spoken, which consists of its internal relationships, contradictions, and categories, and *parole*, or the everyday use and speech of a particular language (Saussure 1983). While recently the study and use of *langue* as an analytical concept has fallen out of favor with many anthropologists, the concept of discourse, which can be seen as a derivative of the concept of *langue*, has become increasingly significant.

The concept of discourse at its most basic can be thought of as the limits of what can be said. Using this as a working definition, discourse can be thought of as the limit not only of possible speech, but also of truth, knowledge, and morality. One of the characteristics of the notion of discourse that makes it so helpful for many social scientists, anthropologists, and philosophers is that while maintaining to some extent the duality between the system and everyday speech of *langue* and *parole*, it also collapses this distinction, such that the system – if discourse can in fact be referred to as a system – manifests itself in the everyday talk, narratives, and utterances of social life. Thus, with the notion of discourse we are able to find not only the limits of speech, but of truth, knowledge, and morality within the everyday use of language.

Assuming for the moment that we can speak of such a discourse, then its very nature allows for what can be possibly considered as moral relationships and responses (Bergmann 1998: 287–8). This is so for a couple of reasons. First, because a discourse is made up of different categories, these are often related to one another not only in terms of an acceptable hierarchy, but also in relation to one another such that certain categories of acceptable speech allow for the articulation of certain other categories of acceptable speech, but perhaps not others. It is the appropriate and acceptable limits of relating certain categories of speech, then, that often allow for moral acceptability of speech and the interpretation of morally acceptable acts and beings (Londoño Sulkin 2005: 8).

Second, and related to the first, is that discourse in its very nature as the limits of acceptable speech made up of interrelated categories allows for tension, ambiguity, and contention. Thus, discourse always allows for the possibility of questioning and response to what is said. To speak within any discourse, and according to discourse theorists we are always speaking within a discourse, entails a risk of being morally questioned. It is this possibility of questioning and dissent, it has been suggested, that allows discourse to maintain a kind of moral order for its speakers (Mageo 1991: 405). It is for this reason – and this is something I have been trying to suggest in different ways throughout the book – that I prefer to speak of discourse as allowing for a range of possibilities, rather than a limit, of certain ways of speaking, acting, and being in the world. While it can rightly be pointed out that a range has limits, and thus one could claim that I am essentially speaking of the same thing, I do not think this is quite so. For to speak of a range of possibilities places in the forefront of the concept of discourse its creative, ambiguous, and contentious nature. Thus, while to some extent limiting, discourse is far from deterministic.

Unfortunately, sometimes it seems that discourse is used to suggest a deterministic-like structure. Take for example Carol Greenhouse's interesting article on the discourse and cultural logic of individualism and the avoidance ethic in American culture (1992). Based on her own fieldwork in a suburban Atlanta town and analysis of research done in other parts of the United States, Greenhouse suggests that American culture can be partly characterized as having what she calls an avoidance ethic, which is closely related to the American discourse and ideal of individualism. Thus, contrary to its popular image of being a country and culture of confrontation and debate, Greenhouse argues that most Americans attempt to avoid confrontation, legal and otherwise, and tend to defend this principle on the grounds of individual differences in experience and other such distinctions.

Be this as it may, what is particularly important for our purposes is Greenhouse's claim that this avoidance ethic is a logic, or we can say a discursive logic, and not a behavior (1992: 248). By this I believe Greenhouse means that while avoidance may not always express itself in behavior, it is one of the foundational discursive categories that provides a limit for American self-understanding and explanatory descriptions of behavior. Thus, while Greenhouse is sure to point out that the discursive logic of avoidance does allow for contradictions and for the potential of switching to its antithesis of confrontation, as surely any good structuralist account of discourse will maintain, she clearly suggests that to some extent the avoidance ethic is a deterministic discursive logic for American culture, self-understanding, and explanation, as well as, to some extent, behavior. For in its very discursive and structural relationship to the category of individualism, the logic, or the bounded and necessary limits, of the avoidance ethic plays a significant role in what it means to be American.

Similarly, but from a completely different perspective, Carolyn Pope Edwards (1985) suggests that discourse is to some degree determining, not for any particular culture or society, but for humans in general. According to Edwards, what she calls ethical discourse is defined as "a string of statements or arguments containing 'moral statements' (statements about *what* actions or attitudes are obligatory or virtuous) and/or 'ethical statements' (statements about *why* those actions or attitudes are morally right or wrong" (1985: 319).

Notwithstanding the ambiguity of this definition, it is clear that Edwards is pointing to the centrality of language for understanding how cultures, societies, and persons utilize morality in their everyday lives. And while she agrees that every culture has a particular kind of ethical discourse, she is clear to point out that these discourses are not radically incommensurable and "that human beings from different cultural traditions can *quite easily* understand one another's ethical discourse" (1985: 336). Thus, for Edwards, if morality is understood, expressed, and communicated through ethical discourse, that is language, and persons from different ethical discourses can "quite easily" understand one another, then to some extent there must be an all-humanly shared morality that has its foundations in language. And if this is so, it is clear that particular ethical discourses, and thus particular expressions and acts of morality, are at least to some extent determined by this all-human morality founded in the possibility of language. Indeed, this is the position taken by Bergmann (1998) who claims that language provides the very basis for morality in that that which is spoken invokes a response from others, and thus, the response that is necessary in language is the basis for the response-ability that he claims is central to the notion of morality. This is something to which we will return briefly.

As I have already said, the notion of discourse can be quite fruitful for the study of local moralities. However, when it is utilized as such a deterministic-like structure as these studies suggest, it loses some of what I see as its strengths as an analytical concept: that is, its flexibility, creativity, possibilities, ambiguity, tension, and contradiction. Rather than seeing discourse as providing the limits of acceptability, as these studies seem to do, I suggest viewing discourse as providing the range of possibilities for acceptable speech and acts. In doing so we can better emphasize these latter characteristics over the more deterministic approach. As such, discourse as a range of possibilities, I suggest, more closely resembles the negotiable nature of moral interactions in everyday life. It is to these interactions, then, that we will now turn.

One of the things I have been trying to emphasize throughout this book is the ways in which moral understandings are negotiated in the course of everyday life. For the rest of this section I will show some of the ways this happens through the use of everyday forms of speech, or what has sometimes been called *parole*, and for our purposes can be understood as the verbal manifestation of discourse in everyday communicative interactions. In other words, through such everyday, language-utilizing practices as conversation, gossip, and instructional interactions – for example, advice giving – and verbal performances, speaking individuals negotiate, construct, and come to agree on their moral ways of being. While sometimes it may be the case that this moral way of being extends well beyond the moment of communicative interaction, it is also necessary to recognize that sometimes these interactions create a unique moral moment in which a particular moral relationship and way of being is constructed and beyond which these do not extend.

Linell and Rommetveit (1998) contend that there are potentially two moral aspects of communicative interactions. First is what they call the discourse-internal ethics of these interactions. By this they mean that every communicative interaction "involves taking on and assigning obligations, entitlements, and responsibilities" to the speaker and her interlocutors (1998: 466). Thus, for example, they argue that there are moral implications in these interactions by means of obliging others to talk or impeding others from doing so, as well as the power relations involved in influencing how others think, speak, and act. While it may be true that some communicative interactions can certainly take on this moral aspect, I suggest, however, that it is not entirely clear that all do. Let's consider some simple examples. I am having a conversation with a friend in which I am trying to convince him that Babe Ruth was a better homerun hitter than Hank Aaron despite the fact that the latter hit more lifetime homeruns than Ruth. At a certain point my passions get the better of me and I continually cut off my friend's attempts to respond to my arguments. In the end, my friend without having had a chance to respond as he would have liked, claims that he is now convinced that Babe Ruth was in fact the better homerun hitter. Now, in this imaginary conversation I both influenced the thoughts and claimed beliefs of my friend, and repeatedly impeded him from responding to me. While he and many others may consider me rude for not having let him respond as he liked, I do not see this being construed as a moral issue. This is particularly so because the conversation was about baseball. Further, the fact that my friend claims that I influenced his thoughts and beliefs on this baseball topic also does not appear to have constituted a moral concern. Thus, while some communicative interactions may have an internal ethics to them, it does not appear that all do. In other words, we should not confuse communicative etiquette with ethics.

It does, however, seem likely that there is some kind of internal ethics when the second moral aspect of communicative interactions is concerned, that is the addressing of particular moral issues. For it would seem that when a moral issue is being addressed, whether implicitly or explicitly, the communicative mode of interacting, in terms of grammar, rhetoric, vocabulary, and tactics, shifts. Indeed, it is this shift that several of the authors I will engage with in this section focus their research upon.

Linell and Rommetveit also point out the centrality of what they call responsibility to the link between morality and communicative interactions (1998: 466–8). However, they seem to conflate two distinct ways of using this important and controversial concept. While on the one hand, they reference the philosopher Charles Taylor (1989) and his use of the concept as the capability "of answering for oneself," they also reference the Russian linguist and literary critic M. M. Bakhtin (1981) and his more dialogical form of responsibility. While the former use of the concept of responsibility is limited in that it focuses primarily on one subjective agent, the latter may more accurately describe communicative interaction and its potential internal ethics. Thus, conceived as response-ability, the concept does not, as Taylor's version does, suggest that a subjective agent must stand up and answer for all that he says and does, but rather suggests that all communicative interactions, and in fact, possibly all social interactions, necessitate a kind of empathetic give and take between those involved. Persons engaged in these kinds of interactions must be "able to respond" to the other in a way that is notionally acceptable to the other, to oneself, and the context of the interaction. In this sense, response-ability has more to do with an ethics of being aware of particular kinds of social and communicative interactions than with an ethics of subjective guilt or innocence. Response-ability, then, may have little to do with answering for oneself, and instead denote the ability to answer others and the interaction context.

If response-ability designates the ability to answer to one's interlocutors in a particular interaction context, then this raises the question of just what is meant by context. This has become a central question and concern of some linguistic anthropologists. While there certainly is no precise and agreed upon definition of context, and in fact, there may never be one, Goodwin and Duranti (1992) provide what I consider an acceptable working definition that could prove particularly helpful in the anthropological study of moralities.

By pointing out context's Latin origin of *contextus*, which means "a joining together," Goodwin and Duranti focus on the centrality to the concept of context of a relationship between two or more phenomena that mutually inform one another, and in so doing constitute a larger whole (1992: 4–6). These phenomena can be conceived at different levels. First, there is the level, or the perspective, of the participant or participants in the interaction. Thus, when considering context it is vital to take into account the interpretations of the participants and the ways in which they situate themselves in the moment of interaction. This goes far beyond coming to an understanding of how each of the participants interpret what it is they are communicating about. For example, in trying to understand the perspective of the participants it is also important to understand the power relations between those involved, the power structures that help shape the interaction itself, and closely related to this, the spatial and placial setting of the interaction, which goes a long way in establishing the context of communicative, social, and moral interactions.

This leads into the second level of mutually constituting phenomena of context. That is, the particular practices and activities being performed at the moment. As with the perspective of the participants, these practices and activities are, for the most part, shaped by socio-historic-cultural interpretations. Thus, for example, one is never simply taking a walk with a friend, for what it means to "take a walk" differs in different socio-historic-cultural worlds, not to mention how these interpretations influence the bodily movements of walking, hand gesturing, and word choice, among other things, as well as the ways in which the participants map out their place within the physical environment. All of this is there, in the context, and thus influencing the interaction, before any conversation occurs, whether this conversation is the amoral baseball discussion I introduced above, or a morally contested debate on abortion.

Lastly, context is continually and quickly shifting. In this sense, it is impossible to speak about participants being in only one context. It is more likely that they are always situated within multiple contexts which are continuously shifting and altering as the interaction is taking place. Indeed, it may be important to consider in the analysis of what Linell and Rommetveit call the internal ethics of communicative interactions how and when participants shift, alter, and adjust to different interaction contexts, for in tracking these, it is likely that one would be able to gain insight into the negotiation of moral understanding in the moment of interaction.

All of this leads to perhaps the most significant contribution that a focus on context can contribute to an anthropological study of local moralities. That is, the dynamic and creative aspect of the context. Because these very interactions are playing back into the context at hand, the multiple contexts that were already there are themselves continually changing as the interaction continues. It is this continuous interplay and creativity that not only provides for the altering of contexts, but so too allows for the dynamic nature of social interactions and the creative and negotiating character of local moralities. For while in most cases it appears to be the case that there is a range of possibilities of what counts as morality in any given context, there is room for creativity and negotiation within this range, as well as there always is the possibility that the range itself can be enlarged or narrowed. It is for this reason, then, that a concern with context should be central to an anthropology of moralities.

Alessandro Duranti (1992) has done a particularly interesting study of the relationship between communicative interactions and context. In his study of Samoan respect vocabulary, Duranti takes as his starting point the assumption "that words do not simply reflect a taken-for-granted world 'out there,' they also help constitute such a world by defining relations between speaker, hearer, referents, and social activities" (1992: 80). He goes on to argue against those who have claimed that the notion of respect is about saving face and freedom of action. Instead, utilizing ethnographic and linguistic data from his research in Samoa, he goes on to argue that respect, and more particularly respectful words, in Samoa is better understood as "a pragmatic force that coerces certain behaviors or actions upon people and thus indexes speakers' control over addressees rather than addressees' 'freedom' of action" (1992: 95–6). Thus, the choice of respectful words a speaker may use, on the one hand, depends upon the context of the speech event, for example, the status of the person to whom the speaker is speaking and where this speaking is taking place, and on the other hand, alters this context by influencing the behavior or action of the addressee.

One of the more interesting findings of Duranti's research is that the use of respectful words is not always predictable. Often on those occasions when one would expect, according to local expectations of respect and status, a speaker to use a respectful word – for example, when addressing a person of higher status in a formal meeting – Duranti found that these words were not used. Conversely, in certain moments when the use of these words would not be expected, for example, in the private interaction between family members when one of them is of higher status, they were used. It is for this reason that Duranti argues that a better understanding of just what constitutes context and how it is related to language-use will help us better understand these kinds of morally imbued interactions. On this point, I agree entirely with Duranti.

Indeed, it was by being particularly concerned with context that Duranti was able to see that these respectful words are often used, not "to pay respect" as it were, but to influence the behavior of others. Thus, for example, respectful words could be used to invoke generosity or to prompt one to act in a controlled demeanor when one might not otherwise so desire. Or, they could be used prior to giving an apology in order that the addressee feels properly situated to accept the apology. These examples strongly suggest that context both provides certain opportunities for choosing from a possible respect vocabulary, and is also altered by this choice by the way in which it influences the addressees' behavior and action. It seems very likely that cross-cultural research would find similar situations where both moral vocabulary and ethical action are both shaped by the context of a particular communicative and social interaction, and in turn, alter this context.

Although a close concern with context provides the best opportunity to observe the creative and dynamic aspects of communicative interaction, such dynamism can be studied in other ways. Take for example Nancy Ries's (1997) insightful study of everyday forms of talk in late 1980s' Moscow. Although this study is not meant to be an anthropological study of moralities, she does provide some important insights into how everyday talk is an important aspect of the creation of moral values. According to Ries, "in Russia talk in all its manifestations is a markedly significant domain of value creation – perhaps, in part, because other domains of action have been so restricted" (1997: 21). By value Ries does not intend any kind of abstract or codified notion of morality, but instead a situationally negotiated and perpetually altering exchange of values by which persons can live together. These values are negotiated by means of everyday forms of talk. As Ries puts it, "Russian talk is not just an activity during which value creation is described, but one in which, during which and through which value is actually produced" (1997: 21).

Ries particularly focused her research upon the various speech genres she found to be especially common in late Soviet Moscow. Speech genres can be described as the conventions and patterns that play a significant role in shaping the form and words of everyday talk (1997: 34). These speech genres, over time, come to be embedded in our personal and collective ways of talking by means of years, decades, and perhaps centuries of repetition. In a sense, they can be seen as the templates we use in our everyday conversations. As such, Ries argues, "values and beliefs are well protected and effectively transmitted through culturewide observance of the basic protocols of genre – an observance which is automatically socialized as part of the acquisition of language" (1997: 35). Likewise, Ries continues, these genres serve to protect cultural values and beliefs from non-native ones.

While to a great extent I agree with Ries that the study of speech genres can provide important insights into the ways in which moral values and beliefs are communicated and performed, I hesitate to conceive of these genres as so tightly bound as Ries here portrays them. To be fair, she does say that genres are "blurry" and "unfixed," but yet she also compares them to "cell walls" that "corral and contain the various elements of culture, ideology, and value" (1997: 35). Whatever the case may be, I suggest that it is important to realize that such speech genres can at one and the same time reflect not only a collective or a shared pattern, but also a personal pattern of experience. As such, it becomes very difficult to speak of *a* speech genre, and thus, perhaps, it is more appropriate to speak of a range of possibilities of speech, and thus it is the *range* and the *possibilities* that constitute the genre. In this way, then, a range of possible moral values and beliefs can be repeated and communicated by means of this genre, and yet remain the kind of blurry and unfixed genre that Ries sometimes describes, while at the same time remaining open to the further possibility of being influenced by "alien" values and beliefs.

One speech genre that has proven particularly interesting to study is that of complaints. While Ries has studied litanies and laments, which are genres very similar to complaints, and showed how these were especially important for creating values through Russian talk, Paul Drew has focused his attention on complaints as such. Drew studies what he and linguists call the natural language of conversation as it was recorded from phone conversations in both the United States and Britain (1998). Similar to Linell and Rommetveit, Drew claims that these conversations can carry both implicit and explicit moral aspects, and although it is quite possible to trace the implicit moral work of many of these conversations, he instead focuses on what he calls the explicit moral work of complaints.

Drew argues that in revealing the transgression of an other, and thus, warranting the offense of the speaker, complaints have three general aspects that can be analyzed as doing moral work (1998: 303–11). First, what Drew calls complaint sequences are bounded within the conversation. In other words, the explicit moral work of complaints is intentionally marked by the speaker, and thus can be easily identified by the listener, from other parts of the conversation. This is important for our purposes because it suggests that when what Drew calls moral work, or what I would call ethical work, is being done, it is often, if not always, bracketed off, or outside, the normal flow of the conversation. Again, this reminds us of the notion of moral breakdown that I have been suggesting throughout this book.

The second aspect of complaints is that they entail an explicit formulation of the transgression. In other words, the one who is complaining about an other is quite clear in articulating just what it is that the other person did that has been interpreted as a transgression. Again, this is important because it is a way of marking off the space for focusing on a moral question, and indeed does so by very clearly stating what is at question, and therefore, implicitly stating the moral expectation that was transgressed. This is always done for the listener and it is a way of bringing the listener into the context of the transgressive moment.

The third aspect is that the speaker expresses moral indignation. In expressing how the transgression made her feel, the speaker is also expressing the seriousness of the offense. It is quite important that these expressions of indignation are always expressed in the first person, e.g. "I was so angry," for as such they reveal the personal quality of moral transgressions. That is, moral transgressions are not simply a transgression of a moral expectation, but they are very often also a transgression against another person and that person's expectations of the transgressor. Drew also points out the significant finding that the listener of the complaint often reciprocates the indignation, thus showing that while the transgression is indeed personal, it is also collectively noted and condemned as a transgression as well.

These general features, then, show how the speech genre of complaints is particularly ripe for moral analysis. Indeed, it seems to have several characteristics of what we might look for in order to find a subject for an explicit anthropological study of local moralities. As I have already pointed out, this speech genre clearly entails a kind of stepping-away from the everyday flow of life and talk, or what I have called a moral breakdown, that marks it as a sequence of talk particularly focused on ethical work. Further, it reveals a process of confirming, if you will, with others that what was perceived by an individual as a personal transgression against themselves is in fact recognizable by others as in some sense a collectively recognizable moral transgression. Indeed, this seems to be one of the most significant aspects of the moral creativity of communicative interactions. And finally, it is also important to note that moral transgressions are often followed by and expressed with indignation. For in evoking such strong feelings within a person and among different people, moral transgressions disclose their potentially damaging effect on personal and social relations. Indeed, all of this seems to support Geurts's view that the particular words used during a moral judgment (and she stresses the sound of these words not their meaning) are marked with a particular style, and as such they are recognizable to others and alter the affective being of those involved in the communicative interaction (2003).

If in the midst of intersubjective communicative interactions moral values are created and moral transgressions are judged, then this entails the necessity of conceiving of communication as an interpretive act. As Kockelman (2004) points out, utterances often allow for "a range of interpretations," and how they are finally interpreted in the communicative moment depends a great deal on the interpretive horizon, or what is often called the stance, of the listener. But this interpretive stance should not be thought of as simply based on the subjective perspective of the listener, rather it may be more appropriate to say that stances are intersubjectively created within the context of the communicative interaction so that between the speaker and the listener some kind of agreed upon understanding becomes possible. Shortly I will turn to the problem of understanding, but for now let us assume that speakers and listeners for the most part understand one another.

It is precisely this kind of intersubjective and dialogical approach to stance that Robin Ann Shoaps takes in her study of the construction of moral personhood in Mayan wedding counsels (2004). These wedding counsels, or *pixab'* in Mayan, are meetings between the soon to be married couple and their parents and closest relatives. The main purpose of the *pixab'* is to instruct the young couple about their future obligations and responsibilities both as a married couple and as gendered married persons. It is, if you will, a moral lesson on how to be properly married.

Shoaps chose to study the *pixab'* because it is a context of the explicit use of what she calls "deontic stance-taking." She chooses this term because during the *pixab'* the parents and relatives linguistically perform their moral personhood in at least two ways. First, they take up a stance, that is, they take a certain interpretive position from which they assume moral authority. From this stance of moral authority they proceed to attempt to intersubjectively create new moral beings in the persons of the soon to be married couple. Here, then, we once again see the dialogical character of communicative interactions, and, in particular, that of morally imbued communicative interaction. That is to say, it is not simply a matter of communicating information from speaker to listener, but instead a creative process in which new moral ways of being a person are made possible. As Shoaps puts it, these dialogical stance-taking interactions have pragmatic and social functions (2004: 73).

In the case of the *pixab'*, the pragmatic and social function is deontic. This is the second reason Shoaps chose the term deontic stance-taking to describe these meetings, for the main purpose of the *pixab'* is to communicate the moral obligations and responsibilities of marriage to the young couple. As we discussed in Chapter 1, the term deontic refers to a particular concern with such obligations and responsibilities. Thus, for example, during the *pixab'* the man will be reminded of his responsibilities to the family, and the woman will be given advice on how to avoid tension with her new mother-in-law, advice which is particularly important considering they will soon be living together according to the patrilocal residence pattern.

What is important to notice in this example is once again how not only the context of communicative interactions, but also the particular stance that a speaker takes within this context each contribute to the way both speakers and listeners interpret what is being said and what is being done. Similar advice given to a young man about to be married may be interpreted in different ways in another context. Consider, for example, if this advice were given by his father (the person probably giving it during the *pixab'*) in the context of an afternoon meal, the young man could simply interpret it as annoying fatherly advice rather than a serious moral lesson. Or if given by a friend late in the evening over a drink, it could then, perhaps, be interpreted as an ironic joke. The point is that the moral seriousness of the communicative interaction is significantly bolstered or decreased in relation to context and stance.

This can be seen in the example of jokes. While some have argued that jokes are inherently deconstructive, disruptive, and disorganizing of social categories and expectations (Douglas 1975; Oring 1992), Susan Seizer has argued that in fact jokes reinscribe that which they flaunt (1997: 63). That is to say, jokes affirm what is "right" by portraying what is "wrong." In considering the moral work of jokes, Seizer asks a very compelling question: how does one tell a joke without morally offending others? The answer is that it all depends on one's stance, or what she calls footing, and the context of the joke.

Seizer studied the comedians in Special Dramas, which are live performances given in villages in India, in order to see how they go about achieving this precarious art of verbally transgressing moral expectations without morally offending their audience, and particularly their female audience. In this case it is obvious that at its simplest level the context is that of a live performance where there is an expectation that jokes will be told. But this is not enough for the comedians to "get away" with their verbal transgressions via jokes. For even in this context it would be inappropriate for the comedians (who are men) to address the jokes directly to the female audience members; therefore, they take advantage of their linguistic footing, or for our purposes, their stance. Thus, while telling the joke, which often takes the form of a narrative, the comedian begins by clearly addressing the entire, mixed-gender audience in the form of a monologue. This part of the joke is not offensive and is only meant to set the scene. But shortly thereafter the comedian turns slightly and begins to address one of the musicians in the theater's band; the musician, in turn, responds to the story with the local Tamil utterance of "Unh," which is commonly used in everyday conversations to acknowledge that one is listening. Thus, the comedian has shifted his stance from addressing the mixed-gender audience with a monologue to having a conversation with one other man, and in so doing has reenacted a typical street scene where men gather and are free to tell such kinds of jokes and use such language. Only intermittently throughout the narrative joke, when the unoffensive parts are being told, does the comedian return to his original stance of monologically addressing the main audience. By shifting his stance in such a way, the comedian at one and the same time is able to "get away with" telling a dirty joke in the presence of women and also to reinscribe the already held moral expectations of what is proper to say in mixed-gender company. In this example, then, it is clear to see how both context and stance help shape what is morally appropriate communicative behavior, define the limits of a transgressive act, and help reinscribe, or in other examples potentially create new, ranges of possibilities of what counts as morally appropriate or inappropriate.

Before this section comes to a close, I would first like to address the assumption of understanding that to some extent stands at the basis of all of these studies and to a great extent much of anthropology in general. As described in the introduction, in response to Enlightenment ideas of the universal foundations of human knowledge and morality, anthropologists have generally adhered to a more or less strict notion of cultural relativism. In doing so, they generally deny, for the most part, universally human shared understandings of meaning, truth, morality, and taste, among other things, and instead posit culturally shared understandings of these categories. Thus, anthropologists generally posit what they call diversity rather than universality, but this diversity, at least in their analyses, generally stops at the limits of some pre-defined border of groups of people. Therefore, despite the critiques of the culture concept that took place during the 1980s, many anthropologists today still share many of the assumptions that underlie compartmentalized cultures, which are bounded and cut off from other cultures. One of the most steadfast of these assumptions is that of a shared understanding between members of a certain culture, which persists despite recent analytic trends of interpretation and creative dialogism. For the result of any negotiation or creativity as these analytic trends see it only results in shared understandings between those involved.

This notion has been importantly critiqued by Unni Wikan (1992), who argues that we should go beyond the particular words and meanings used by persons and instead focus on the intentions and similar experiences of speakers and listeners. Wikan's concern is to argue that an anthropological focus on meaning tends to cut off groups of people from one another arbitrarily, which, she claims, does not happen in everyday life, and she uses the example of Hindus and Muslims in Bali to illustrate this. Instead, she argues, people all over the world, and she provides several examples, are able to transcend the kinds of cultural, social, religious, ethnic, and linguistic boundaries that anthropologists set up in their analyses by focusing on the intentions of speakers, charitably interpreting their words, and relying on similar experiences shared between speakers and listeners to come not so much to a shared understanding, but to an agreement.

Such a notion of understanding as charitable agreement is borrowed from the philosopher Donald Davidson (1984), who argues that speakers are perfectly able to get along in the world and do things together without necessarily sharing the same understanding of what they mean or what they are doing. Thus, rather than focusing on meaning and congruence, Davidson focuses on what he calls the charity of the listener to try to make sense of what the speaker is saying even if it is not the exact same sense the speaker intends to make. The test of understanding, then, is not whether meaning or moral concepts are precisely shared or not, but whether the speaker and the listener can live and act together in the world. Similarly, Jackson has pointed out in his comparative study of peoples from Sierra Leone and Australia, that intersubjectivity does not necessarily lead to mutual understanding, but is perhaps better understood as the process of being able to be together (1998: 4).

In doing research in Moscow, Russia on the connection between personal experience and moral conceptions, I encountered just this dilemma raised by the assumption of shared understanding (Zigon 2006). This research consisted of taking the life histories and stories of several different Muscovites. Two of my interlocutors had been best friends since their teenage years; thus, I often interviewed them together. Once, while doing an interview together, a semi-argument and debate broke out between the two of them concerning a recently perceived moral transgression of one of the young women (both now in their late twenties) against the other. Of course it was finally resolved, but not before the one who was transgressed against said she forgave her friend because she "understood" why the other had acted the way she did. This claim was immediately responded to by her friend with a rather aggressive "No!," indicating that in fact she had not understood her. Nevertheless, the topic was then dropped and not discussed again until I brought it up again about a year later.

I found this very interesting because like so many of my colleagues I assumed that this claim of understanding meant a claim of shared meaning or shared values or some such thing. After spending much time considering this interaction, I brought it up with them again. It became clear to me at this point that it was not about shared meanings and values, but instead about similar experiences and what they called "knowing the character" of the other person. Indeed, what I had come to find so interesting about these two best friends is that they are so different – one a very strict Russian Orthodox Christian and the other a non-believing business-minded woman eagerly seeking success in the new Russian economy – in many of their beliefs and moral values. Thus, when one claimed to understand the other and that it was this understanding that allowed her to forgive a transgression, it was not a shared belief or moral value that she understood, but instead it was a charitable interpretation of the other's intentions based on similar experiences that allowed her to make this claim of "understanding."

This ethnographic encounter was essential for shifting my own assumptions and way of considering social and communicative interactions, and especially for the way I conceptualize and analyze moral relations. I will close this section, then, with the suggestion that an anthropology of local moralities not look for bounded and shared moral understandings and conceptions within groups of people and cultures, but instead undertake the much more trying but realistic endeavor of revealing the ways that people in their everyday interactions act charitably with one another so as to live together and, in so doing, charitably enact morality with one another.

Narrative

In the last chapter we saw how medical anthropologists have been at the forefront of utilizing narratives in their analyses of medical encounters, and how these narratives are particularly helpful in revealing the moral assumptions, understandings, and expectations of these encounters. In this section we will take another look at narrative and consider more closely how it is a primary means for the communication and articulation of moral worlds.

Before we go any further, let me very briefly and simply define narrative as those stories persons tell one another (or themselves) in order to create and maintain meaning and order in one's (or a community's) life. These stories may or may not be fictional, and, in fact, can often combine the two. These narrative stories are also limited by certain socio-historic-cultural expectations and understandings of, among other things, what constitutes a story and how and to whom it can be told. As I mentioned in the last chapter, it is often noted by anthropologists that narratives, as part of their meaning-making function, disclose a causal order to events and activities. Again, to a great extent I agree with this. However, it must be recognized that narratives do not always, and indeed often do not, provide a logical and coherent causal order. In other words, one damn thing does not always follow another in narrative utterances. Thus, it is often up to the listener – and in our case the listener is often the anthropologist – to interpret the meaning of these stories. While in everyday life such interpretation poses little problem, since all communicative interaction is a matter of interpretation and is more or less easily resolved through the give and take of interpretive negotiations that is common in all spoken forms of communication, there is more danger for the interpreting anthropologist. Therefore, for anthropologists who use narrative analysis it is imperative that they do long-term fieldwork with their interlocutors so that they too can engage in the kind of interpretive negotiations that are characteristic of everyday forms of communicative interaction.

As was also mentioned in the last chapter, narratives are the articulation of the interaction between a person and her social world. For this reason narratives provide a particular perspective on events and actions, and as Ochs and Capps have argued, and similar to what was discussed in the last section, central to these narrative perspectives is the moral stance they provide (2001: 45–6). According to these authors, a moral stance is "[r]ooted in community and tradition [and aims] towards what is good or valuable and how one ought to live in the world" (2001: 45). Because of this moral stance that is central to many narratives, everyday narrative articulations are significant for the perpetuation of local moral worlds. This is so because in taking a moral stance within a narrative telling, a speaker provides an opportunity for a public clarification, reinforcement or revision of locally held moral beliefs (2001: 46).

One of the reasons the analysis of narratives is so important to the anthropological study of moralities is that it provides a rare instance to see and hear the articulation of competing and contested moral perspectives, for what often becomes clear in the analysis of these narratives is that the teller is setting up her own moral position over and against another position. In doing so through the public forum of narrative, she is often looking to gather or persuade others to join in sharing her own moral perspective rather than the other. As such, narrative often works as a kind of public debate on local moral issues. This can be seen in the way that narrative speakers often take a position of moral superiority over and against that of the other position, and in so doing attempt to convince their interlocutors of the rightness of their moral perspective (2001: 47).

Although Ochs and Capps claim that to some degree all narratives take a moral stance (2001: 50), I would hesitate to go so far. It seems that in making this claim the authors begin to fall into that error of so many anthropologists who take such things as subjective perspective, social values, and certain expectations as morally laden positions. This is something we must avoid as anthropologists of moralities who are attempting to provide focused and concise explications of local moralities. What is clear, however, is that one of the benefits of the study of narratives is that their constituent parts are separated by frames. That is to say, the constituent parts of a greater narrative, one of which may be a moral stance, can be read as stories within a story that are separated from each other by means of the use of certain words or phrases that indicate a shift in focus or perspective. Examples of such frame utterances that mark moral stances may be: "Oh, you won't believe what he did the other day," "Wait until you hear this one," and "The other day I got so angry." Similar to how these shifts work in the complaints we discussed in the last section, these kinds of utterances communicate to the speaker's interlocutors that she is about to shift the focus of the narrative and, perhaps, to that of a moral stance. It is for such frames and shifts that anthropologists of moralities must look.

Because narratives are a primary means for persons to give meaning and order to their lives, they provide important insights into the ways in which persons conceive of themselves as moral persons. That is to say, narratives reveal the relationship between selfhood, identity, and moral dispositions. And because narratives are structured by the socio-historic-cultural range of what is sayable, they also reveal local notions of this relationship. Again, then, in narratives it is possible to see the intersection of the subjective processes of this relationship and the structures of the socio-historic-culturally possible.

Chris McCollum provides an interesting look at this intersection. Using a combination of anthropological narrative analysis and psychodynamic theory, McCollum (2002) shows how middle-class Americans articulate a contradictory definition of self-agency in their narrative descriptions of how they met their current romantic partner. While the central theme throughout these narratives is that the romantic partners did not meet through any significant personal agency of their own – that is to say, they met by fate or some other force that was out of their hands – the majority of these narratives also reveal that the persons involved in these partnerships needed to first be ready for such an encounter. In other words, McCollum argues, the persons involved in these romantic relationships needed to have first achieved a certain degree of personal autonomy and self-sufficiency before they could open themselves up to being seriously romantically involved with others.

McCollum contrasts this seeming contradiction of romantic encounters depending upon the achieving of autonomy in order to give it up so that one can "find" their partner, with the choice-of-profession narratives collected by Charlotte Linde. Linde (1993) found that in middle-class American accounts of how they came to their particular current jobs, there is a strict emphasis on the personal agency of the narrator. In order for these choice-of-profession narratives to have meaning – indeed, for the tellers of the story to have a meaningful life – they must articulate their story of finding their current job in a way that suggests they themselves were responsible for finding the job and that it is the job they wanted to do. Contrasted to the theme of autonomy that must be yielded to fate which is central in McCollum's romance narratives, then, Linde contends that choice-of-profession narratives reveal the importance that a sense of personal agency has for middle-class Americans' sense of self.

Both of these authors argue that these narratives not only tell us about middle-class Americans' sense of self, but also about their sense of moral self. This moral self is closely related to that of the expectations of the local moral world, for as Linde puts it, these narrative accounts are deemed socially adequate because they adhere to local notions of "the nature of proper lives, proper sequences of events, and proper reasons for professional choices" (1993: 128). Thus, because choice-of-profession narratives emphasize the ability of the person to make his own way in the world without the help of others, a value highly prized in American society, and romance narratives emphasize the necessity of gaining autonomy before giving oneself over to fate, and therefore showing that the person was not needy or lonely, these narratives both articulate different versions of the American sense of the good person. In this way, these narratives can be seen as articulations of the good American (McCollum 2002: 113–15).

While these narratives articulate middle-class notions of the good American, they or similar narratives can be used, as we have already said above, to take a stance against other moral perspectives. In doing so, those who articulate this stance are claiming, whether they consciously intend to or not, a moral superiority over other moral perspectives and social and self-identities. Sofia Villenas (2001) shows how this happens in a small town in North Carolina and how the Latina mothers who are narratively placed in the position of inferiority articulate their own counter-narratives that call into question the dominant values of Americans. Thus, for example, while the moralizing narratives of the native (predominantly white) North Carolinians call into question the Latina mothers' ability to raise their children properly, the Latina mothers counter that they have raised good children back in their home countries and if they are not doing so now it is more a result of the inherent difficulties within the American social structure than their own motherly practices.

Villenas argues that these counternarratives show the agency of these mothers and their resistance to racist and moralizing discourse, narratives, and practice (2001: 19–22). But, as I have already cautioned, we as anthropologists should not be so quick to award the characterization of agency and resistance, for it is becoming increasingly clear, as Mahmood and Asad among others have pointed out, that these concepts are often more representative of the assumptions and hopes of the anthro-pologist than of the people we study. While the counternarratives of the mothers may not lead to the "future mobilization" that Villenas envisions (2001: 22), they certainly do show that everyday life and its communities are filled with competing and contested narratives. And while it certainly is true that the narratives of the native North Carolinians stand in a position of power over and against those of the Latina mothers, both are equally characterized by taking a position of moral superiority over the other, which at the same time places the other in a position of immorality. It is clear that the Latina mothers' narratives do this just as much as the native North Carolinians. Both structurally and socially, then, both narratives do the same moral work. In other words, from a perspective of narrative analysis, both narratives are equally demeaning of the other, as each claims the moral high ground.

So far we have focused on the way in which moral worlds are articulated, negoti-ated, and created through narratives. But it is also possible to speak of the ways in which moral worlds themselves shape narratives. That is to say, by doing in-depth interviewing – for example, life historical research – it is possible to see how the moral outlook of the persons with whom we do our research helps shape the stories they tell us. This is what Jennifer Cole (2003) calls the role of moral projects in shaping narratives. By using the term "moral project," Cole attempts to connect what she sees as the centrality of striving for the good in self-formation with particular sociopolitical circumstances. Therefore, she defines moral projects as referring to those "local visions of what makes a good, just community, and the ways in which these conceptions of community reciprocally engage people's notions of what constitutes a good life, and their efforts to attain that life" (2003: 99). For the most part I find this a compelling concept, for there is no doubt that persons engage in projects of making themselves into certain kinds of moral persons. Indeed, my own research, as we will see in the third case study, shows how individuals go through this very process. Nevertheless, I would hesitate to say that the "local vision" and the "community" are as widespread as Cole seems to indicate. For it also seems clear that all societies are made up of a diverse range of moral perspectives, and that even those who might constitute a so-called moral community still differ from one another to some degree. Still, I think that Cole has hit on an important way of conceptualizing the relationship between individual persons, their immediate moral community, and the kind of work it takes for these persons to make themselves and the community into the kind of moral beings they hope to be. This work is very nicely captured in the concept of moral projects.

Cole uses her concept of moral projects to show how persons' moral visions of their world shape their memories and their narrative telling of events in the past. She does this by showing how different generations of people living in both rural and urban Madagascar differently remember the 1947 rebellion, which took place there against the French colonizers. She claims that the differences in the narrative tellings are not simply accounted for by various deviations from a supposed truth of the rebellion, but instead are shaped by the difference in moral projects between generations and urban and rural residents. Not only narrative, but memory as well, is shaped by moral projects.

How particular moral projects shape memory and narrative can also be seen in Gilbert Quintero's (2002) study of drinking on a Navajo reservation in Arizona. Quintero does not use the concept of moral project, but instead chooses to use that of moral economy. Unfortunately, and as we have already seen is often the case with this concept of moral economy, it is used in a way completely unlike its original intent. Indeed, in defining moral economy as "the norms, values, relationships and expectations that have traditionally shaped and organized" Navajo society (2002: 12), Quintero seems to be simply giving a basic definition of morality. Be that as it may, it is certainly clear that the concept of moral projects would have been a more useful one to utilize. This is so because in his study Quintero shows that in many of the narratives he collected about drinking on the reservation there is a clear focus on how drinking goes against the traditional moral ways of Navajo society. This is done through recollections of the past when Navajo society was supposedly well ordered, controlled, and responsible. The past, then, is memorialized as a morally superior time when it is remembered and narrated through the lens of a present-day moral project that holds drinking as a central moral problem to be overcome in contemporary Navajo society. The immoralities of the present must be overcome, so it is claimed by Quintero's interlocutors, by a return to an imagined morally superior past. A past, that is, which is imaginatively created in opposition to and by the very fact of the so-called immoral present.

Indeed this is often the case when societies are going through what I would call a societal-wide moral breakdown. My own research has shown that many Russians today remember the Soviet past as a time of moral superiority, order, and responsibility when compared to the supposed widespread immorality of the present. This is widely considered true despite historical evidence that the public and the government in Russia and the Soviet Union have been bemoaning the supposed immorality of the present when compared to the moral past for at least the last sixty years. A similar kind of memory created through moral projects can be seen in Joel Robbins's research with the Urapmin of Papua New Guinea. Memory, the past, and its narratives, then, are often nostalgically created through the lens of the moral projects of the present.

Arthur Kleinman (2006) also considers the relationship between memory, narrative, and what he calls moral experience. By considering the case studies of seven individuals, some of whom he worked with very closely as a psychiatrist, he explores the ways in which memory is both constituted through and helps to construct the moral lives of these individuals, and how their memories and moral lives are articulated through narratives. What I find particularly useful in Kleinman's work, and something very close to what I have been calling the moral breakdown, is his claim that "[o]rdinary experience frequently thrusts people into troubling circumstances and confounding conditions that threaten to undo our thin mastery over those deeper things that matter most" (2006: 4). It is both Kleinman's and my own contention that it is these breakdowns and the ways that we negotiate them that are primarily responsible for making us into the kind of moral persons we become.

Kleinman's work, then, offers anthropologists of moralities a significant example of just how we can, with great compassion and concern for the everyday lived experiences of real people, articulate and describe their moral experiences and lives. It is too often thought that a focus on individual lives denies their essential sociality and the role of history, politics, and culture in shaping their lives. Kleinman shows that this is clearly not the case. By paying particular attention to the intersection of person's experiences with greater socio-historic-cultural structures, we are offered a rare glimpse at the subtle struggles and joys of living a human and moral life. In the case study that follows this chapter, I will present my own research, which is very similar to Kleinman's, and describe the ways in which I have tried to offer moral portraits of individuals who are striving to live moral lives in post-Soviet Moscow.

Before we end this section, however, I would like to briefly touch upon one last aspect of narrative that makes it a significant part of moral communication between persons cross-culturally. Narratives are not only the stories that people tell one another about their own lives, they are also stories that they tell one another about other people and the kinds of lives they have or do live. These stories are often of particular historical figures, who in fact may be fictional or semi-fictional, who offer a kind of moral exemplar for people to try to live up to today. No doubt many of us are familiar with these stories, and in fact, a good deal of these stories are about characters central to religious traditions.

Take, for example, Patrice Ladwig's (2005) insightful analysis of the most famous of Buddhist donor stories, *The Perfect Generosity of Prince Vessantara*. This story is the last in a series of 547 that recount the various rebirths and the virtuous acts of the protagonist that eventually lead to the birth of the Buddha. In this story, Prince Vessantara exemplifies the virtue of giving and generosity by giving away his possessions, including his wife and children. In doing so, the prince achieves ethical self-perfection and will therefore be reborn in the next life as the Buddha. What is particularly interesting about this story is that the prince's excessive generosity is upheld in the narrative as a virtuous act despite it going against not only our own moral expectations (ask yourself, do you consider it moral to give away your wife and children to strangers?) but also the moral expectations of his own contemporaries within the story. One lesson of the story, then, is that what counts as moral within the community may not always be so from another perspective.

This contradiction, however, gives the story a sense of moral ambiguity, to which its listeners generally have an emotional response. It is this emotional response to the narrative, so Ladwig argues, that is central to the way in which narratives work as a source of moral education. For unlike Humphrey's (1997) discussion of Mongolian exemplar narratives, where she seems to suggest they provide moral guidance by offering examples for listeners to embody themselves, Ladwig claims that the Vessantara narrative offers no clear ethical resolution so that it cannot stand as a guide for what to do in one's life (2005: 14–15).

Instead, the narrative of the prince's excessive generosity held up as ethical perfection is meant to evoke an emotional response from its listeners, and it is this emotional response that does moral work. Because the narrative does not present an example of ethical resolution, but instead a case of moral ambiguity, it evokes within listeners the emotions of such ambiguity. The listeners, then, must learn to manage and work through this state of the moral emotions of ambiguity, which, in fact, are part of any serious ethical dilemma. The narrative, then, does not provide an exemplar of what to do in any particular case of a moral problem, but instead provides an exemplar of how to work through the emotions that will necessarily arise within the context of any ethical dilemma. Therefore, the narrative can be seen as a lesson in how to, if you will, deal with the existential crisis of a moral breakdown.

Some Final Words

In this chapter I have tried to show the central role that language-use plays in the shaping of local moral worlds. As I said at the outset, language is not only vital because it is how moral understandings and expectations are communicated between persons and between institutions and persons, but also, and more importantly, because it is through everyday language-use that moralities are negotiated, reevaluated, and enacted. By looking at the ways in which language is utilized and performed in particular contexts through discourse, speech genres, and narratives, we have seen how it allows for the enactment of a certain range of possible moral worlds. In a very real way it seems possible to say that morality, as we tend to understand the concept, would not be possible without the all too human capability of language and the particular kind of communicative interactions this capability allows for. It is for this reason that special attention to forms of everyday language-use is essential to anthropological studies of local moralities.

Case Study 3

Narratives of Moral Experience in Moscow

Unlike the previous two case studies, my own research has focused on the ways in which the personal experiences of some Muscovites have led them to hold their own particular moral conceptions (Zigon 2006). By utilizing life historical research and narrative analysis I have tried to show that a person's claimed moral conceptions and beliefs are closely related to the kinds of moral experiences they have had through-out their life. In other words, I have tried to show that a personally held morality is constructed throughout one's life in a continuous process of negotiating with others in particular contexts, reevaluating previously held beliefs, and then enacting new or revised moral practices based on this process of negotiation and reevaluation. The result of this research shows that morality is better thought of as a continuous dialogical process during which persons are in constant interaction with their world and the persons in that world, rather than as a set category of beliefs from which one picks appropriate responses according to particular situations.

My work, then, is an attempt to show how a few Muscovites articulate their subjective moral positions. By interpreting their narrative articulations I provide examples of how persons "theorize" morality through their narratives. In this analysis I look for certain patterns, regularities, and recurrent themes of my inter-locutors' narratives. While such consistencies are important for understanding persons' narratives, it is also important to look for inconsistencies, gaps, shifts, and contradictions, for these can also tell us much about a person's moral conception. In analyzing my interlocutors' narratives, I attempt to show the process by which some Muscovites go about creating their moral worlds.

Because my research is limited to the explication of the moral conceptions of a few Muscovites, I make no claim to describe Russian morality in general. While it is important to recognize that personal experience is intimately intertwined with social experience, and that one's socio-historic-cultural world always provides a range of possible experiences outside of which it may be impossible to step, nevertheless, it remains important to recognize that all persons have a certain perspective on social life and for this reason each lives within a unique moral world. This remains true even if these unique moral worlds are recognizable or even partly shared by others. This approach, then, recognizes what Rogers has called the shades of similarity and difference in local moral worlds (2004: 36).

This tension between shared and personal experience is often revealed and
covered over in my interlocutors' narratives. While at times this is intentionally
done, it should also be noted that this is what narrative as a form of speech does.
Narrative is a social form of speech. This is so not only because narrative is done
with others, but also because it is ripe with shared values and meanings. But sociality
is not a simple sharing; it is a dialog within a range of possibilities of understanding.
It is often through narrative that persons negotiate this understanding, in doing so
they navigate the potentially dangerous semiotic waters of difference and similarity,
ambiguity and coherence, unfamiliarity and recognizability. In other words, through
narrative persons perform sociality. They can also perform and articulate their moral
conceptions, and do so in ways that are both personal and socially recognizable.
Thus, in presenting the moral portraits of my Muscovite interlocutors, I show how
through narrative they negotiate the tension between personal and shared experiences
of living-through a particular socio-historic-cultural world. This allows them, in
turn, to conceive of and articulate morality in a way that may not be entirely unique,
but also may not be entirely shared.

This fuzzy line between the unique and the shared is to a great extent dependent
on just how different personal experiences are between individuals. Thus, for
example, two of my interlocutors, Olya, a dedicated Russian Orthodox Christian
in her mid twenties, and Aleksandra Vladimirovna, a 51-year-old strict Orthodox
Christian and ex-Communist, despite their many differences, have shared similar
kinds of experiences in terms of their relationship to the Church, referencing the
same foundational literature, most specifically the Bible, reading similar secondary
literature, and participating in the same Church rituals and practices – because of
this they also share similar conceptions of morality. Most obviously is their shared
distinction between what they both call God's morality and social morality, the
former being superior to the latter.

On the other hand, there is a much greater difference of moral conceptions
between, for example, Aleksandra Vladimirovna and Dima, a musician and institutionally agnostic man in his early thirties. Although Dima does on occasion reference
God and considers himself a "religious person," he does not speak of God and
religion in Russian Orthodox terms, as does Aleksandra Vladimirovna. More importantly, however, is the real difference that exists between the two of them in terms
of motivation for acting "morally." I mark morally here in scare quotes because
one similarity that does exist between the two of them is that both seem to reject
a social notion of morality. For Aleksandra Vladimirovna, true morality is godly
morality, which is acquired when what she calls one's heart and will are in harmony
with God's will. For Dima, on the other hand, morality as social expectation is
for the most part rhetorically rejected, and instead he focuses on a personal ethics
of self-interest. That is, an ethics of doing what he wants for himself as long as it
doesn't hurt others. As can be seen, then, the greater or lesser differences between
individuals can ebb and flow not only across individuals, but also throughout their

various narratives so that at different times people can be more or less similar in their way of speaking about their moral conceptions.

Because of this, I have concluded from my research that narratives and what they reveal about persons' everyday lives, experiences, and conceptions force us to reconsider the very idea of morality. Indeed, they force us to ask why it is that we even believe there is something like a unified concept of local morality. For if narratives force us to recognize the diversity in local moralities, shouldn't they also force us to question our own conceptual view of the world? Shouldn't they force us to question the very idea of morality? Perhaps, what narratives do is force us to recognize that the One Big Idea concepts such as morality, culture, and history do little to help us understand the ways in which actual lived life, the kind of life that every human being must wake up to every morning, can never be boxed into such singular and totalizing concepts. Because they raise such important questions not only about how our interlocutors live their lives, but also about the ways in which we as anthropologists do our own research and analyze our research data, narratives are an important and significant methodological resource for anthropologists of moralities.

Part V
Closing

–7–

Some Closing Words

In closing I will not summarize what I have tried to cover in this book, nor will I attempt to draw any conclusions. Instead I will take an opportunity to outline some of my own thoughts on how anthropologists can approach the study of local moralities with the kind of focus, precision, and subtlety they bring to many of the traditional concepts of anthropological research. This is important, I believe, because without such an approach there is a real danger that morality as both a research and analytic concept can too easily be used in ways that are at best confusing and at worst distorting. The manifestation of this danger is clear in several of the works discussed in this book.

Douglas Rogers has claimed that the anthropological study of moralities allows us to move past some of the totalizing social scientific analytical concepts that have been prevalent in anthropology (2004: 397). This is something with which I entirely agree. However, as we have seen throughout this book, too often in the work of anthropologists morality seems to step in as a convenient replacement for such totalizing concepts as culture, society, history, or power, without really replacing the totalizing presence of these latter concepts. That is to say, while morality is intended to invoke a sense of everyday life and intersubjective interactions, it is, with a few very important exceptions, often used to represent a deterministic or nearly deterministic structure within which persons have little choice to deviate without the threat of societal penalty. The analytical concept, then, may have changed, its totalizing structure, however, seems not to have done so.

Is it possible to utilize morality within anthropological research in another way? I think it is. Michael Fischer claims that his own work and writings focus on the interaction of individual persons, what he calls the locus of ethical struggles, and the moral systems of societies and institutions (2003: 11). In following this approach, I suggest, anthropologists can best undertake the task of an anthropology of moralities. For it is through this approach that: (1) we can make a coherent distinction between morality and ethics, which will help us be more focused and subtle in our research and analysis; and (2) the concepts of morality and ethics can actually do away with the traditional social scientific totalizing concepts of, for example, culture and society, and focus on the everyday acts and practices of persons in a context that does not need to reference outside itself for determining structures. Let us, then, see how this is possible by turning to the distinction between morality and ethics.

Morality and Ethics

A focused anthropology of moralities is best brought about by beginning with a distinction between morality and ethics. Before turning to a discussion of ethics, I will begin with morality. Morality can be considered in at least three different, but certainly interrelated, spheres: (1) the institutional; (2) that of public discourse; and (3) embodied dispositions. I will take each of these in turn.

Institutions, for our purposes, can be very loosely defined as those formal and non-formal social organizations and groups that are a part of all societies and that wield varying amounts of power over individual persons. It can be said that all human persons have at least some nominal contact with or participation in some of the institutions that make up their respective societies. However, most human persons are intimately entwined within the overlapping spheres of influence of several different institutions within and beyond their own society. Lastly, it can be said that most, if not all, institutions proclaim the truth or the rightness of a particular morality. Some examples of such institutions are governments, organized religions, village elder councils, the workplace, international organizations such as the UN or the IMF, and local clubs, organizations, or orders.

Part of what it is to be an institution is to claim that it is the bearer and securer of the truth or rightness of a particular kind of morality. And while institutions have varying levels of power available to them in order to propagate and enforce their version of morality, it is generally a formal prerequisite of interacting with the institution that one, at least publicly, adheres to this morality. Thus, for example, the Roman Catholic Church has a particular moral view on sexuality, which is part of the Church's larger moral system, and it is expected that all Roman Catholics should believe and live according to this moral doctrine. Another example would be that of a council of village elders, which in one form or another is common in many small-scale societies, which claims to uphold the traditions of the ancestors and it is expected that all members of that society or community are to follow these traditions.

It is obvious that not all members, if any, of these small-scale societies and communities, or Roman Catholic believers, or participants in any institutional sphere for that matter, always follow to the letter the claimed morality of the institution. It is also obvious that those who do not follow the institutional morality are not always punished or reprimanded for not doing so. In fact, it may often go unnoticed. It is also clear that all societies, including small-scale societies, are made up of a plurality of institutional moralities. Despite the fact of the plurality of institutional moralities within all societies and that persons do not always precisely adhere to one or any of these institutional moralities, the influence that institutional moralities have on individual persons is clearly real and substantial. For this reason it is not uncommon that when asked what morality is, a person will often give you some version of, for example, the Ten Commandments, the law, societal tradition, or something like these.

Institutional morality, then, is a significantly influential moral discourse, which is often supported by very real expressions of power, but which, nevertheless, is not totalizing and is more akin to a very persuasive rhetoric than it is to a truth. Institutional morality, while it should never be mistaken for a local morality as such, is a significant sphere for anthropological research because it is at the intersection of this sphere of morality and individual persons that it becomes possible to see how institutions and power play a large part in the making of moral persons.

Closely related to institutional morality, but yet not quite the same is what I will call the public discourse of morality. This distinction is very similar to the distinction Vološinov (2000) made between official ideology and behavioral ideology, where the former is that which is upheld by official and state institutions and the latter is the result of the everyday dialogical interactions between persons. Although these two kinds of ideologies, like the institutional and public discourse of morality, are separate and distinct from one another, they are in constant dialogue with one another. Thus, both of the ideologies about which Vološinov speaks, and the two moralities about which I am here speaking (as well as the third kind I will discuss next), not only support and authorize one another, but at times they also undermine and subvert one another (Caton 2006: 51). The public discourse of morality, then, is all those public articulations of moral beliefs, conceptions, and hopes that are not *directly* articulated by an institution. Some examples of the public discourse of morality are the media, protest, philosophical discourse, everyday articulated beliefs and opinions, the arts, literature and stories, and parental teachings.

As is clear from some of these examples, and as I have already said, the public discourse of morality can be very closely related to institutional morality, but need not be. Whatever the case may be, the two types of moralities are always in a dialogical relationship with one another. Thus, for example, certain television news networks may articulate a moral discourse that is very similar to that of the institutional morality of the government, yet when the network is not itself run by the government, it cannot be said to be a part of that institutional moral voice. This is so because given even relative independence from the institution of the government, there is always the possibility of dissent and debate within the network and by speakers on its broadcasts. Indeed, it has become a trademark of most modern media outlets to provide some diversity of moral voices on their broadcasts or in their pages.

Because in the contemporary world the media has become so entwined with many institutions, perhaps it is better to consider some other examples of the public discourse of morality to see how it is a distinct, yet dialogically interacting, sphere of morality from institutional morality. Take, for example, the arts, literature, and other stories. In the so-called Western world these have provided an alternative moral vision to institutional morality since at least the time of ancient Greece – Sophocles, Shakespeare, Dostoevsky, Stravinsky, Picasso, among many others have all provided, in their own ways, distinct moral views of the world. The same can be said of the arts, literature, and everyday stories of non-Western countries, and I have no reason to think the same cannot be said for some of the oral stories and arts of small-scale societies around the world. Likewise, it cannot be forgotten that the arts, literature, and stories also often support institutional moralities. Thus, they provide a ripe area of research for anthropologists of moralities to discern the often subtle support and subversion that can take place in one creative act or piece.

Similarly, it is very clear that people in their everyday articulations of their moral beliefs and concepts also offer an alternative moral voice to that of institutional morality. Above I said that it is not uncommon that one would reference, for example, the Ten Commandments or the law when asked what morality is. In my own research I have found this to be certainly true. This shows the pervasive influence of institutional morality, but it is by no means the end of the story, for once one begins to press a person a bit more – for example, in the kinds of moral debates that arise on occasion in everyday life or in the context of anthropological interviews and conversation – here you often find moral articulations that differ, sometimes radically, from the dominant institutional moralities of a society. Such moral articulations are a part of what I have been trying to describe as the public discourse of morality.

They are also, I suggest, an articulation, or a reflected verbalization of the third kind of morality, that is, morality as embodied dispositions. This third kind of morality can be described as what Mauss called a kind of habitus, or unreflective and unreflexive dispositions of everyday social life attained over a lifetime of what Mauss (1973) called socially performed techniques. Morality in this third sense, then, unlike the way morality is so often considered as rule-following or conscious reflection on a problem or dilemma, is not thought out beforehand, nor is it noticed when it is performed. It is simply done. Morality as embodied dispositions is one's everyday way of being in the world.

It is because all persons are able to embody their morality in this unreflective and unreflexive way that most persons most of the time are able to act in ways that are, for the most part, acceptable to others in their social world seemingly naturally. My own research in post-Soviet Russia, a place where morality is on a daily basis questioned by the government or the Russian Orthodox Church or the media or people in their daily conversations, found that despite this constant cacophony of moral questioning, most of my interlocutors claim that they are able to act in ways that are morally appropriate most of the time without ever considering their actions. I suggest this holds true for all persons and that it is this ability to be nonconsciously moral that allows humans to be social beings. Thus, it is the rare occasion in everyday life when one actually has to stop and consider how to act or be morally appropriate. These moments are what I call ethics.

Ethics, then, is a kind of stepping-away from this third kind of morality as embodied dispositions. In stepping-away in this ethical moment, a person becomes reflective and reflexive about her moral way of being in the world and what she must do, say, or think in order to appropriately return to her nonconscious moral mode of being. What must be done is a process of working on the self, where the person must perform certain practices on herself or with other persons in order to consciously be and act morally in the social world. Ethics, then, is a conscious acting on oneself either in isolation or with others so as to make oneself into a more morally appropriate and acceptable social person not only in the eyes of others but also for oneself.

This working on oneself in what I call the ethical moment is brought about by a moral breakdown or what Foucault called problematization. This occurs when some event or person intrudes into the everyday life of a person and forces them to consciously reflect upon the appropriate ethical response (be it words, silence, action or non-action). Once one has experienced this moral breakdown, they work on themselves by utilizing certain ethical tactics not merely to return to the unreflective and unreflexive disposition of morality, but in so doing, to create a new moral dispositional self. Thus, this moment of ethics is a creative moment, for by performing ethics, persons create, even if ever so slightly, new moral selves and enact new moral worlds.

This ethical moment, similar to what Fischer (2003) calls the ethical plateau, is a moment in which the multifarious aspects of local moralities, which are all part of the three spheres of morality I described above, come together to *inform* the ways in which a person works on herself. I say *inform* because none of the aspects that belong to the institutional moralities, the public discourses of morality, or the person's own embodied dispositional morality determine how this person will work on herself in this ethical moment. While it may be true that one or several of these aspects, for example, Roman Catholic morality, the moral teachings of one's parents, or one's own moral experiences, will often play a very significant role (so significant that some might be tempted to say instead that it or they are determinant) in the workings of the ethical moment, nevertheless, because this is a moment of conscious reflection and dialogue with one's own moral dispositions, as well as with the other two spheres of morality, it is also a moment of freedom, creativity, and emergence.

It is because of this moment, and the way it feeds back into the social world, that not only one's own embodied moral dispositions change throughout a lifetime, but so too does the possibility arise for shifts, alterations, and changes in the spheres of institutional morality and the public discourse of morality. For this reason, then, I suggest that it is ethics and the ethical moment brought about through the moral breakdown that should draw the most attention of anthropologists of moralities. For it is by studying ethics and the ethical moment that we can see the intersection of the various spheres of morality in the daily lives of individual persons, and also the multifarious ways in which human persons work on themselves not only to enact, but also to alter the moralities of their social worlds.

In this book we have seen many examples of how anthropologists have either approached the study of local moralities or have used the concept of morality as an analytic concept. Some of these examples have and will make a significant contribution to an anthropology of moralities. It is my contention that what sets these examples apart is that they have each, in their own way, focused their research methodology and analysis on either one of the three spheres of morality that I have described here, or ethics and the ethical moment, or, in most cases, the intersection of two or all of these. It is to these examples that a future anthropology of moralities should look for guideposts to future research on this increasingly important topic both within the discipline and within our world.

References

Abrahams, Ray (1996), "Vigilantism: order and disorder on the frontiers of the state," in O. Harris, ed., *Inside and Outside the Law: Anthropological Studies of Authority and Ambiguity*, London: Routledge.

Alter, Joseph S. (1997), "Seminal Truth: A Modern Science of Male Celibacy in North India," *Medical Anthropology Quarterly* 11(3): 275–98.

Aquinas, Thomas (1988), "The Summa Theologica," in Paul. E. Sigmund (ed.), *St. Thomas Aquinas on Politics and Ethics*, New York: W. W. Norton & Co.

Asad, Talal (1993), *Genealogies of Religion: Discipline and Reasons of Power in Christianity and Islam*, Baltimore: The Johns Hopkins University Press.

Asad, Talal (2003), *Formations of the Secular: Christianity, Islam, Modernity*, Stanford: Stanford University Press.

Bakhtin, M. M. (1981), *The Dialogical Imagination*, Austin: University of Texas Press.

Bauman, Zygmunt (1993), *Postmodern Ethics*, Oxford: Blackwell.

Benedict, Ruth (1956), "Anthropology and the Abnormal," in Douglas Haring (ed.), *Personal Character and Cultural Milieu*, Syracuse, NY: Syracuse University Press.

Bergmann, Jörg R. (1998), "Introduction: Morality in Discourse," *Research on Language and Social Interaction* 31(3&4): 279–94.

Boas, Franz (1911), "Introduction," *Handbook of American Indian Languages*, Washington DC: Smithsonian Institute.

Bourdieu, Pierre (2001), *Masculine Domination*, Stanford: Stanford University Press.

Brandt, Richard B. (1954), *Hopi Ethics: A Theoretical Analysis*, Chicago: University of Chicago Press.

Brandtstädter, Susanne (2003), "The Moral Economy of Kinship and Property in Southern China," in C. Hann and the "Property Relations" Group, *The Postsocialist Agrarian Question: Property Relations and the Rural Condition*, Münster: Lit Verlag.

Briggs, Jean L. (1998), *Inuit Morality Play: The Emotional Education of a Three-Year-Old*, New Haven, CT: Yale University Press.

Brodwin, Paul (1996), *Medicine and Morality in Haiti: the Contest for Healing Power*, Cambridge: Cambridge University Press.

Burchhardt, Marian (2005), "The Moral Orders of Sexuality: Advancing Positions in Contemporary Social Theory," presented at the workshop on "Rethinking Morality" at the Max Planck Institute for Social Anthropology.

Caldwell, Melissa L. (2005), "The Russian Orthodox Church, the Provision of Social Welfare, and Changing Ethics of Benevolence," presented at the workshop on "Eastern Christianities in Anthropological Perspective" at the Max Planck Institute for Social Anthropology.

Cassell, Joan (1980) "Ethical Principles for Conducting Fieldwork," *American Anthropologist* 82: 28–41.

Caton, Steven C. (2006), "What Is an 'Authorizing Discourse'?" in D. Scott and C. Hirschkind (eds), *Powers of the Secular Modern: Talal Asad and His Interlocutors*, Stanford: Stanford University Press.

Cicero (1999), *On the Commonwealth and On the Laws*, Cambridge: Cambridge University Press.

Cole, Jennifer (2003), "Narratives and Moral Projects: Generational Memories of the Malagasy 1947 Rebellion," *Ethos* 31(1): 95–126.

Cook, John W. (1999), *Morality and Cultural Differences*, Oxford: Oxford University Press.

Cowan, Jane K. (2006), "Culture and Rights after *Culture and Rights*," *American Anthropologist* 108(1): 9–24.

Davidson, Donald (1984), *Inquiries into Truth and Interpretation*, Oxford: Oxford University Press.

Dickson-Gómez, Julia (2003), "Growing Up in Guerilla Camps: The Long-Term Impact of Being a Child Soldier in El Salvador's Civil War," *Ethos* 30(4): 327–56.

Dilger, Hansjörg (2003), "Sexuality, AIDS, and the Lures of Modernity: Reflexivity and Morality among Young People in Rural Tanzania," *Medical Anthropology* 22: 23–52.

Douglas, Mary (1975), *Implicit Meanings: Essays in Anthropology*, London: Routledge.

Drew, Paul (1998), "Complaints About Transgressions and Misconduct," *Research on Language and Social Interaction* 31(3&4): 295–325.

Dupret, Baudouin (2004), "The Person and the Law: Contingency, Individuation and the Subject of the Law," in B. Dupret (ed.), *Standing Trial: Law and the Person in the Modern Middle East*, London: I. B. Tauris.

Duranti, Alessandro (1992), "Language in context and language as context: the Samoan respect vocabulary," in A. Duranti and C. Goodwin (eds), *Rethinking Context: Language as an Interactive Phenomenon*, Cambridge: Cambridge University Press.

Durkheim, Emile (1953), "The Determination of Moral Facts," in *Sociology and Philosophy*, Glencoe, IL: The Free Press.

Durkheim, Emile (1961[1925]), *Moral Education: A Study in the Theory and Application of the Sociology of Education*, Glencoe, IL: The Free Press.

Edel, May and Edel, Abraham (2000[1959]), *Anthropology and Ethics: The Quest for Moral Understanding*, New Brunswick: Transaction Publishers.

Edelman, Marc (2005), "Bringing the Moral Economy back in … to the Study of 21st-Century Transnational Peasant Movements," *American Anthropologist* 107(3): 331–45.

Edwards, Carolyn Pope (1985), "Rationality, Culture, and the Construction of 'Ethical Discourse': A Comparative Perspective," *Ethos* 13(4): 318–39.

Ellison, Marcia A. (2003), "Authoritative Knowledge and Single Women's Unintentional Pregnancies, Abortion, Adoption, and Single Motherhood: Social Stigma and Structural Violence," *Medical Anthropology Quarterly* 17(3): 322–47.

Evans-Pritchard, E. E. (1968[1937]), *Witchcraft, Oracles and Magic Among the Azande*, London: Oxford University Press.

Factor, Regis A. and Turner, Stephen P. (1979), "The Limits of Reason and Some Limitations of Weber's Morality," *Human Studies* 2: 301–34.

Farmer, Paul (1988), "Bad Blood, Spoiled Milk: Bodily Fluids as Moral Barometers in Rural Haiti," *American Ethnologist* 15(1): 62–83.

Farmer, Paul (1992), *AIDS and Accusation: Haiti and the Geography of Blame*, Berkeley: University of California Press.

Faubion, James D. (2001a), "Toward an Anthropology of Ethics: Foucault and the Pedagogies of Autopoiesis," *Representations*, 74.

Faubion, James D. (2001b), *The Ethics of Kinship*, Lanham, MD: Rowman & Littlefield Publishers.

Fine, Gary Alan (1993), "Ten Lies of Ethnography: Moral Dilemmas in Field Research," *Journal of Contemporary Ethnography* 22(3): 267–94.

Firth, Raymond (1951), *Elements of Social Organization*, London: Watts.

Fischer, Michael M. J. (2003), *Emergent Forms of Life and the Anthropological Voice*, Durham, NC: Duke University Press.

Fiske, Alan Page and Mason, Kathryn F. (1990), "Introduction," *Ethos* 18(2): 131–9.

Fordham, Graham (2001), "Moral Panic and the Construction of National Order," *Critique of Anthropology* 21(3): 259–316.

Foucault, Michel (1984), "Polemics, Politics, and Problemizations: An Interview with Michel Foucault," in P. Rabinow (ed.), *The Foucault Reader*, New York: Pantheon Books.

Foucault, Michel (2000a), "Technologies of the Self," in P. Rabinow (ed.), *Ethics: Subjectivity and Truth*, London: Penguin Books.

Foucault, Michel (2000b), "On the Genealogy of Ethics: An Overview of Work in Progress," in P. Rabinow (ed.), *Ethics: Subjectivity and Truth*, London: Penguin Books.

Foucault, Michel (2000c), "The Ethics of the Concern of the Self as a Practice of Freedom," in P. Rabinow (ed.), *Ethics: Subjectivity and Truth*, London: Penguin Books.

Frank, Gelya, Blackhall, Leslie J., Michel, Vicki, Murphy, Sheila T., Azen, Stanley P., and Park, Kye-young (1998), "A Discourse of Relationships in Bioethics:

Patient Autonomy and End-of-Life Decision Making among Elderly Korean Americans," *Medical Anthropology Quarterly* 12(4): 403–23.

Fuller, Lon L. (1969), *The Morality of Law*, New Haven, CT: Yale University Press.

Galanter, Marc (2005), "Law and Society in Modern India," in S. F. Moore (ed.), *Law and Anthropology*, Oxford: Blackwell.

Geertz, Clifford (1984), "Distinguished Lecture: Anti Anti-Relativism," *American Anthropologist* 86(2): 263–78.

Geertz, Clifford (1989), *Local Knowledge*, New York: Basic Books.

Geurts, Kathryn Linn (2003) "On Rocks, Walks, and Talks in West Africa: Cultural Categories and an Anthropology of the Senses," *Ethos* 30(3): 178–98.

Gilligan, Carol (1982), *In a Different Voice: Psychological Theory and Women's Development*, Cambridge, MA: Harvard University Press.

Gledhill, John (1998), "Liberalism, Socio-economic Rights and the Politics of Identity: From Moral Economy to Indigenous Rights," in R. A. Wilson (ed.), *Human Rights, Culture and Context: Anthropological Perspectives*, London: Pluto Press.

Good, Byron J. (1994), *Medicine, Rationality, and Experience: An Anthropological Perspective*, Cambridge: Cambridge University Press.

Goodale, Mark (2006a), "Introduction to 'Anthropology and Human Rights in a New Key,'" *American Anthropologist* 108(1): 1–8.

Goodale, Mark (2006b), "Ethical Theory as Social Practice," *American Anthropologist* 108(1): 25–37.

Goodin, Robert E. (2000), "Utility and the good," in P. Singer (ed.), *A Companion to Ethics*, Oxford: Blackwell Publishers.

Goodwin, Charles and Duranti, Alessandro (1992) "Rethinking context: an introduction," in A. Duranti and C. Goodwin (eds), *Rethinking Context: Language as an Interactive Phenomenon*. Cambridge: Cambridge University Press.

Greenhouse, Carol J. (1992), "Signs of Quality: Individualism and Hierarchy in American Culture," *American Ethnologist* 19(2): 233–54.

Hallpike, C. R. (2004), *The Evolution of Moral Understanding*, London: The Prometheus Research Group.

Hann, Chris (2003), "Introduction: Decollectivisation and the Moral Economy," in C. Hann and the "Property Relations" Group, *The Postsocialist Agrarian Question: Property Relations and the Rural Condition*, Münster: Lit Verlag.

Hann, Chris and the "Property Relations" Group (2003), *The Postsocialist Agrarian Question: Property Relations and the Rural Condition*, Münster: Lit Verlag.

Hart, H. L. A. (1961), *The Concept of Law*, Oxford: Oxford University Press.

Hatch, Elvin (1983), *Culture and Morality: The Relativity of Values in Anthropology*, New York: Columbia University Press.

Heald, Suzette (1999), *Manhood and Morality: Sex, Violence and Ritual in Gisu Society*, London: Routledge.

Heidegger, Martin (1996), *Being and Time*, Albany, NY: State University of New York Press.

Heritage, John and Lindström, Anna (1998), "Motherhood, Medicine, and Morality: Scenes From a Medical Encounter," *Research on Language and Social Interaction* 31(3&4): 397–438.

Hernández-Truyol, Berta Esperanza (ed.) (2002), *Moral Imperialism: A Critical Anthology*, New York: New York University Press.

Herskovits, Melville (1958), "Some Further Comments on Cultural Relativism," *American Anthropologist* 60(2): 266–73.

Herzfeld, Michael (1985), *The Poetics of Manhood: Contest and Identity in a Cretan Mountain Village*, Princeton: Princeton University Press.

Hirschkind, Charles (2001) "The Ethics of Listening: Cassette-Sermon Audition in Contemporary Egypt," *American Ethnologist* 28(3): 623–649.

Hoffmaster, Barry (2001), "Introduction," in B. Hoffmaster (ed.), *Bioethics in Social Context*, Philadelphia: Temple University Press.

Howell, Signe (1997), "Introduction," in S. Howell (ed.), *The Ethnography of Moralities*, London: Routledge.

Howell, Signe (2003), "Kinning: The Creation of Life Trajectories in Transnational Adoptive Families," *Journal of the Royal Anthropological Institute* 9: 465–84.

Humphrey, Caroline (1997), "Exemplars and rules: aspects of the discourse of moralities in Mongolia," in S. Howell (ed.), *The Ethnography of Moralities*, London: Routledge.

Hunt, Linda M. (1998), "Moral Reasoning and the Meaning of Cancer: Causal Explanations of Oncologists and Patients in Southern Mexico," *Medical Anthropology Quarterly* 12(3): 298–318.

Jackson, Michael (1998), *Minima Ethnographica: Intersubjectivity and the Anthropological Project*, Chicago: The University of Chicago Press.

Jackson, Michael (2005), *Existential Anthropology: Events, Exigencies and Effects*, New York: Berghahn Books.

James, Wendy (1999), *The Listening Ebony: Moral Knowledge, Religion, and Power among the Uduk of Sudan*, Oxford: Oxford University Press.

Just, Peter (2001), *Dou Donggo Justice: Conflict and Morality in an Indonesian Society*, Lanham, MD: Rowman & Littlefield.

Kant, Immanuel (1949), *Fundamental Principles of the Metaphysics of Morals*, New York: Macmillan Publishing Co.

Kant, Immanuel (1996), *Critique of Practical Reason*, Amherst, NY: Prometheus Books.

Kaufman, Sharon R. (2001), "Clinical Narratives and Ethical Dilemmas in Geriatrics," in B. Hoffmaster (ed.), *Bioethics in Social Context*, Philadelphia: Temple University Press.

Kelly, Raymond C. (2002), "Witchcraft and Sexual Relations: An Exploration in the Social and Semantic Implications of the Structure of Belief," in M. Lambeck (ed.), *A Reader in the Anthropology of Religion*, Oxford: Blackwell.

Kleinman, Arthur (2006), *What Really Matters: Living a Moral Life Amidst Uncertainty and Danger*, Oxford: Oxford University Press.

Kockelman, Paul (2004), "Stance and Subjectivity," *Journal of Linguistic Anthropology* 14(2): 127–150.

Ladd, John (1957), *The Structure of a Moral Code: A Philosophical Analysis of Ethical Discourse Applied to the Ethics of the Navaho Indians*, Cambridge: Harvard University Press.

Ladwig, Patrice (2005), "Narrative ethics: The excess of giving and moral ambiguity in the Lao Vessantara-Jataka," presented at the workshop on "Rethinking Morality" at the Max Planck Institute for Social Anthropology.

Laidlaw, James (1995), *Riches and Renunciation: Religion, Economy, and Society Among the Jains*, Oxford: Oxford University Press.

Laidlaw, James (2002), "For an Anthropology of Ethics and Freedom," *Journal of the Royal Anthropological Institute* 8(2): 311–32.

Lambek, Michael (2000), "The Anthropology of Religion and the Quarrel between Poetry and Philosophy," *Current Anthropology* 41(3): 309–20.

Lambek, Michael (2002), "Nuriaty, the Saint and the Sultan: Virtuous Subject and Subjective Virtuoso of the Postmodern Colony," in R. Werbner (ed.), *Postcolonial Subjectivities in Africa*, London: Zed Books.

Lambek, Michael and Solway, Jacqueline S. (2001), "Just Anger: Scenarios of Indignation in Botswana and Madagascar," *ethnos* 66(1): 49–72.

Leavitt, Judith Walzer (1987), "The Growth of medical Authority: Technology and Morals in Turn-of-the-Century Obstetrics," *Medical Anthropology Quarterly* 1(3): 230–55.

Linde, Charlotte (1993), *Life Stories: The Creation of Coherence*, Oxford: Oxford University Press.

Linell, Per and Rommetveit, Ragnar (1998), "The Many Forms and Facets of Morality in Dialogue: Epilogue for the Special Issue," *Research on Language and Social Interaction* 31(3&4), 465–73.

Linton, Ralph (1952), "Universal Ethical Principles: An Anthropological View," in R. N. Anshen (ed.), *Moral Principles of Action: Man's Ethical Imperative*, New York: Harper.

Linton, Ralph (1954) "The Problem of Universal Values," in R. F. Spencer (ed.), *Method and Perspective in Anthropology*, Minneapolis: University of Minnesota Press.

Lock, Margaret (2001a), "The Tempering of Medical Anthropology: Troubling Natural Categories," *Medical Anthropology Quarterly* 15(4): 478–92.

Lock, Margaret (2001b) "Situated Ethics, Culture, and the Brain Death 'Problem' in Japan," in B. Hoffmaster (ed.), *Bioethics in Social Context*, Philadelphia: Temple University Press.

Londoño Sulkin, Carlos D. (2005), "Inhuman Beings: Morality and Perspectivism among Muinane People," *ethnos* 70(1): 7–30.

Luckmann, Thomas (2002), "Moral Communication in Modern Societies," *Human Studies* 25: 19–32.

Lukes, Steven (1977), *Emile Durkheim His Life and Work: A Historical and Critical Study*, New York: Penguin Books.

MacIntyre, Alasdair (1966[1998]), *A Short History of Ethics*, Notre Dame: University of Notre Dame Press.

Mageo, Jeannette Marie (1991), "Samoan Moral Discourse and the Loto," *American Anthropologist* 93(2): 405–20.

Mahmood, Saba (2003), "Ethical Formation and Politics of Individual Autonomy in Contemporary Egypt," *Social Research* 70(3): 837–66.

Mahmood, Saba (2005), *Politics of Piety: The Islamic Revival and the Feminist Subject*, Princeton: Princeton University Press.

Malinowski, Bronislaw (1926), *Crime and Custom in Savage Society*, London: Paul Kegan.

Marshall, Patricia A. (1992), "Anthropology and Bioethics," *Medical Anthropology Quarterly* 6(1): 49–73.

Mattingly, Cheryl (1998), "In Search of the Good: Narrative Reasoning in Clinical Practice," *Medical Anthropology Quarterly* 12(3): 273–97.

Mauss, Marcel (1973), "Techniques of the body," *Economy and Society* 2: 70–88.

Mauss, Marcel (1997), "A Category of the Human Mind: The Notion of Person; The Notion of Self," in M. Carrithers (ed.), *The Category of the Person: Anthropology, Philosophy, History*, Cambridge: Cambridge University Press.

McCollum, Chris (2002), "Relatedness and Self-Definition: Two Dominant Themes in Middle-Class Americans' Life Stories," *Ethos* 30(1/2): 113–39.

Melhuus, Marit (1997), "The Troubles of Virtue: Values of Violence and Suffering in a Mexican Context," in S. Howell (ed.), *The Ethnography of Moralities*, London: Routledge.

Menon, Usha (2002), "Making Śakti: Controlling (Natural) Impurity for Female (Cultural) Power," *Ethos* 30(1/2): 140–57.

Merry, Sally Engle (2001), "Spatial Governmentality and the New Urban Social Order: Controlling Gender Violence through Law," *American Anthropologist* 103(1): 16–29.

Merry, Sally Engle (2006), "Transnational Human Rights and Local Activism: Mapping the Middle," *American Anthropologist* 108(1): 38–51.

Miller, W. Watts (2002), "Morality and ethics," in W. S. F. Pickering (ed.), *Durkheim Today*, New York: Berghahn Books.

Misra, Kavita (2006), "Politico-moral Transactions in Indian AIDS Service: Confidentiality, Rights and New Modalities of Governance," *Anthropological Quarterly* 79(1): 33–74.

Moore, Sally Falk (2005), "General Introduction," in S. F. Moore (ed.), *Law and Anthropology*, Oxford: Blackwell.

Muller, Jessica H. (1994), "Anthropology, Bioethics, and Medicine: A Provocative Trilogy," *Medical Anthropology Quarterly* 8(4): 448–67.

Munsey, Brenda (ed.) (1980), *Moral Development, Moral Education, and Kohlberg*, Birmingham, AL: Religious Education Press.

Murdock, George Peter (1965), *Culture and Society*, Pittsburgh: University of Pittsburgh Press.

Nordenstam, Tore (1968), *Sudanese Ethics*, Uppsala: The Scandinavian Institute of African Studies.

Ochs, Elinor and Capps, Lisa (2001), *Living Narrative: Creating Lives in Everyday Storytelling*, Cambridge, MA: Harvard University Press.

Oring, Elliott (1992), *Jokes and their Relations*, Lexington: University of Kentucky Press.

Ortner, Sherry B. (1974), "Is Female to Male as Nature Is to Culture?" in M. Z. Rosaldo and L. Lamphere (eds), *Woman, Culture, and Society*, Stanford: Stanford University Press.

Pardo, Italo (2004), "Introduction: Corruption, Morality and the Law," in I. Pardo (ed.), *Between Morality and the Law: Corruption, Anthropology and Comparative Society*, Aldershot, UK: Ashgate.

Parish, Steven M. (1991), "The Sacred Mind: Newar Cultural Representations of Mental Life and the Production of Moral Consciousness," *Ethos* 19(3): 313–51.

Parish, Steven M. (1994), *Moral Knowing in a Hindu Sacred City: An Exploration of Mind, Emotion, and Self*, New York: Columbia University Press.

Parkin, David (1985) "Introduction," *The Anthropology of Evil*, Oxford: Blackwell.

Paxson, Heather (2004), *Making Modern Mothers: Ethics and Family Planning in Urban Greece*, Berkeley: University of California Press.

Pence, Greg (2000), "Virtue theory," in P. Singer (ed.), *A Companion to Ethics*, Oxford: Blackwell.

Perry, Richard (2000), "Governmentalities in City-Scapes: Introduction to the Symposium. Symposium on City-Spaces and Arts of Government," *Polar: Political and Legal Anthropology Review* 23(1): 65–73.

Pettit, Philip (2000), "Consequentialism," in P. Singer (ed.), *A Companion to Ethics*, Oxford: Blackwell.

Pfeiffer, James (2004), "Condom Social Marketing, Pentecostalism, and Structural Adjustment in Mozambique: A Clash of AIDS Prevention Messages," *Medical Anthropology Quarterly* 18(1): 77–103.

Piaget, Jean (1965), *The Moral Judgment of the Child*, New York: Free Press.

Pirie, Fernanda (2006), "Secular morality, village law, and Buddhism in Tibetan societies," *Journal of the Royal Anthropological Institute* 12(1): 173–90.

Pocock, D. F. (1986), "The Ethnography of Morals," *International Journal of Moral and Social Studies* 1(1): 3–20.

Povinelli, Elizabeth A. (2002) *The Cunning of Recognition: Indigenous Alterities and the Making of Australian Multiculturalism*, Durham, NC: Duke University Press.

Quintero, Gilbert (2002), "Nostalgia and Degeneration: The Moral Economy of Drinking in Navajo Society," *Medical Anthropology Quarterly* 16(1): 3–21.

Rapport, Nigel (1997), "The morality of locality: On the absolutism of landownership in an English village," in S. Howell (ed.), *The Ethnography of Moralities*, London: Routledge.

Rasmussen, Susan (1998), "Ritual Powers and Social Tensions as Moral Discourse among the Tuareg," *American Anthropologist* 100(2): 458–68.

Read, K. E. (1955), "Morality and the Concept of the Person Among the Gahuku-Gama," *Oceania* 25(4): 233–82.

Rebhun, L. A. (2004), "Sexuality, Color, and Stigma among Northeast Brazilian Women," *Medical Anthropology Quarterly* 18(2): 183–99.

Redfield, Robert (1957), "The Universally Human and Culturally Variable," *Journal of General Education* 10: 150–60.

Ries, Nancy (1997), *Russian Talk: Culture and Conversation during Perestroika*, Ithaca, NY: Cornell University Press.

Ries, Nancy (2002), "'Honest Bandits' and 'Warped People': Russian Narratives about Money, Corruption, and Moral Decay," in C. J. Greenhouse, E. Mertz, and K. B. Warren (eds), *Ethnography in Unstable Places: Everyday Lives in Contexts of Dramatic Political Change*, Durham, NC: Duke University Press.

Rivkin-Fish, Michele (2005), *Women's Health In Post-Soviet Russia: The Politics of Intervention*, Bloomington: Indiana University Press.

Robben, Antonius C. G. M. and Sluka, Jeffery A. (2007), *Ethnographic Fieldwork: An Anthropological Reader*, Malden, MA: Blackwell.

Robbins, Joel (2001), "God Is Nothing but Talk: Modernity, Language, and Prayer in a Papua New Guinea Society," *American Anthropologist* 103(4): 901–12.

Robbins, Joel (2004), *Becoming Sinners: Christianity and Moral Torment in a Papua New Guinea Society*, Berkeley: University of California Press.

Robbins, Joel (2005), "Morality, Value, and Radical Cultural Change," presented at the workshop on "Rethinking Morality" at the Max Planck Institute for Social Anthropology.

Robbins, Joel (2007), "Between Reproduction and Freedom: Morality, Value, and Radical Cultural Change," *ethnos* 72(3): 293–314.

Robins, Steven (2006), "From 'Rights' to 'Ritual': AIDS Activism in South Africa," *American Anthropologist* 108(2): 312–23.

Rogers, Douglas J. (2004), "An Ethics of Transformation: Work, Prayer and Moral Practice in the Russian Urals 1861–2001," Doctoral Dissertation, Department of Anthropology, University of Michigan.

Rowe, Christopher (2000), "Ethics in ancient Greece," in P. Singer (ed.), *A Companion to Ethics*, Oxford: Blackwell.

Rydstrøm, Helle (2003), *Embodying Morality: Growing Up in Rural Northern Vietnam*, Honolulu: University of Hawaii Press.

Salvatore, Armando (2004), "The 'Implosion' of *Shari'a* within the Emergence of Public Normativity: The Impact on Personal Responsibility and the Impersonality of Law," in B. Dupret (ed.), *Standing Trial: Law and the Person in the Modern Middle East*, London: I. B. Tauris.

Sapir, Edward (1921), *Language*, New York: Harcourt, Brace and World.

Saussure, Ferdinand de (1983), *Course in General Linguistics*, La Salle, Illinois: Open Court.

Scott, James C. (1976), *The Moral Economy of the Peasant: Rebellion and Subsistence in Southeast Asia*, New Haven, CT: Yale University Press.

Seizer, Susan (1997), "Jokes, Gender, and Discursive Distance on the Tamil Popular Stage," *American Ethnologist* 24(1): 62–90.

Shoaps, Robin A. (2002) "'Pray earnestly': The Textual Construction of Personal Involvement in Pentecostal Prayer and Song," *Journal of Linguistic Anthropology* 12(1): 34–71.

Shoaps, Robin A. (2004), "Morality in Grammar and Discourse: Stance-taking and the Negotiations of Moral Personhood in Sakapultek (Mayan) Wedding Counsels," Doctoral Dissertation, Department of Linguistics, University of California, Santa Barbara.

Shore, Bradd (1990a), "Human Ambivalence and the Structuring of Moral Values," *Ethos* 18(2): 165–79.

Shore, Bradd (1990b), "Afterword," *Ethos* 18(2): 219–23.

Shweder, Richard A. (1990), "Ethical Relativism: Is There a Defensible Version?" *Ethos* 18(2): 205–18.

Simpson, Bob (2004), "Impossible Gifts: Bodies, Buddhism and Bioethics in Contemporary Sri Lanka," *Journal of the Royal Anthropological Institute* 10: 839–59.

Sivaramakrishnan, K. (2005), "Some Intellectual Genealogies for the Concept of Everyday Resistance," *American Anthropologist* 107(3), 346–55.

Stoler, Ann L. (1989), "Making Empire Respectable: The Politics of Race and Sexual Morality in 20th-Century Colonial Cultures," *American Ethnologist* 16(4), 634–60.

Strathern, Marilyn (1997), "Double Standards," in S. Howell (ed.), *The Ethnography of Moralities*, London: Routledge.

Svašek, Maruška (2006), "Postsocialist Ownership: Emotions, Power and Morality in a Czech Village," in M. Svašek (ed.), *Postsocialism: Politics and Emotions in Central and Eastern Europe*, New York: Berghahn Books.

Taylor, Charles (1989), *Sources of the Self: The Making of Modern Identity*, Cambridge, MA: Harvard University Press.

Thiele, Steven J. (1996), *Morality in Classical European Sociology: The Denial of Social Plurality*, Lewiston: The Edwin Mellen Press.

Thompson, E. P. (1991), *Customs in Common*, New York: The New Press.

Thompson, Ken (2002), *Emile Durkheim*, London: Routledge.

Torsello, Davide (2003), "Trust and Property in Historical Perspective: Villagers and the Agricultural Cooperative in Kiralyfa, Southern Slovakia," in C. Hann and the "Property Relations" Group, *The Postsocialist Agrarian Question: Property Relations and the Rural Condition*, Münster: Lit Verlag.

Uhl, Sarah (1991), "Forbidden Friends: Cultural Veils of Female Friendship in Andalusia," *American Ethnologist* 18(1), 90–105.

Vallely, Anne (2002), "Moral Landscapes: Ethical Discourses among Orthodox and Diaspora Jains," in M. Lambeck (ed.), *A Reader in the Anthropology of Religion*, Oxford: Blackwell.

Villenas, Sofia (2001), "Latina Mothers and Small-Town Racisms: Creating Narratives of Dignity and Moral Education in North Carolina," *Anthropology and Education Quarterly* 32(1): 3–28.

Vološinov, V. N. (2000), *Marxism and the Philosophy of Language*, Cambridge, MA: Harvard University Press.

von Benda-Beckmann, F. (2002), "Who's afraid of legal pluralism?" *Journal of Legal Pluralism* 47: 37–82.

von Fürer-Haimendorf, Christoph (1964), *The Sherpas of Nepal: Buddhist Highlanders*, London: John Murray.

von Fürer-Haimendorf, Christoph (1967), *Morals and Merit: A Study of Values and Social Controls in South Asian Societies*, Chicago: The University of Chicago Press.

Wanner, Catherine (2005), "Money, Morality and New Forms of Exchange in Postsocialist Ukraine," *ethnos* 70(4): 515–37.

Weber, Max (1958) "Politics as a Vocation," in H. H. Gerth and C. Wright Mills (eds), *From Max Weber: Essays in Sociology*, New York: Oxford University Press.

Weber, Max (1999[1930]), *The Protestant Ethic and the Spirit of Capitalism*, London: Routledge.

Westermarck, Edward (1906), *The Origin and Development of the Moral Ideas*, Vol. 2, London: MacMillan.

Whorf, Benjamin (1956), *Language, Thought and Reality: Selected Writings*, Cambridge, MA: MIT Press.

Widlok, Thomas (2004), "Sharing by Default?: Outline of an Anthropology of virtue," *Anthropological Theory* 4(1): 53–70.

Wikan, Unni (1992), "Beyond the Words: The Power of Resonance," *American Ethnologist* 19(3): 460–82.

Wilson, Richard Ashby (2006), "Afterword to 'Anthropology and Human Rights in a New Key': The Social Life of Human Rights," *American Anthropologist* 108(1): 77–83.

Wolfram, Sybil (1982), "Anthropology and Morality," *Journal of the Anthropological Society of Oxford* 13: 262–74.

Wynn, L. L., and Trussell, James (2006), "The Social Life of Emergency Contraception in the United States: Disciplining Pharmaceutical Use, Disciplining Sexuality, and Constructing Zygotic Bodies," *Medical Anthropology Quarterly* 20(3): 297–320.

Zigon, Jarrett (2006), "Five Muscovites: Narratives of Moral Experience in Contemporary Russia," Doctoral Dissertation, Department of Anthropology, City University of New York, Graduate Center.

Zigon, Jarrett (2007), "Moral Breakdown and the Ethical Demand: A Theoretical Framework for an Anthropology of Moralities," *Anthropological Theory* 7(2): 131–50.

Zigon, Jarrett (2008), "Moral Responses to an HIV/AIDS Epidemic: A Comparison of Russian Orthodox Church, Secular NGO and Russian Government Discourse and Practice," in Patricia Cholewka (ed.), *Health Capital and Sustainable Economic Development*, Boca Raton, FL: CRC Press.

Index

179